MANAGEMENT INFORMATION SYSTEMS AND DATA PROCESSING

*To Derek, Nigel, John, Rick, Brian and Ian,
from whom I learned a great deal*

Management Information Systems and Data Processing

Second Edition

TREVOR J. BENTLEY, PhD, FCMA, FMS, MIDPM

HOLT, RINEHART AND WINSTON
LONDON · NEW YORK · SYDNEY · TORONTO

Holt, Rinehart and Winston Ltd: 1 St Anne's Road,
Eastbourne,
East Sussex.
BN21 3UN.

British Library Cataloguing in Publication Data

Bentley, Trevor J.
   Management information systems and data processing.
   — 2nd ed.
   1. Electronic data processing—Management
   I. Title
   004'.068   QA76.9.M3

ISBN 0–03–910688–8

Typeset by Photographics, Honiton, Devon
Printed in Great Britain by Mackays of Chatham Ltd

Copyright © 1982, 1986 by Holt, Rinehart and Winston
All rights reserved. This book is protected by copyright. No part of it may be reproduced, stored in a retrieval system, or transmitted in any form or by any means, electronic, mechanical, photocopying or otherwise, without written permission from the publisher.

Last digit is print no: 9 8 7 6 5 4 3 2 1

Contents

TO THE STUDENT IX
TO THE LECTURER X

PART ONE   MANAGEMENT INFORMATION SYSTEMS 1

1 Systems Theory

1.1 *Definition of systems* 3;   1.2 *Systems hierarchy* 4;   1.3 *The nature of systems* 5;   1.4 *The nature of organizations* 6;   1.5 *Control systems* 6;   1.6 *Models and simulation* 8;   1.7 *Summary and revision notes* 9;   *Questions* 10;   *Case study exercise* 10

2 Information 11

2.1 *Definition of information* 11;   2.2 *The value of information* 11;   2.3 *Information and organizations* 13;   2.4 *Information handling* 15;   2.5 *Information flows* 15;   2.6 *Information loops* 17;   2.7 *Summary and revision notes* 19;   *Questions* 20;   *Case study exercise* 20

3 Information Systems 21

3.1 *Decisions and information* 21;   3.2 *Establishing information needs* 22;   3.3 *The system framework* 22;   3.4 *System objectives* 24;   3.5 *Accuracy and timeliness* 26;   3.6 *The adaptive information system* 27;   3.7 *Presentation of information* 28;   3.8 *Summary and revision notes* 29;   *Questions* 30;   *Case study exercise* 31

4 Information Systems Strategy 31

4.1 *The need for a strategy* 31;   4.2 *Systems strategy survey* 32;   4.3 *Information technology developments* 33;   4.4 *Organizing and controlling information systems* 33;   *Summary and revision notes* 34

v

5 Systems Design 36

5.1 *Principles of systems design* 36;   5.2 *Project life cycle* 38;   5.3 *The stages of systems design* 38;   5.4 *Project management and control* 42;   5.5 *Systems analysis* 43;   5.6 *Flowcharting* 43;   5.7 *Batch and interactive processing* 49;   5.8 *Summary and revision notes* 50;   *Questions* 51;   *Case study exercise* 52

6 Systems Selection 53

6.1 *The right approach* 53;   6.2 *Dealing with manufacturers and suppliers* 56;   6.3 *Contracts* 57;   6.4 *Tailor-made software* 58;   6.5 *Packages* 58;   6.6 *Benchmark tests* 59;   6.7 *Evaluation and ranking* 59;   6.8 *Summary and revision notes* 60;   *Questions* 61;   *Case study exercise* 62;   *Critical criteria for assessing computer systems proposals* 62

7 Systems Installation 66

7.1 *Justification* 66;   7.2 *Management agreement* 69;   7.3 *Report writing* 70;   7.4 *User education and training* 71;   7.5 *Systems testing* 72;   7.6 *Changeover* 76;   7.7 *Data conversion* 77;   7.8 *Manuals* 77;   7.9 *Implications of change* 79;   7.10 *Summary and revision notes* 79;   *Questions* 80;   *Case study exercise* 80

PART TWO DATA PROCESSING 82

8 The Role of Computers 83

8.1 *Computers in business* 83;   8.2 *Computer categories* 84;   8.3 *Computer strengths* 88;   8.4 *Computer weaknesses* 89;   8.5 *Computer-based systems* 90;   8.6 *Distributed processing* 92;   8.7 *Networks* 92;   8.8 *Summary and revision notes* 94;   *Questions* 95;   *Case study exercise* 96

9 Computer Hardware 97

9.1 *Elements of the computer* 97;   9.2 *Digital and analog computers* 98;   9.3 *Operating functions* 99;   9.4 *Input devices* 100;   9.5 *Storage facilities* 103;   9.6 *Communications* 106;   9.7 *Output* 106;   9.8 *Summary and revision notes* 108;   *Questions* 110;   *Case study exercise* 110

10 Software 111

10.1 *What is software?* 111;   10.2 *Stored instructions and languages* 111;   10.3 *Levels of software* 112;   10.4 *Principles of programming* 116;   10.5 *Modular and structured programs* 120;   10.6 *Batch processing programs* 120;   10.7 *Interactive software* 120;   10.8 *Data base software* 121;   10.9 *Summary and revision notes* 121;   *Questions* 122;   *Case study exercise* 123

11 Data Generation and Processing 124

11.1 *Data: a definition* 124;   11.2 *Forms of data* 124;   11.3 *Data hierarchies and networks* 126;   11.4 *File structures* 127;   11.5 *File organization* 129;   11.6 *Data manipulation* 131;   11.7 *Data base design principles* 134;   11.8 *Data administration* 136;   11.9 *Summary and revision notes* 137;   *Questions* 138;   *Case study exercise* 139

12 Data Collection and Communication — 140

12.1 *Data collection: the foundation* 140; 12.2 *Methods of data collection* 141; 12.3 *Coding* 143; 12.4 *Input devices* 145; 12.5 *Data transmission* 147; 12.6 *Data validation and control* 151; 12.7 *Data collection: the key to good systems* 153; 12.8 *Cost of data collection* 153; 12.9 *Summary and revision notes* 154; *Questions* 155; *Case study exercise* 156

13 Computer Operations — 157

13.1 *Organization of the data processing function* 157; 13.2 *Computer management and control* 158; 13.3 *Planning and scheduling* 159; 13.4 *Computer runs* 161; 13.5 *Multi-programming* 163; 13.6 *Multi-processing* 164; 13.7 *Control procedures* 165; 13.8 *Performance monitoring* 167; 13.9 *Efficient computer management* 168; 13.10 *Summary and revision notes* 169; *Questions* 170; *Case study exercise* 170

14 Computer Output — 171

14.1 *Principles of usable output* 171; 14.2 *Methods of computer output* 174; 14.3 *Printed reports* 176; 14.4 *Terminal output* 179; 14.5 *Graphics* 179; 14.6 *Computer output microfilm* 180; 14.7 *Designing computer output* 180; 14.8 *The user-DP conflict* 184; 14.9 *Summary and revision notes* 185; *Questions* 186; *Case study exercise* 187

15 System Standards — 188

15.1 *The need for standards* 188; 15.2 *Hardware standards* 189; 15.3 *Software standards* 190; 15.4 *System design standards* 190; 15.5 *Documentation* 194; 15.6 *Maintaining the systems investment* 201; 15.7 *Operating standards* 202; 15.8 *Enforcing standards* 205; 15.9 *Summary and revision notes* 205; *Questions* 207

PART THREE SYSTEMS EVALUATION AND AUDIT — 210

16 System Evaluation — 211

16.1 *Assessing system performance* 211; 16.2 *Performance analysis* 213; 16.3 *Key success criteria* 214; 16.4 *Evaluating design techniques* 215; 16.5 *Evaluating operating techniques* 217; 16.6 *Computer efficiency audit* 218; 16.7 *Summary and revision notes* 220; *Questions* 221

17 Systems Audit — 222

17.1 *Information: a vital resource* 222; 17.2 *Systems dependency and vulnerability* 222; 17.3 *Physical protection and security* 223; 17.4 *System controls and security* 225; 17.5 *Operational controls* 228; 17.6 *Auditability* 228; 17.7 *Audit path* 230; 17.8 *Summary and revision notes* 231; *Questions* 232

CASE STUDY — 234

INDEX — 248

To The Student

I have written this book to meet the syllabus requirements of the ICMA and the IMS examinations. It is not, however, a textbook in the conventional sense. When you have passed your examinations and are qualified you will need to apply your knowledge to the design of management information systems. This book, therefore, is also a guide to the new practitioner in the application of his or her knowledge in the real world.

The theory of management information systems is, therefore, explained in the context of its application in a working environment. There are numerous examples showing how this has been done.

The content of every chapter is summarized in the form of revision notes which should make your revision easier and more comprehensive.

There are approximately 60 figures in the book, most of which are original and unique explanations of some part of the text. These, together with the examples, should make the book interesting and readable, both important features of a useful textbook.

My objective is simply to help you pass your examinations and provide a book which you will find of interest and use long after you have qualified. If in addition you enjoy the book, then I shall be doubly satisfied.

T.J.B.

To The Lecturer

As a lecturer in information systems and data processing, I have often wanted a book which linked theory and practice so that my students could learn in a realistic way. I have, therefore, written this book to fill the gap. The primary aim is to meet the syllabus of the ICMA and the IMS, but the secondary aim is to provide the lecturer with a teaching tool which treats the subject in a logical, thorough and interesting way.

There are, of course, sample questions and chapter summaries, but in addition there are two features which should make the book a valuable addition to your tool-kit. These are: a case study covering the first 14 chapters of the book; and approximately 60 figures, many of which will provide material for use as visual aids.

It is also hoped that the approach taken in the book, using practical examples, will provide both an interesting and an informative basis for your course.

If, in addition to finding the book useful, you also find it interesting and readable, then I shall be well satisfied.

T.J.B.

PART ONE

Management Information Systems

1

Systems Theory

1.1 DEFINITION OF SYSTEMS

The word 'system' is used in many different ways, and mostly in some specific context which provides a definition; e.g. the solar system is taken to mean the system of planets and associated satellites which move in orbit round the sun. Each component of the system moves in some relationship to the other components.

Because of the many uses of the word 'system', some of which are quite specific in a scientific sense, it is difficult to produce a generally applicable definition. The one below will provide a suitable basis for this book.

> A system comprises a number of things which are connected or related, and which are organized, either naturally or by design, to achieve some purpose.

A system must have a purpose or objective and it functions with the achievement of that purpose as its overriding control mechanism. To achieve the purpose the system will have a number of parts or activities, each of which manipulates and feeds off the resources available to the system.

The system receives inputs, works upon them, and converts or transforms them into outputs which meet the objectives of the system. This process is not carried out in isolation, but within an environment alongside or linked with other systems.

A purchasing system in a business can be used as an example of a typical system (Figure 1.1). The system is linked to a variety of other systems including the supplier's sales order processing system, the stores control system (which probably generated the order in the first place), the accounting system and the quality control system.

Each separate purchase is a transaction which flows through the system, which can be described as a continuous system. Systems of this kind are referred to as 'open systems' because they interact with other systems around them, with information flowing in and out at various points in the system.

Closed systems, where there is no interaction with the environment or other

4 — *Management information systems and data processing*

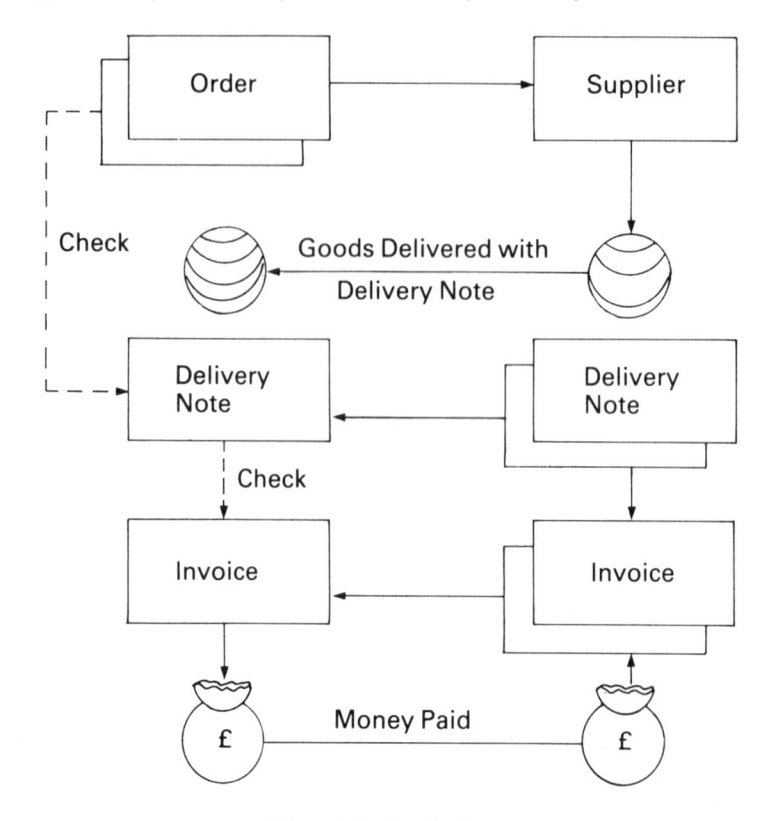

Figure 1.1 *Purchasing system*

systems, are rare, especially in the business environment. A closed system will have no input or output points and would not react to control information from outside.

A business can be seen, therefore, as an open system with an objective, possibly the satisfaction of its customers' needs at a reasonable profit, a number of activities, e.g. production, sales, administration, and resources of materials, manpower, energy and money, working within an environment and linked to other systems, suppliers, customers, banks, etc.

1.2 SYSTEMS HIERARCHY

The individual business is an open system and is also a sub-system of the industry in which it operates, and the economy of the country, which is itself a sub-system of the world economy. Yet within the business there are a variety of sub-systems, each of which is an open system linked to several others.

The enterprise is therefore constructed of a hierarchy of sub-systems and is itself part of an even larger framework. Within the business the sub-systems fit together rather like a jigsaw (Figure 1.2).

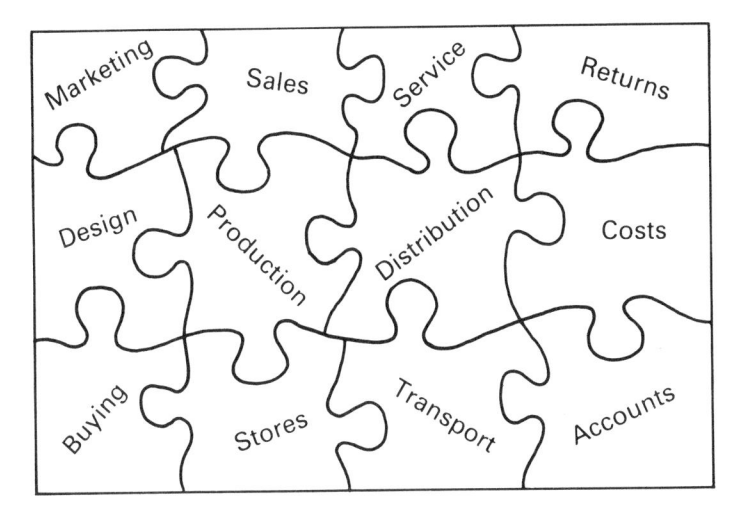

Figure 1.2 *Systems jigsaw*

The importance of the various sub-systems depends on the nature of the business. In a quarrying company, production and distribution are crucial to success, whereas in a construction company design and buying could the the main activities. In retailing, buying is crucial, and in vehicle manufacture, stores and material control, linked to production, are vital. Marketing is, of course, vital for all business enterprises.

The particular systems structure of a business is very important to the design of good systems, placing emphasis on those sub-systems which have the greatest impact on the achievement of the business objectives.

1.3 THE NATURE OF SYSTEMS

Individual systems tend to have a nature of their own: they can be deterministic or probabilistic, adaptive or rigid.

Deterministic systems are those which act in a definite way, devoid of uncertainty. If a certain signal is received by the system, then it can be predicted exactly what the system will do (assuming it works in accordance with its basic rules); e.g. a central heating system will be switched on when the room temperature falls below the setting on the room thermostat.

Probabilistic systems are those in which the outcome is uncertain, where predictions can be made only with the qualification that they are *likely* outcomes or reactions. Most of the broader business systems fall into this category.

Adaptive systems are those which can be adapted to suit the environment when changes take place. All business systems should be adaptive, but it is possible, through poor design, for systems to be rigid.

A rigid system is one which does not adapt to change and is therefore of limited value. There are some instances, such as systems for handling dangerous materials, or maintenance procedures on aircraft, in which the discipline of a rigid system is of value. However, both natural and man-made systems must adapt if they are to survive, and survival is one of the primary objectives of the business organization.

1.4 THE NATURE OF ORGANIZATIONS

An organization is a group of people working towards a common objective, within a framework devised to ensure co-operation and co-ordination. This framework or structure is created to allocate authority and responsibility and to prescribe the activities to be undertaken by the people within the organization.

The structure of an organization evolves, adapting to change in the environment, in the objectives of the organization and in the people. In theory the structure should be designed and then the required people fitted in, but in practice the structure is usually designed to fit the people who exist within the organization.

Organization structures, though very real, have no physical form. They are an abstract concept that can be only partly depicted graphically. The formal relationships are overlaid by informal ones, and though the people are working towards the same overall objective, they have many subsidiary and conflicting objectives.

The systems within the organization, both formal and informal, provide the means for co-operation and co-ordination. Though there are many different systems at work, most, if not all, business systems can be grouped into one of three main categories:

1. Planning systems.
2. Operating systems.
3. Control systems.

Planning systems are concerned with the future of the organization, with predicting the need for change, which in turn is used as a basis for adapting the other systems. Planning systems, both long-term and short-term, are probabilistic and adaptive.

Operating systems are the systems that are used to get things done. Production systems, material handling systems, administrative systems, for example, are all designed to provide the product or service that the customer needs. They are mainly deterministic and, though they should be adaptive, are often rigid.

Control systems are rather special. They try to ensure that the operating systems perform in such a way that the targets produced by the planning system are achieved or, if they are not, to direct attention to the cause of deviation.

1.5 CONTROL SYSTEMS

The study of control systems in organizations has evolved into the science of cybernetics, defined as:

The study of the theory of control systems with particular regard to the comparison between machines and the nervous systems of animals and man.

The design of a control system is based on the need for information about what is happening, so that when a deviation from the norm is spotted, it can be acted on and corrected. The process is called the control loop and is depicted in Figure 1.3.

```
┌─────────┐    ┌─────────┐    ┌─────────┐
│ Monitor │───▶│ Compare │───▶│   Act   │
└─────────┘    └─────────┘    └─────────┘
     ▲                             │
     │                             ▼
     └─────────────────────────────┘
              Continuous activity
```

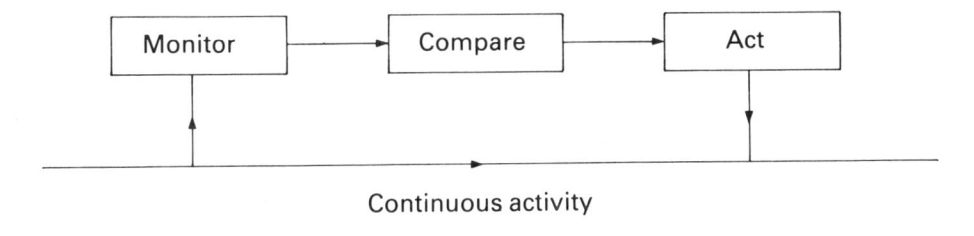

Figure 1.3 *Control loop*

To build effective control loops it is, of course, vital to have a good understanding of the activity or system being controlled, but in addition there are three crucial elements:

1. Measuring devices.
2. Control standards.
3. Regulators.

Measuring devices are needed to monitor what is happening. The accuracy of the information collected depends entirely on the accuracy of the measuring device used. Whether it is temperature, quantity or weight that is being measured, the device used must perform at the required level of accuracy if significant deviations are to be determined.

Control standards are the norms against which the information monitored is compared in order to determine whether or not there is deviation, and whether or not the deviation is significant. When this information is available a decision can be made to do something to correct the activity or system.

Regulators are the means by which action is taken to correct deviations. There are numerous examples of control systems that do not complete the control loop because regulators do not exist or, if they do, cannot be operated in time to be effective.

With the development of microprocessors the potential for designing and building effective control systems has been increased enormously. The accuracy, speed and relatively low cost of the devices are beginning to have a considerable effect on production systems of all kinds.

Control systems operate within different time scales. A quality control system checking glass bottles on a continuous production line is moving through the control loop in fractions of a second, whereas the credit control system is moving through the loop on a monthly interval.

The control loop must therefore be designed to serve the system it controls and must be as fast as is necessary to maintain control at minimal levels of waste.

1.6 MODELS AND SIMULATION

A model is a representation of reality. It might be a physical model such as a model of an aircraft for testing aeroplanes in a wind tunnel, or an abstract model using mathematics to represent size, shape, weight, relationships, etc.

System models are all abstract and are used to simulate reality by feeding in data and predicting likely outcomes. Models, by their very nature, are probabilistic; they are neither true nor false in their predictions. Their usefulness can be established only by comparing the outcome with reality.

A model is built by a process of abstraction from reality, changing attributes and relationships into symbols, the symbols of mathematics. Symbolic models, though the mathematics might seem complex, are often much simpler to construct than physical models.

A model consists of a number of attributes, each of which relates to the others in some way which can usually be described mathematically. When data are fed to the model they are manipulated according to these rules and a result is produced. Both data and rules can be changed so that the model reflects the real world as nearly as possible.

The best known business model is the Budget. Few people appreciate that a Budget is a model, but of course it is, for it seeks to represent the real activities of the business and predicts the likely outcome in the form of a profit. Its success, of course, depends largely on the model builder's knowledge of the business and the way he or she abstracts it. It also depends on the data that are fed in and the accuracy of the rules portraying the relationship of attributes; e.g. what effect does a price increase have on the volume sold?

Models can be improved with experience, but past experience is not always the best guide to future events and so it is not possible to rely on experience alone. Some estimate or forecast of relationships has to be added to experience to make the model a valuable one.

Models are problem-solving tools which are used to try to predict what would happen in the real world if certain events took place. This is why models are often referred to as 'what if' models, the 'if' being the variable data and the 'what' being the outcome. Models of business systems have advantages and disadvantages.

Advantages

1. They provide a framework for examining problems. Though they may not always lead to solutions, they could highlight gaps in information.
2. The process of building the model contributes significantly to a better understanding of the problem.
3. They allow manipulation of both the rules and the data to test a wide variety of possible outcomes.
4. They are easier and less expensive than carrying out a full-scale exercise, saving both time and money.

Disadvantages

1. There is a danger of oversimplification. The model builder may leave out crucial factors for expediency.
2. Symbolic language, though valuable, is limited and not every relationship can be expressed mathematically.
3. Model builders can become so enamoured of their models that they begin to believe they are better than reality, and the model becomes rigid.
4. Models produce only predictions of outcomes. These might be a simple figure, as in a budget, or a range of results with an indication of the one most likely to occur.
5. Models are, of course, never (or extremely rarely) right, and in some people's minds must therefore always be wrong.

The value of models is not in their accuracy, but in the use that is made of them in the problem-solving activities of managers. A model is a tool to be used with skill and understanding.

1.7 SUMMARY AND REVISION NOTES

A system is a group of connected activities organized to achieve some purpose.

There are open systems which interact with the environment and closed systems which are isolated from the environment, with no input or output points.

A business is an open system made up of a hierarchy of sub-systems, the importance of which depends on the type of business.

Systems can be deterministic, devoid of uncertainty or, more likely, probabilistic, where the outcome is uncertain.

They can be adaptive, changing in response to the environment, or rigid.

Systems function within the organization, which is defined as a group of people working towards a common objective within a structure.

The structure, which is abstract, enables authority and responsibility to be allocated to people.

Within the structure systems tend to fall into three main categories: planning, operating and control.

Control systems depend on the efficiency and speed of the control loop and require three elements to exist: measuring devices, control standards and regulators.

Systems can be modelled by representing reality using mathematics in place of actual.

These symbolic and abstract models provide a means of manipulating the rules or parameters, with variable data being input to carry out 'what if' exercises.

Models which simulate reality are not to be taken in place of reality, for they are probabilistic and produce only predictions of likely outcomes. The real test comes in the real world.

The model, like any tool, is valuable only to the craftsman who knows how to use it, understanding both its strengths and its weaknesses.

QUESTIONS

1. Do you consider that the principles of general systems theory (GST) are related to the principles of management? In what way, if any, do GST principles conflict with the practice of management? (ICMA)

2. The financial director has indicated that he wants to do some financial planning using a computer-based model and he has asked you to write a paper on the advantages and disadvantages.

3. Explain what is meant by simulation and give examples using: (a) physical models; and (b) symbolic models.

4. Explain what is meant by systems theory. Show how the theory relates to the management of an organization.

5. 'Oh, it's fine having control information, but what's the point if you can't act?' Discuss.

CASE STUDY EXERCISE

Examine the organization structure in the case study at the end of the book and produce an organization structure identifying the major systems and sub-systems, and commenting on the types and nature of the systems. Comment on the reasons given by the directors for the lack of budgetary control procedures.

2
Information

2.1 DEFINITION OF INFORMATION

It is desirable in the computer age to draw a distinction between data and information. Data processing takes raw, unrelated facts in large quantities, merges, calculates, accumulates, and sorts the data, with the objective of producing information. That is giving form to the data so that it will increase the knowledge of the recipients.

Information can be defined as anything which increases the recipient's knowledge, and an information system can be defined as the means by which the information is generated and communicated to the people involved.

But is this definition adequate? In his book *Management Systems* Peter Schoderbek (1971, Chichester: John Wiley) defines information as follows:

> Whatever contributes to the diminution of ignorance or uncertainty surrounding an impending decision merits the label information. Information, therefore, ranges in value from a position in which it eliminates completely all ignorance and uncertainty surrounding a decision to a position in which it contributes absolutely nothing to the diminution of existing ignorance and uncertainty.

2.2 THE VALUE OF INFORMATION

Information has always been a vital resource for all forms of life. Of all the animals that live on this planet, as far as we know, only man has developed the means of sending information beyond the boundaries of his sight and hearing.

In the early days of man's development, information could be sent for many miles using methods such as drums and smoke signals; however, these still depended on man's ability to see and hear. Messages could be sent over even greater distances by using runners who carried a written message or gave the news in their own words.

Gradually man's ability to communicate over long distances improved and this has continued until the present, when information can be transmitted from the other side of the world and received almost instantaneously. In fact, with the variation in international time zones, it is possible to receive information before it has been sent.

These developments in communications have stemmed from man's need for information in order to survive. At first this was almost entirely concerned with knowing when danger threatened, who the enemy was and how powerful he was. This is the basic level of communication exercised by all living things. But as time went on, information was transmitted and received about many activities apart from the basic survival need, although this has always been, and still is, an area in which vast sums of money are invested to gather, collate and disseminate information as fast as possible. The early warning systems that circle the world are an example; spy satellites are another.

As commerce flourished, merchants found a need to protect their investments and they discovered that if they could find out what their competitors were doing, they could minimize the risk they took. Gradually it was realized that, with more information, it was possible to reduce the risks to both life and investments.

There is always some element of risk that the results of a course of action will be different from those expected; they may be better or worse. Some events can be predicted, e.g. if the fire is not fed with fuel it will go out. Others are completely unpredictable; a new product may be launched without anyone knowing for certain whether it is going to succeed or fail. In order to reduce such a risk, information must be gathered to find out what might happen in the case of a product launch; this is known as market research. Potential customers are asked whether they will buy the new product and what they are prepared to pay for it. This information is then used to try to reduce the risk of failure.

Information is used to reduce the risk attached to making a decision, so information increases knowledge and reduces risk. Just how far is this true? Is there a point at which more information is simply not necessary? In most commercial decisions the answer is yes.

The balance between what is necessary and what is enough is not easy to decide. Sometimes the extra piece of information may have changed the decision. The only way to decide what is enough is to look at each decision and ask:

1. What must be known before action is taken?
2. What ought to be known?
3. What would it be nice to know?

In each case the answer must be related to the cost of providing the information.

Unfortunately, many decisions are made without the benefit of this analysis. This may be due to lack of time or lack of understanding of the decision-making process. Somehow a balance between information and risk seems to exist in every organization. This is perhaps more true of those organizations controlled by entrepreneurs than of others, but nevertheless, it is clear that the need to act forces a balance to be created.

There is no clear proof that more information leads to better decisions, and there are examples of both success and failure in situations where information is readily available, and in others where it is not.

Information is a vital resource, but improving the quality and quantity will create value only if it is used effectively. Just like any other resource, information can be wasted.

2.3 INFORMATION AND ORGANIZATIONS

Every organization requires information in order to survive and grow, particularly when the organization is concerned with making a profit in a competitive environment.

The various sub-systems within the organization feed on information as well as other resources. In fact, information is becoming one of the most vital resources available to the modern organization.

The operation of an organization is based on a hierarchy of systems, each of which consists of a variety of activities or decision points. Each of these decision points has to receive the appropriate information for the activity to continue. The decision points are connected by channels of communication along which information flows both to and from the decision points.

The information which flows along these channels is used for a variety of purposes, but will normally be one of the following: planning, operating or control.

Planning Information

Planning information is of three main types:

1. What is already known. Historic fact, though of limited value, is still one of the prime inputs to the planning process.
2. What is reasonably certain to happen. Orders and contracts have been placed for some future period.
3. The unknown. No matter how disguised, estimates, forecasts and predictions are all trying to state what will happen, and are usually heavily qualified.

The qualification of planning information is a very interesting thing. Statements are made such as the following: 'If things keep going as they are and there are no problems, then such and such will happen.' The one certain thing that can be said about the future is that it is unknown.

No matter how sophisticated the technique might be, or how carefully the data are collected, the outcome predicted is only one of many possibilities. The main advantage of planning is not that the plan works out, but that in the process of planning, problems and difficulties are examined and the likely outcomes of various decisions are tested.

In using information for planning many managers fall back on historic facts. Experience is a great teacher, but only if the events and the environment remain constant is the result of previous experience likely to be repeated. Experienced managers do not always perform better in the planning process than relatively inexperienced managers, since so much of the skill in planning depends on the information available, its source, relevance and accuracy.

Operating Information

Operating information is, of course, essential in order for an activity to be performed. Operating information is information such as the customer supplies with his order, e.g. product or service required, quantity, colour, when it is required, where it is to be delivered, and so on. Without this basic information it would be impossible to meet the order. When asked whether the order can be met, production will need to know the availability of materials, correct capacity levels, manpower available, etc.

The volume, range and complexity of operating information are considerable and yet operating information systems seem to perform adequately. It is because this information has to be available in order for the business to function that systems develop to cope with it. This does not mean that they could not be improved, but at least the information is usually available.

Control Information

Control information is perhaps one of the most difficult types of information to collect and use. Without it control systems cannot function, and yet at times organizations operate with at best very limited controls and at worst none at all.

The effectiveness of control is related to the level of control and the speed with which control data can be gathered. Many control information systems fail because they cannot provide the information in time for action to be taken. It is vital, therefore, that when a system is introduced care is given to collecting data and linking them with the control regulators.

As the activity proceeds the results are monitored, checked and, if necessary, control action is triggered. This, of course, takes time. Control, therefore, is exercised some time after the information which signalled a need for corrective action has been read. This time span increases as the level of control rises in the hierarchy.

Collection of control data cannot be a haphazard operation. It must be done via a carefully designed system which speedily converts the raw data into meaningful control information. Such systems do, however, have to be based on the level of control and the timeliness of the feedback required. This, then, means that there will be a need for local control systems which provide feedback for control action and also provide input to the next level of control system. Only in this way will the overall control system be meaningful to management.

There should be only one source of data for the control system. Numerous examples could be cited where this simple rule is overlooked and where friction is caused.

Kenneth Gee, in his thesis *Specifying and Satisfying the Control Information Requirements of Middle Management* (1971, Manchester University), identified five reasons why the control information was not used:

1. Information came too long after the period to which it related for effective action to be taken on it.
2. The subjects covered in the information were outside the control of managers.
3. The control information provided was insufficiently detailed to help.
4. The information provided was thought to be inaccurate.
5. The information was not presented in a form that could be understood.

This is a considerable condemnation of the control systems in organizations in which the research was conducted.

2.4 INFORMATION HANDLING

It was stated earlier that information is the output of the data processing function, but simply producing schedules of facts or figures, no matter how comprehensive, is of little value until it can be used within the system. This means that the potential information has to be handled, to be moved from the generation point to the consumption point, i.e. it has to be distributed. In addition it has to be distributed in a form that can be understood, i.e. it has to be suitably packaged.

Unfortunately, information is like any other commodity: it deteriorates with repeated handling. It is also a perishable commodity. The value of information, especially control information, is largely dependent on time. The systems that are designed for distributing and packaging information are crucial to the success of the business. Such systems are generally described as management information systems, in that they feed information to management.

If the management process is described as a decision-making process, and if the decision points are linked by communication channels, then a framework exists for the development of effective information systems which provide information in the right form, at the right place, and at the right time. This can be achieved only if information is subjected to the minimum of handling. It is preferable for decisions to be made where the information is generated, which is one of the reasons for the recent developments towards distributed processing systems.

Information must flow through the system in such a way that it can be tapped where it is needed and additional information fed back into the system. The concept of continuous information flows is an important one.

2.5 INFORMATION FLOWS

The word 'flow' implies a smooth movement, a continous movement, which, when related to information, means a regular and consistent supply of the information

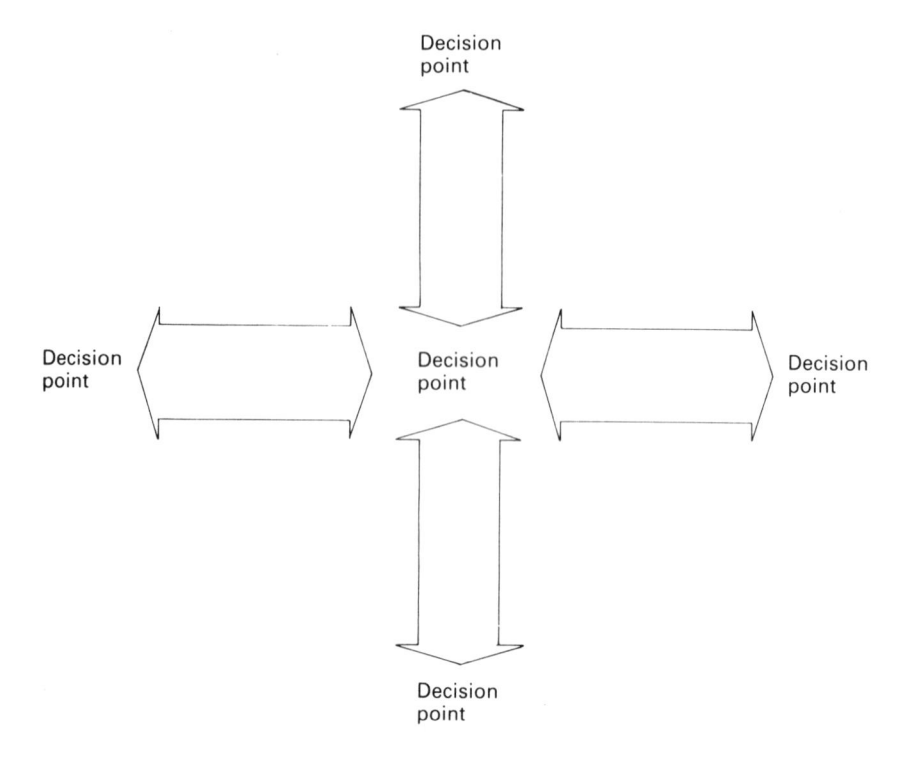

Figure 2.1 *Information flows*

needed for decision making. But information flows in several directions (see Figure 2.1) referred to as:

1. Horizontal.
2. Vertical.

Horizontal information flows are between activities and management at the same level. The vast majority of operational information flows horizontally.

Vertical information flows go both upwards and downwards, and consist almost entirely of planning and control information.

If the organization is looked at, as has been suggested, as decision points linked by communication channels along which information flows, then it is possible to get an idea of the complexity of information system design. If the organization had to rely entirely on the prescribed or formal system, then because of the complexity it would be a rather rigid system, not the kind of adaptive system which is needed.

Fortunately, there is also an informal system superimposed on the formal one. This system consists of managers using their eyes, ears and mouths to observe, listen and pass on information via *ad hoc* correspondence, telephone calls, discussions and meetings. The importance of the informal system should not be underestimated, nor should any attempt be made to remove it. The informal information system is a vital part of any human activity; it is the most adaptive and frequently the most effective way for information to flow.

Information — 17

An example of an effective informal control system was discovered in a quarry.

> As each tonne of material travels along the conveyor it passes over a belt weigher. The weight is recorded and registers in the manager's office on a meter. The meter has been adjusted to make an audible click for each tonne. The speed of the clicks, i.e. the rhythm, changes as production rises and falls. Changes in the rhythm cause a varying response from the manager, ranging from interest to annoyance if the sound should stop. He can act immediately if desirable. Because his men know that he can 'hear' what is happening they are always quick to diagnose and correct any problems.

The system was christened the 'rhythm control method'.

Formal systems consist almost entirely of operating, administration, accounting and management reporting, and depend mainly on the flow of paperwork through the organization. This is changing with the use of computer-based systems, but today and for many years to come, paper will be an important part of information systems.

These routine regular systems have specific objectives. For example, the sales invoicing system has the prime objective of obtaining payment from the customer, but with some additional work it is possible to obtain information on sales as a by-product of the sales invoicing system.

Often the attraction of by-product information is that it is produced without a great deal of additional effort. Unfortunately, the information generated as a by-product has to wait until the primary product of the system has been produced, and this can cause delays. An example of this occurred in a company producing readymixed concrete.

> Data on individual deliveries were written onto a delivery ticket which was used to collect the data for sales invoicing and sales analysis. The delivery ticket also carried data of use in the material control system. It was suggested that the same data collection system could be used for material control. A problem arose because the information was needed daily for material control, but only weekly for sales invoicing, and monthly for sales analysis. It was better in this case to make the data collection system for material control a primary one, rather than a by-product of an existing system.

The choice of whether to use formal or informal systems, primary or by-product flows, will depend on the needs of the systems concerned. Control systems are usually the most time critical, with operating systems coming next and planning last.

2.6 INFORMATION LOOPS

The correct timing of information, especially control information, is crucial. Yet, as was shown in the 'readymix' example, not all information is needed within the same time scale, not even for control.

In Chapter 1 the nature of control loops was discussed and it was mentioned that a

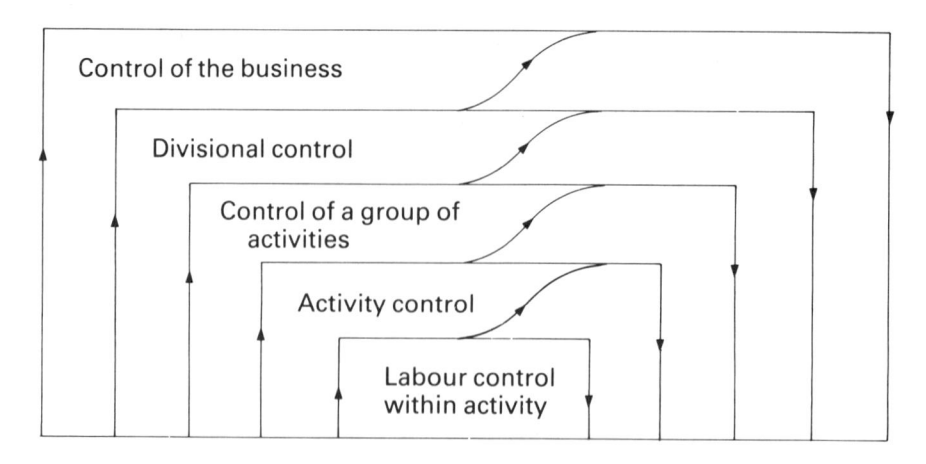

18 — *Management information systems and data processing*

Figure 2.2 *Nest of control loops*

principal feature of the loop was the monitoring and collection of control information. If the operation of control systems is examined, it will be seen that there are loops within loops, depending on what is being controlled. A typical structure (nest) of loops is depicted in Figure 2.2. This structure starts with control of labour within an activity, which is based on the work done within certain time limits. It is measured hourly or daily and acted on within the same time scale.

The next level is the activity or department within which labour is only one element. The information for control might be volume of output, measured daily or weekly. At the next level, a group of activities, the information is probably converted into financial terms and a contribution or profit calculated. This will probably be done monthly.

The fourth level, divisional, will be summarized financial data with ratios such as 'return on net assets' and cash flows. The fifth level in this structure is the company, where the figures will be even more summarized with even more abstract ratios, and will give only the year-to-date information.

For different levels there is both a different level of information and a different time scale. If this is examined further by isolating the simple element of labour the point will be clearer.

	Control
Level one	the amount of work done per hour
Level two	the total hours worked
Level three	the number of people allocated to each activity
Level four	the number of activities
Level five	the number of divisions

The decisions made are also quite different. Within the activity a key decision, over which there could be considerable debate, is how many 'Tocks' should be produced per hour.

At the divisional level the decision might be whether the company should continue to produce 'Tocks', and both decisions could be being considered at the same time at different levels.

It will be noticed in Figure 2.2 that information does not only flow round the loop but 'spins off' into, or is collected by, the next loop up, and so on. In addition, information, usually on changes in the plans or standards, is fed back from the loop above.

This form of information, especially the feedback principle, is important in assessing the results of decisions and in taking corrective action. The process is complex and the further management is from the activity the more difficult it becomes to relate to what is happening. This isolation can lead to poor decision-making unless the information system is good enough to cope.

2.7 SUMMARY AND REVISION NOTES

Information is defined as anything which diminishes the ignorance or uncertainty surrounding an impending decision.

The value of information is dependent on its usefulness in improving decision-making.

Information is the life-blood of an organization and falls into one of three categories: planning, operating and control.

Information is handled within the organization as it moves from the point where it is generated to the point where it can be used.

Information has to be packaged and distributed efficiently and has to flow smoothly, both horizontally and vertically, within the organization.

The systems which enable information to be communicated are both formal and informal. Within formal systems information is often collected for planning and control as a by-product of operating systems, although this is not necessarily the best way to do it.

Timing of information depends on the level of the activity and the decision being made. Information flows round the organization in a series of loops, each feeding information to the next level and in turn receiving feedback.

QUESTIONS

1. Typically information within an organization can be classified into three levels. Using a typical manufacturing company as background, define the three levels and give examples of the information which would be provided at each level. In what way does the destination level influence the presentation of the information? (ICMA)

2. The output of a management information system is, by definition, information. Define information and discuss ways in which a company might assess the value of information to be produced by a new management information system. (ICMA)

3. The managing director has asked you to design a system which gets information to him before he hears it on the grapevine. Prepare a statement on your view of his request.

4. Information flows in several directions. State what these are and comment on the type of information that flows in each direction.

5. 'I don't think much of all the fancy computer-based information systems. What really counts is a manager's experience.' Discuss.

CASE STUDY EXERCISE

The Managing Director complains regularly and bitterly about the control information which he does not receive. Every time something goes wrong, it is because the information was not available to prevent it from happening.

He has asked you to examine the present information that is available, to comment on it and to make suggestions for the kind of information you think should be made available.

Examples of the information available at present can be found under 'Product Information' in the case study at the end of the book.

3

Information Systems

3.1 DECISIONS AND INFORMATION

Whatever the level of decision-making, there is a need for information. Whether or not the interpretation of the information can be structured according to a set of rules, it is essential for the right information to be produced at the right time in the right place.

As the decisions become more complex and more far-reaching, the value of information increases rapidly.

Information is the raw material which the manager needs to make a decision. Without information the manager is unable to carry out his function in the organization.

The manager needs information to help him to select courses of action, i.e. to make decisions, to control the implementation of action, and to record the success or failure of the action taken. It is necessary, therefore, to define the decision-making areas of each manager's job in order to provide information which will be of help.

The relationship of information to decisions is a fundamental and vital consideration in the development of the right approach to the problem. The manager must receive information related to his job, his responsibilities and the decisions which he makes.

The link between decision and information is irrefutable. Decisions *can* be made without information; e.g. when the road forks a decision can be made to go right or left without any information on where the road leads. However, such blind decisions have completely unpredictable outcomes and are pure chance.

In the early days of trading it was largely a matter of chance whether a particular venture was successful or not. However, in modern business nothing should be left to chance, and this means gathering, collating and disseminating information to the points where decisions are made; in other words, it means having an efficient information system.

The relationship between decisions and information can clearly be seen. For example, if a manager is asked what his information needs are, he will find the question difficult to answer. When the question is changed to what information he needs to make a particular decision, he will find it much easier to provide a list of his needs.

A good information system is one which provides the information that managers need in order to make decisions. To design such a system it is obvious that the starting point is an analysis of management's information needs.

3.2 ESTABLISHING INFORMATION NEEDS

Some of the information the manager needs will be available and some will not. The information available will be obtained from both internal and external sources. Managers already have sources of information which they use for making decisions and any research on information needs must start from the present position and examine:

1. The information used at present.
2. The information needed but not available.
3. The information which cannot be obtained.

The first step can be made by examining the information produced at present and asking the following questions:

1. Why is this information produced?
2. Who receives it?
3. Why do they receive it?
4. What do they do with it when they receive it?
5. What decisions is it used for?

From this analysis it will be possible to obtain an indication of the relevance and usefulness of the existing information.

The second step, defining what is needed, is much more difficult and calls for a detailed survey which answers the following questions:

1. What decisions does the manager take?
2. What type of decisions are they? Are they:
   (a) Complex: made infrequently, unstructured, depending largely on current circumstances, unknown information requirement, i.e. cannot be predetermined.
   (b) Routine: made more frequently, but still structured with known data requirement, e.g. producing a production schedule.
   (c) Mechanical: made regularly, highly structured, with easy access to the data required, e.g. authorizing the weekly bonus payments.
3. What information is needed for each decision?

Such a survey can be carried out only by someone who understands the business and the way it is organized and controlled.

The third step, deciding what information cannot be obtained, may seem to be a negative approach, but it is important to know and understand the limits of the information system that is being designed. As Drucker says in his book, *The Practice of Management* (1955, London: Heinemann):

> The manager will never be able to get all the facts he should have. Most decisions have to be based on incomplete knowledge – either because the information is not available or it would cost too much in time and money to get it. To make a sound decision, it is not necessary to have all the facts – but it is necessary to know what information is lacking in order to judge how much of a risk the decision involves, as well as the degree of precision and rigidity that the proposed course of action can afford. For there is nothing more treacherous – or alas, more common – than the attempt to make precise decisions on the basis of coarse and incomplete information.

Perhaps it is not possible to meet all the manager's needs, but at least an attempt can be made to define what they are.

3.3 THE SYSTEM FRAMEWORK

The system framework is made up of a hierarchy of systems rather like a jigsaw (Chapter 1). Each sub-system relates to and links with the next system so that information flows smoothly through the organization. In theory it should be possible to analyse the sub-systems, the decision points and the information flows, and produce a totally integrated information system. The computer offered the processing power and the storage facilities to make it possible. Yet there are few, if any, totally integrated information systems.

The reason for the failure to build such systems is that organizations are not stable, predictable entities. They are changing constantly, in objectives, people and direction. They are influenced by the environment and have to adapt to survive. To cope with this constant movement, information systems must themselves be adaptable, both in form and content, changing to meet the demands placed upon them by management.

The systems framework is, then, the structure of systems indicating how each interacts with the others. Within each sub-system it is possible to produce formalized information flows for operating, planning and control. The system could be a sales system receiving customers' orders and processing them, making sure the goods are delivered and paid for, analysing sales for future planning and controlling prices to match demand to production capability and to costs. Such a system could be designed and could operate efficiently regardless of whether or not the production system was as efficient, though there would, of course, be some effects in production, lost orders, etc.

The independence of systems is both an advantage and a disadvantage. It is an advantage because the specific system objectives can be identified and a system

24 — *Management information systems and data processing*

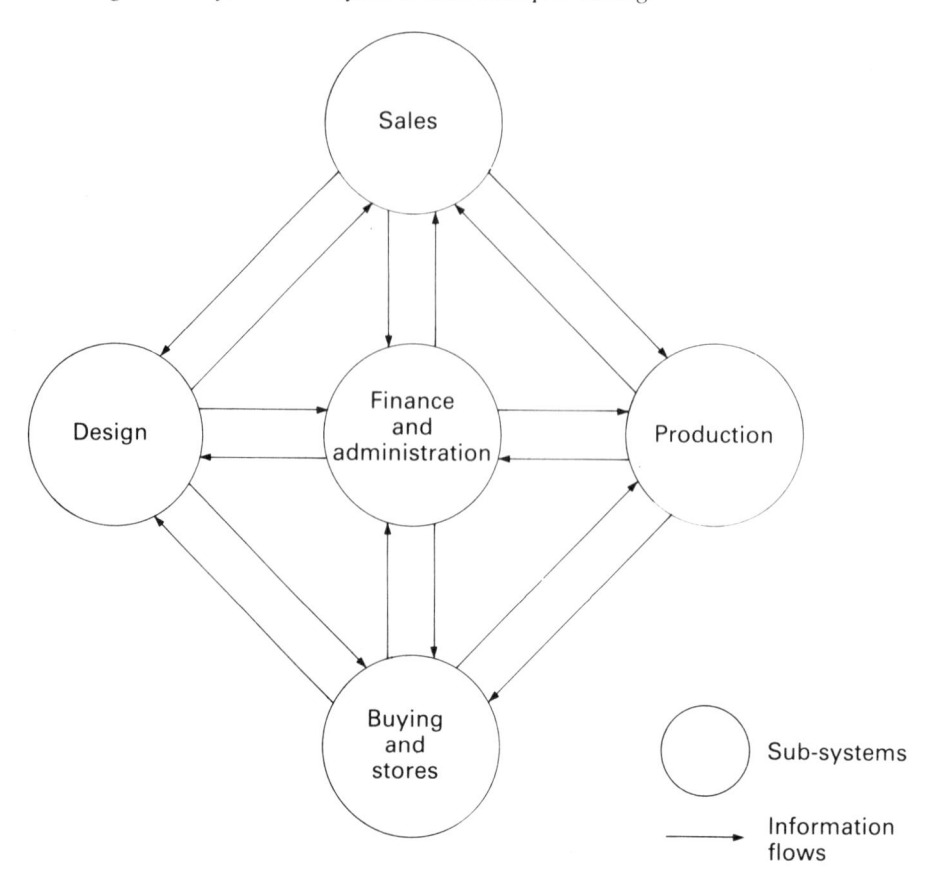

Figure 3.1 *Systems framework*

designed. It is a disadvantage because the system could become isolated and introverted, concerned only with its own performance and efficiency. This problem is frequently encountered in comments such as 'It's not production control you want to look at; it's sales and distribution that let us down.'

The systems framework ensures that the dependence of each sub-system on the others is recognized and built into the information flows. This is shown in Figure 3.1. The diagram is, of course, an over-simplification in both the number of such systems and the information flows, but it serves to indicate how the framework can be envisaged.

3.4 SYSTEM OBJECTIVES

Few systems, if any, work at the best possible level of performance, and this is particularly true of information systems. However, there is no reason to design systems to operate below their best. This happens because the systems designers trade off the finer points for convenience or expediency. When this occurs, managers tend to develop their own systems, or they use the informal channels of communication.

Failure of the system to perform effectively (known as sub-optimization) can occur in very simple ways, as the following example of material control in a building company shows:

A material schedule for the contract was prepared and the buyer placed orders with suppliers. Copies of the orders went to the site to inform the site manager what to expect, from whom and when. The site manager recorded receipts on a weekly record sheet which was sent to accounts. The accounts clerk received the purchase invoice and checked the receipts on the site record. The invoice was sent to accounts for payment. Nobody recorded or checked the quantities received against the original schedule. The only way to check total materials received was to laboriously go through all the site record sheets.

A solution to the above problem is not difficult to find, but because the system was designed to check receipts and prices, which it did, it missed the important element of quantity. It was operating below its best because it was designed to meet limited objectives.

It is possible to avoid such failure by examining each sub-system within the framework and deciding on:

1. The primary objectives.
2. The secondary objectives.

Table 3.1 *Purchasing system elements*

Element	Purchasing System Objective	Information
Requisitioning	1. To authorize buyer to place an order	1. What is required 2. By whom 3. When
Ordering	1. To authorize supplier to deliver goods 2. To inform requisitioner of action 3. To inform accounts	1. What is required 2. By whom 3. When 4. At what price
Goods received	1. To check receipts 2. To record receipts 3. To inform buyer 4. To inform accounts	1. What is received (Item, quantity) 2. When 3. By whom
Purchase accounts	1. To check and agree suppliers' invoices 2. To pay suppliers 3. To take as much credit as possible 4. To analyse purchases	1. Goods received (Item, quantity) 2. By whom 3. Where 4. What for 5. Price to pay
Material control	1. To see that only the materials necessary are bought and paid for	1. What is needed 2. What is bought

When this is done it is often necessary to subdivide the system into further elements. For example, a purchasing system might be a sub-system within the framework, but within the purchasing system there will be a number of distinct elements (see Table 3.1). There could be even more elements if stores control procedures were to be included as part of the purchasing system. It could be that purchasing is an element of the material control system, and this, of course, depends on individual organizations and terminology.

For the system to perform at its best it must meet all its objectives and generate the necessary information required in the operating, planning and control levels of the specific system.

It is not surprising, therefore, that many systems operate below their best, and this failure has to be attacked by good systems analysis and design, particularly with regard to accuracy and timeliness of the information that flows between the various sub-systems.

3.5 ACCURACY AND TIMELINESS

Accuracy and timeliness are both relative and subjective evaluations of information. If you were told that Bluebird would win the 3.30 race, the information would be timely only if you had the opportunity and time to place a bet; the information would be accurate if Bluebird won the race. It wouldn't be necessary to know whether he would win by a nose or by ten lengths.

The key is the ability to make use of the information to improve the result of the decision being made. Information systems must be designed to meet both the accuracy and the timeliness needs of the decisions. This means that when information needs are being established it is also important to ask two questions:

1. How accurate must the information be?
2. When is it required?

When managers say that information is inaccurate, they do not mean that it is wrongly calculated, but that it is unreliable. This is caused by three things:

1. Missing data, which means the resulting information is incomplete.
2. Wrong coded data, which means that the analysis is incorrect even if the totals are correct.
3. Badly formulated, e.g. producing average prices for product groups with widely differing price ranges; the information is mathematically correct but meaningless.

It can be seen, therefore, that the design of the information system is a crucial factor in ensuring that the data are complete, correctly coded and properly formulated. Management must be able to rely on the information they receive, and this is what is meant by accuracy. Mathematical accuracy is, of course, important, but information which adds up does not always make sense.

Even if information is reliable it still has to be received in time for action to be taken. This need for speed can conflict with the idea of accuracy just put forward. Making sure data are complete, correct and properly formulated takes time, and time can be of the essence. The answer lies in achieving a balance. The more accuracy the less timeliness and vice versa, though with modern computer technology it is possible to achieve high levels of accuracy very fast indeed. Sometimes, however, system designers create a false illusion of accuracy. This occurred in a stock control system.

> The system operated in a readymixed concrete company. The receipts of materials, sand, gravel and cement were carefully recorded and input to the computer. Deliveries of concrete were recorded and the theoretical usage of the various materials calculated by the computer. Waste was then calculated. The calculation was:
>
> $$\text{opening stock} + \text{receipts} - \text{closing stock} = \text{usage}$$
>
> This was compared with the theoretical usage figure and the wastage percentage was calculated to one decimal place.
>
> When a problem occurred a systems analyst visited the plant and discovered that the stock figures were guessed by such crude techniques as banging the cement silo with a spanner to see how empty it was, judged by the sound produced.
>
> The apparent accuracy of the computer records was quite illusory.

3.6 THE ADAPTIVE INFORMATION SYSTEM

To be effective the information system must be capable of adapting to change. If it cannot, then it will become a rigid system serving needs which no longer exist.

This problem is not new to management. Edward T. Elbourne recognized it in 1914, in his book *Factory Administration and Accounts*, when he wrote:

> It is quite possible for the Management to collect more information than it can use to advantage, or which is more costly, or hinders production more, than the information is worth. This is a real danger that has to be guarded against continuously, for routine that serves a valuable purpose when initiated may cease to be useful by some later change in conditions.

The information system should be flexible in respect of three areas which are all likely to demand changes;

1. The user will almost certainly want to change the format, content and possibly timing of the information he or she receives. This should be possible without any difficulties and should be a service that can be provided quickly and simply. Users will change and the new user's needs will almost certainly vary.
2. The organization will change via acquisitions, re-organizations, product changes, diversification, etc. The system must recognize this and be able to adapt within reason to cope with these changes.

28 — *Management information systems and data processing*

3. The environment will affect the system, particularly in respect of external factors. Recent examples are VAT changes, price controls, etc. The need to provide ways of catering for such factors should be accepted and even if the initial design is extended, this should be done. Many firms have been caught out on VAT rate changes, although this was a certainty and should have been catered for.

Flexibility is a key to efficient operation. Without flexibility, systems have to be amended and have additions grafted on in such a way that, when looked at as a whole, the system has become unwieldy, inefficient and wasteful of time and effort.

3.7 PRESENTATION OF INFORMATION

The form in which information is packaged is very important. It is not sufficient for the information to be accurate and timely: it must also be understandable. Imagine reading a newspaper that uses just a mass of printing, without columns or headlines. The words would still be there, but the process of understanding would be much more difficult.

A good example of this problem can be seen in the many computer-produced reports which contain masses of numerical information. The computer processes data using numerical codes for speed and convenience, but human beings prefer words to numbers. It is quite easy to convert material codes, site codes and payroll numbers to real names, and the appearance and usefulness of the reports improve accordingly.

Effective presentation is concerned with three vital things:

1. Layout.
2. Relevance.
3. Significance.

Layout is concerned with the appearance and receptivity of the form in which the information is presented. The human eye records what it sees with amazing precision, and passes the message to the brain, where it has to be unscrambled and interpreted. The simpler the layout the easier this process becomes, and as the objective is to communicate, it is sensible to help the process as much as possible. Though the eye records what it sees, the brain can be confused, as Figure 3.2 shows.

Relevance means making sure that only the information which is necessary is presented on the report and that all superfluous facts and figures are removed. Just because the other data are present during the processing sequence, this does not mean that they should be reproduced in the report. Yet often managers are expected to search through computer-produced haystacks of irrelevant data for the pertinent needle of fact.

Significance is, or should be, the keyword for the presentation of information. Deciding what is significant is not always easy. Should information be presented to the nearest £100, £1000 or £1 million? It depends of course on the scale of the informa-

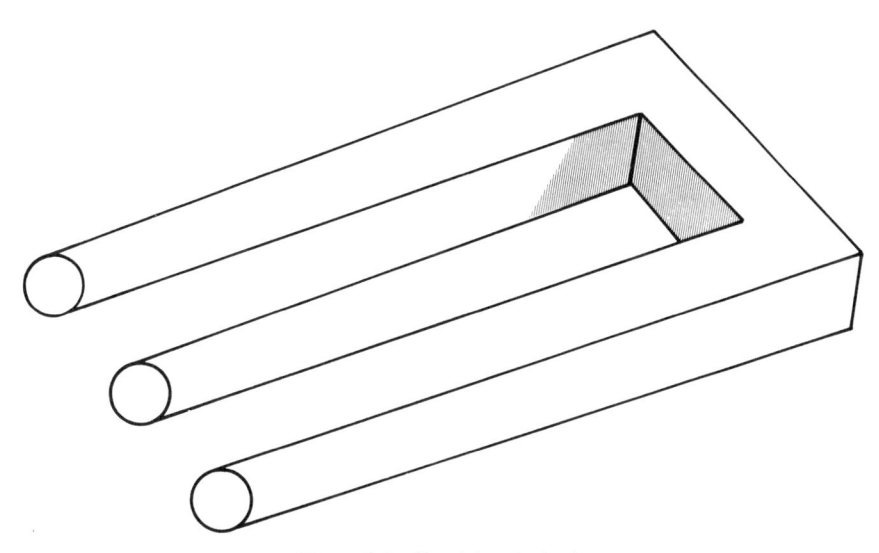

Figure 3.2 *Deceiving the brain*

tion, but careful attention to significance can considerably reduce the amount of data included on a report and the effort of the reader in deciphering the meaning.

The information system has not achieved its objective until the recipient has received and understood the message; it is only then that he is in a position to act.

3.8 SUMMARY AND REVISION NOTES

Information is vital to decision-making. Decisions can be made without information, but the outcome is only a matter of chance.

Management's information needs can be defined if the analysis of needs is related to decision-making.

When needs have been established, the methods of meeting them depend on the system framework and the way information flows between systems.

There is a danger of sub-optimization if the objectives of each sub-system are not carefully analysed and systems designed to achieve them.

Accuracy and timeliness of information are linked, and the critical balance has to be achieved for the information system to be effective.

The information system has to be adaptive to react to change. If it is not, then it becomes rigid and ceases to meet the needs of management.

The presentation of information is the final stage, which is critical to the ease with which the manager reads and comprehends the message.

QUESTIONS

1. One of the pitfalls a system designer must avoid is that of sub-optimality.
   (a) Define what is meant by sub-optimality and explain how it might be avoided.
   (b) Give a practical example of sub-optimality.
   (ICMA)

2. Why is information linked to decision-making and what are the key steps in identifying information needs?

3. Accuracy is fundamental to an effective information system. Explain what is meant by accuracy and indicate the factors which affect the levels of accuracy in the system.

4. What are the main factors in good presentation of information, and why is presentation so important?

5. Customers have been complaining that they are not receiving exactly what they order. The managing director has asked you to produce a report indicating what might be going wrong and how you might correct it.

CASE STUDY EXERCISE

Following your comments on the information available at present (Case Study Exercise in Chapter 2), you have been asked to carry out a survey to identify management's information needs.

Set out exactly how you would tackle such a survey, indicating the main questions you would need to ask and how you would analyse responses.

4

Information Systems Strategy

4.1 THE NEED FOR A STRATEGY

The need for a coherent systems strategy is both widespread and of growing importance. During the last twenty-five years organizations of all shapes and sizes have developed accountancy-based information systems. The management accountant has played a major role in providing effective information to management.

In the last five years the information technology developments have been so far-reaching that few people have been able to comprehend the enormous changes that will have to take place.

The technological developments have almost overnight changed the way that data can be collected, processed and disseminated as information. The problems that have plagued the management accountant in the past can now be overcome relatively easily. The three major problems are relevance, timeliness and accuracy.

These problems can be overcome because we can place the necessary elements of the technology close to where things happen and in the blinking of an eyelid, collect, process and feed back to the operative and manager the pertinent information they need for decision-making. That same data can then be collated, summarized and stored with enormous accuracy and passed to the next level of need. This continues with higher levels of concentration and aggregation until at the end of the same day the board of directors have a summary of the organization activities.

This scenario is not only theoretically feasible, it is technically possible at the present time. If organizations see a need for this form of integrated systems approach, and most advanced efficient organizations do, then a start must be made immediately to formulate a strategy for achieving it.

Such a strategy cannot start from a 'greenfield site'. It must start from the present existing situation, for whilst change takes place the organization must continue to function effectively.

The first important step is the carrying out of an information systems strategy survey. This is best done by a small dedicated team of people with a representative from each of the major areas of the business.

4.2 SYSTEMS STRATEGY SURVEY

The survey should follow a series of steps in a logical way as follows:

1. *Activity analysis.* Carry out an activity analysis seeking to establish the key business activities. This divides the business into logical strategic business units, each of which is attacking specific markets with clearly identified products. Within each of these units there is usually a number of key business activities which need to be defined.
2. *Decision analysis.* Examine the decision-making that takes place in each activity. Within each of the business activities analysed it is necessary to establish the decisions that are made. This is carried out by developing a dialogue with the managers concerned. (See *Making Information Systems Work*—Trevor J. Bentley, 1981, London: Macmillan.)
3. *Information needs analysis.* This step relates information needs to specific decisions and leads to the development of a complete set of information requirements related to individual business activities.
4. *Information levels.* The information requirements are categorized into the three primary levels of operational, planning and control and the appropriate frequency and timeliness of the information is assessed.
5. *Data flows.* In order for information to be created data have to be collected, processed, stored and disseminated. This step in the survey determines how the data flows have to be organized.
6. *Systems framework.* With all this information to hand it is possible to construct a systems framework, which has to be created to meet the information needs of the business.

From this survey it is then possible to determine how the systems framework can be constructed by:

(a) changing existing systems;
(b) developing new systems.

This approach goes into all areas of the business and treats the monthly accounting system as the information system for the financial planning and control activities of the business, rather than as at present, the information system for the whole business.

In the systems strategy of the year 2000, marketing, production, distribution, technical, research and design and finance will all have their own information systems. All these sub-systems will be linked by the overall systems framework to provide the corporate information system for top management.

The idea of spasmodic reporting on a monthly basis will be replaced by continuous monitoring with a series of review points. At these review points comparisons with plans will be made and adjustments made to the directional impetus from top management. Regular financial statements, valuing assets and performance, will be necessary to provide an overview of business success. These will probably be perfectly adequate on a quarterly basis.

Day-to-day information will signal potential problems well in advance of their becoming serious. This will demand a much more vigorous identification of control criteria at all levels of business activity. With the technology available this can now be done.

4.3 INFORMATION TECHNOLOGY DEVELOPMENTS

Three major developments taking place at the present time will make the idea of continuous monitoring a reality. These are:

(a) multi-connection networks;
(b) new memory chips;
(c) new processing chips.

The multi-connection networks will make it possible to plug any device into the system and to send and receive data, pictures and voice, to any other device. Each device plugged in will have a memory to hold information relevant to the particular user.

New memory chips are being built which will provide a capacity of thousands of millions of characters of information on the smallest desk-top device. These new memory chips will provide almost unlimited capacity to hold information.

New processing chips are being built which contain complete printed circuit boards. They promise to be more powerful, more reliable and considerably faster than conventional computers.

If we add to these three developments those of voice recognition and two-way visual communication, we can see that the future requires radical new ways of looking at the way we do things and the things we do.

4.4 ORGANIZING AND CONTROLLING INFORMATION SYSTEMS

Perhaps the question of organizing and controlling this important resource is the most difficult one to answer.

1. Can it be controlled centrally?
2. Will local systems development cause problems?
3. Who is the best person to manage the resource?
4. Who owns the data?
5. How can we protect it from misuse?

6. What is the size of the investment?
7. Where does the return come from?

All these questions and many more are being asked concerning the new information resources of the present and future. There is, of course, no one best answer. People take up positions in favour of one or other approach. They develop sensible-sounding arguments to support their views, but whatever they may think there is no one answer.

The answer undoubtedly lies in a combination of approaches properly balanced to meet local needs whilst maintaining the consistency of information flows through the organization. Each organization depending upon its philosophy, organization, management style, location, etc., will devise its own approach. The technology will enable this to happen without there being any overriding cost pressure in a particular direction. The overriding consideration will be the needs of the organization and the people who make the decisions at all levels.

It will, however, be desirable to have a nucleus of skilled information specialists who can advise management on the best way to meet their needs. Such a group should operate as a consultancy service with its leader represented on the board of directors, and responsible for the cost-effectiveness of the advice given.

The information systems (IS) director should not be responsible for the investment in the technology. This is the prerogative of local divisional activity managers. Nor should the IS director be responsible for the people collecting, processing and disseminating information. These should also report directly to the managers they service. His responsibility would be to see that the organization had a group of people who, through their knowledge of the business and the technology, could ensure that the system strategy of the organization changes to meet the changing needs of the environment in which it functions.

This is a vital role for the future and appropriate people should be trained to fill the role and to carry out the information systems strategy survey so necessary for success.

SUMMARY AND REVISION NOTES

Based upon a careful analysis of needs a systems strategy should be developed.
There are six steps to follow:

(a) activity analysis;
(b) decision analysis;
(c) information needs analysis;
(d) information levels;
(e) data flows;
(f) systems framework.

The rapid developments in IT make such a strategy vital.
Three major developments will have a big impact:

(a) multi-connection networks;

(b) new memory chips;
(c) new processing chips.

The organization and control of information systems is becoming a serious consideration for senior management and should be a key element in the strategy.

QUESTIONS

1. Explain why a company needs to develop an information systems strategy.
2. How would the information systems strategy relate to the identification of management's information needs?
3. What are the implications for an organization which does not have an information systems strategy?
4. Describe the way you would approach the development of an information systems strategy for a medium-sized retailing company.

CASE STUDY EXERCISE

In the previous exercise you were asked to identify management's information needs. Now you are required to convert this into an information systems strategy, highlighting the key systems areas for the commercial success of Reward Chemicals Ltd.

5

Systems Design

5.1 PRINCIPLES OF SYSTEMS DESIGN

Systems design is the generic term applied to all those activities which go together to produce the system which meets its objectives. The starting point of systems design is therefore the definition of the objectives of the system being designed.

We have already seen that systems have primary and secondary objectives and that these can differ according to individual managers' viewpoints; e.g. from the accountant's viewpoint the sales accounting system has the primary objective of collecting cash from customers, while from the salesman's view the objective might be the calculation of his commission.

In establishing objectives these different viewpoints must be considered and the perfect system is one which achieves all its objectives in the eyes of all the people concerned with the system. This is very difficult to achieve.

When defining the objectives of the system it is essential to establish what everybody expects from the system. This might include customers and/or suppliers. When designing a purchasing system it is important to establish what the supplier needs from the system.

One example of good design stemming from this careful analysis of needs is described below.

> The system was a sales system in a quarrying company. One of the primary objectives was to present information to customers so that they would pay quickly. This meant producing sales invoices as soon as possible after the delivery of the materials. The system designer visited a number of large customers to ask if payments would improve if they received invoices more quickly, and the answer was not encouraging. While visiting one customer the designer asked what the customer wanted on the invoice. He discovered that the invoice would be passed more quickly if it showed deliveries of each type of material in

chronological order for each site, with a daily total. The reason for this was quite simple: the customer recorded receipts at the site on separate documents for each type of material ordered. These documents were totalled daily and sent to the office to be checked with invoices. If the invoices were produced in the same sequence as the receipt documents, they would be agreed much more easily and hence faster. The designer visited several more customers and discovered that they had very similar systems. The invoice was produced in this way and the speed of payments improved by an average of six days.

In this example the customer's purchasing system affected to a significant degree the supplier's sales system, and though the designer was concerned primarily with the sales system, he had to examine the supplier's purchasing system to identify an objective of the sales system. This objective fits into the general objective of providing information not only when and where it is needed, but in the right form for it to be used.

Systems design is therefore concerned with defining objectives and finding ways of meeting these objectives. There are five guiding principles for good systems design:

1. Flexibility.
2. Reliability.
3. Economy.
4. Simplicity.
5. Helpfulness.

Flexibility is important if the system is to be adaptive in order to meet changing circumstances and changing demands. Ways of ensuring flexibility are dealt with later in more detail.

Reliability has already been mentioned (Chapter 3) in terms of timeliness and accuracy. The system must also be robust and stand up to misuse, both deliberate and accidental (Chapter 17).

Economy is always important. It is linked to simplicity because simple systems are always economic. It is interesting that, where money has been plentiful, complex and artistically beautiful systems have been built which are rarely flexible, often unreliable and consequently not very helpful.

Simplicity is the key to success. There is a saying that the best ideas are always the simple ones, and this is very true of systems.

Helpfulness is not just the achievement of the objectives, but also the usefulness of the system to those who have to work with it.

In a garage the mechanic complained bitterly about completing a 'record of work done'. It was no use to him and meant extra work. It didn't matter to the mechanic that it was useful to someone else. He said, 'If it's useful to them, let them do it'. The problem was overcome by combining the 'record of work done' with the mechanic's time-sheet, which was useful to him, as it was used to calculate his wages.

When a system is being designed these principles have to be kept in mind throughout the project, from the definition of objectives to the evaluation of the working system.

5.2 PROJECT LIFE CYCLE

A systems design project starts with the definition of the objectives and continues until the system is operational. It is important to consider the elements of the project as a life cycle which covers a varying period of time depending on the system and the circumstances.

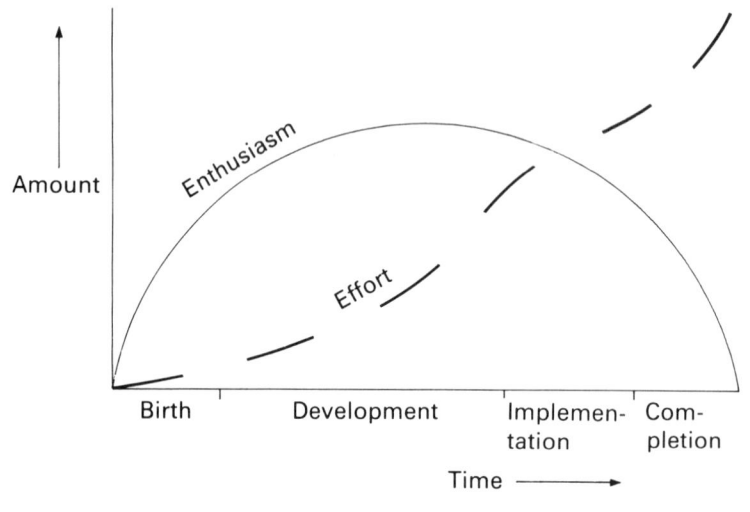

Figure 5.1

The phases of this life cycle are depicted in Figure 5.1. This shows two important factors during the project life cycle: enthusiasm and effort. When the project starts, enthusiasm is high and effort low; as the project continues through the development stage, enthusiasm increases until a point is reached near the end of the development phase when the design has to be made to work. Effort increases slowly but then jumps towards the end of the development, just at the point where enthusiasm is beginning to fade. Effort is further increased to get the system working, until at the completion of the project, effort is at its highest and enthusiasm just about exhausted.

Understanding this life cycle is crucial to project management and to the way systems design projects are subdivided into separate elements over time periods of less than one year, so that enthusiasm can be maintained and effort more easily balanced.

5.3 THE STAGES OF SYSTEMS DESIGN

System design should be carried out in a number of stages which enable the designer to constantly check that the principles are being followed and that the objectives are being achieved. This is a process of iteration, constantly returning and reviewing what is being done, and making changes in the design to ensure that the objectives are achieved.

The stages of systems design are shown in Figure 5.2, which indicates the way management are involved in the process of approving each stage of the design. There are 12 stages in the overall system design process, and these are discussed below.

The Initial Review

This is the problem definition phase and involves an examination of the new system concerned, with the aim of establishing its objectives.

Systems Proposal

This is the outcome of the initial review and should contain:

1. The objectives of the system.
2. The approach to a solution.
3. The benefits.
4. The project team.
5. The time scale.

If the systems proposal is agreed, then we proceed to the third stage. If not, we return to a re-examination of the problem.

Detailed Survey and Preliminary Design

The system is analysed in detail, bearing in mind the five principles of good design.

Design Report

The design report is the outcome of the third stage and should contain:

1. Reiteration of objectives.
2. Reiteration of benefits.
3. Basis of the system (description and flowchart).
4. Output (reports, layout, frequency).
5. Input (types and volumes).
6. Operation of the system.
7. Implementation proposals.

The design report goes for approval. If it is approved we proceed. If not, we return to re-examine the preliminary design.

Detailed Design

The detailed design phase includes the preparation of the full specification, including detailed form design, file design and detailed operating procedures. The outcome is the systems specification.

Systems Specification

This sets out precisely how the system is to be built. It is the blueprint for the construction team, and should contain:

1. General description of the system.
2. Detailed input forms.
3. Systems flowcharts.
4. Controls.
5. Output details.
6. File specification.
7. Program overview.
8. Appendices containing additional material such as code lists.

Construction

When the systems specification is approved the actual construction of the system can take place, and this involves all the work necessary to produce an operational system, including programming and, of course, testing.

Test Report

The outcome of the construction phase is the test report, which sets out the tests that have been carried out, with examples, and includes a statement of 'readiness' of all concerned. When approved the system moves to Stage 9.

Implementation

The implementation phase includes the installation of equipment, printing of documents, training of personnel, generation of files, transfer of data and everything necessary to get the system into an operational state.

Operational

Once the system has been implemented and monitored for a period of time it is considered operational and the responsibility is handed over to the users.

Systems design — 41

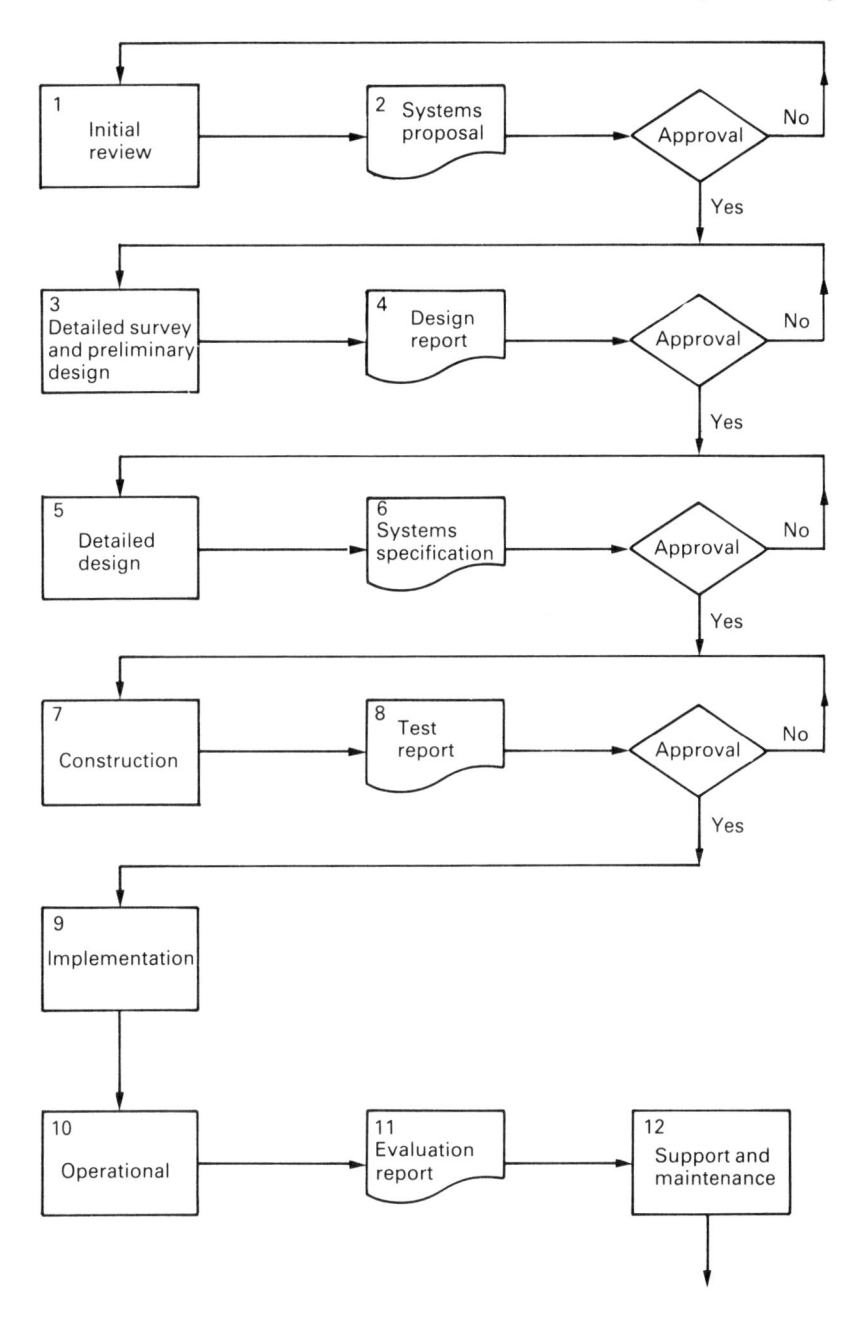

Figure 5.2 *System design stages*

The Evaluation Report

To complete the system design an evaluation report is prepared, indicating whether the system is meeting the objectives as set out in the systems proposal and the design report. If not, then the reasons are established and the system changed.

Support and Maintenance

If the system is to be adaptive then it must be changed as necessary, and this is handled in the continuing phases of support and maintenance.

Documentation is required at every stage of the systems design process. Systems documentation is not a stage on its own, though it is often handled this way. It should be an inherent part of the systems design process. (See section 15.5 for documentation standards.) The 12 stages of systems design are all important and should be carried out as individual steps with the clear involvement of the users as well as the approval points shown in Figure 5.2. This process requires good management and control.

5.4 PROJECT MANAGEMENT AND CONTROL

The successful completion of a systems design project depends largely on the way it is managed and controlled. Subdividing the project into the 12 phases indicated is important, but in addition specific performance targets have to be set and carefully monitored.

The design process is a creative one and the management and control of creative effort is always difficult. The answer lies in three key activities:

1. Planning.
2. Resource scheduling.
3. Control.

Planning involves deciding what will be done, when it will be done and how long it will take. This provides the basic information required for deciding the resources needed.

Resource allocation usually means allocating work to people and this means deciding not only who has the time, but also who is best suited to the work to be done.

Control is exercised by measuring individual performance with the plan and establishing clear reasons for variations.

When a project stretches ahead for several months it is tempting for the people involved to take it easy in the early stages, believing that they will have scope to make up time later. Of course this never happens and time lost at the beginning of a project is rarely, if ever, made up. The manager in charge of the project must keep the pressure on from the start, and experience shows that one of the phases which should be monitored most closely is the systems analysis phase.

5.5 SYSTEMS ANALYSIS

Analysis is defined as 'the resolution of anything complex into its simple elements' (OED). It is hoped that the system design is not complex, but even a simple system needs to be broken down into specific elements which can be programmed.

The OED defines systems analysis as:

> The technique of analysing an activity, process, organization, etc., in order to determine how a computer may be employed to achieve the desired end more efficiently or conveniently.

System analysis is often taken to mean the total design process, which it is not. Systems analysis is concerned with taking the design report and producing the systems specification, then guiding the construction stage. The term is generally used in relation to computer-based systems although the process is also required for non-computer systems.

The systems analyst takes the design and the primary and secondary objectives and decides how this can best be achieved, using the people and equipment available. It is rare for the analysis to be carried out without the people and equipment constraints.

The analyst's starting point is the desired result of the system. From this point he or she has to work out the best way for that result to be achieved, including the data content of files, the way the data are processed, the data that have to be input, the controls, the checks and the operating procedures.

In doing this the analyst has to check constantly to ensure that he or she is keeping the objectives of the system clearly in mind. It is easy when working very close to a detailed analysis to forget what the desired result is. There is a well known piece of graffiti which appears in most systems design departments. It reads:

> The objective of all staff should be to analyse thoroughly all situations, anticipate all problems prior to their occurrence, have answers for these problems, and move swiftly to solve these problems when called upon...
> However –
> when you are up to your arse in alligators, it is difficult to remember that your initial objective was to drain the swamp.

One of the ways that the analyst can ensure that the objectives are kept in mind is to write them in large letters on a card hung on the wall where he or she can see it clearly.

5.6 FLOWCHARTING

The reasons for using charts are:

1. They force consideration of the procedure in a logical, step-by-step sequence.
2. They clearly indicate missing steps.

44 — Management information systems and data processing

3. They indicate deficiencies and duplication in the system.
4. They eliminate the variable interpretation which can be placed on narrative procedures.
5. They clearly show the path the procedures follow, on one piece of paper.

Flowcharting techniques and styles vary, though the approach used for systems and programming flowcharts indicated here is fairly common. In addition to these two techniques there are a number of other types of flowcharts, which are explained in the author's book, *Information, Communication and the Paperwork Explosion*.

Systems Flowcharts

Systems flowcharts are used to provide the systems designer with a means of constructing a logical and systematic approach to the problem with which he or she is dealing. They are usually drawn at two levels of detail:

1. Overview (Figure 5.3);
2. Detailed systems flowchart (Figure 5.4).

The overview seeks to show the broad picture of the whole system or a major section. It is an over-simplified flowchart and is used mainly for presentation to management and for basic systems structuring. This is the type of flowchart that appears in the design report. The symbols used below are now recognized as the standard in accordance with the British Standards Institute BS 4058:1973.

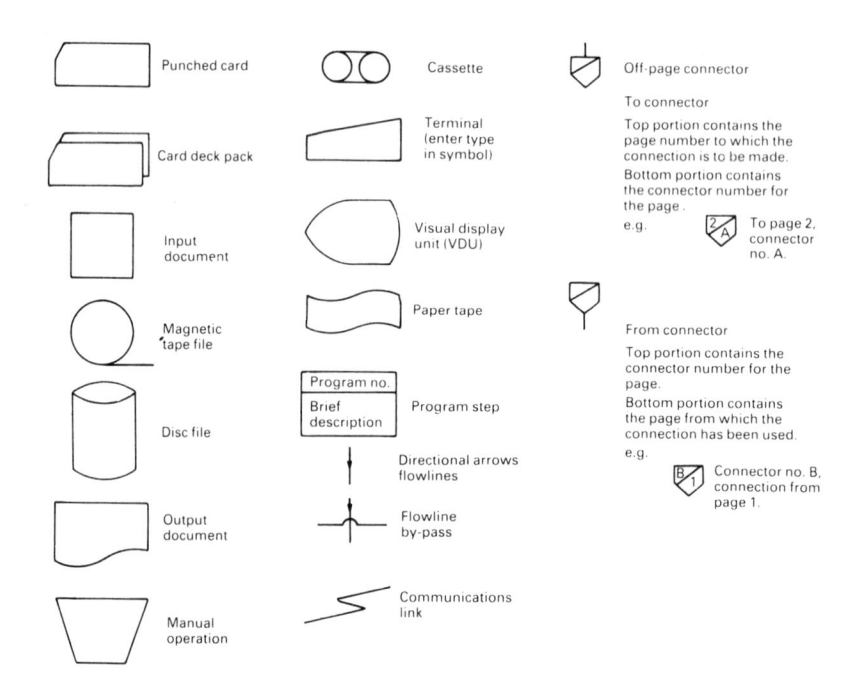

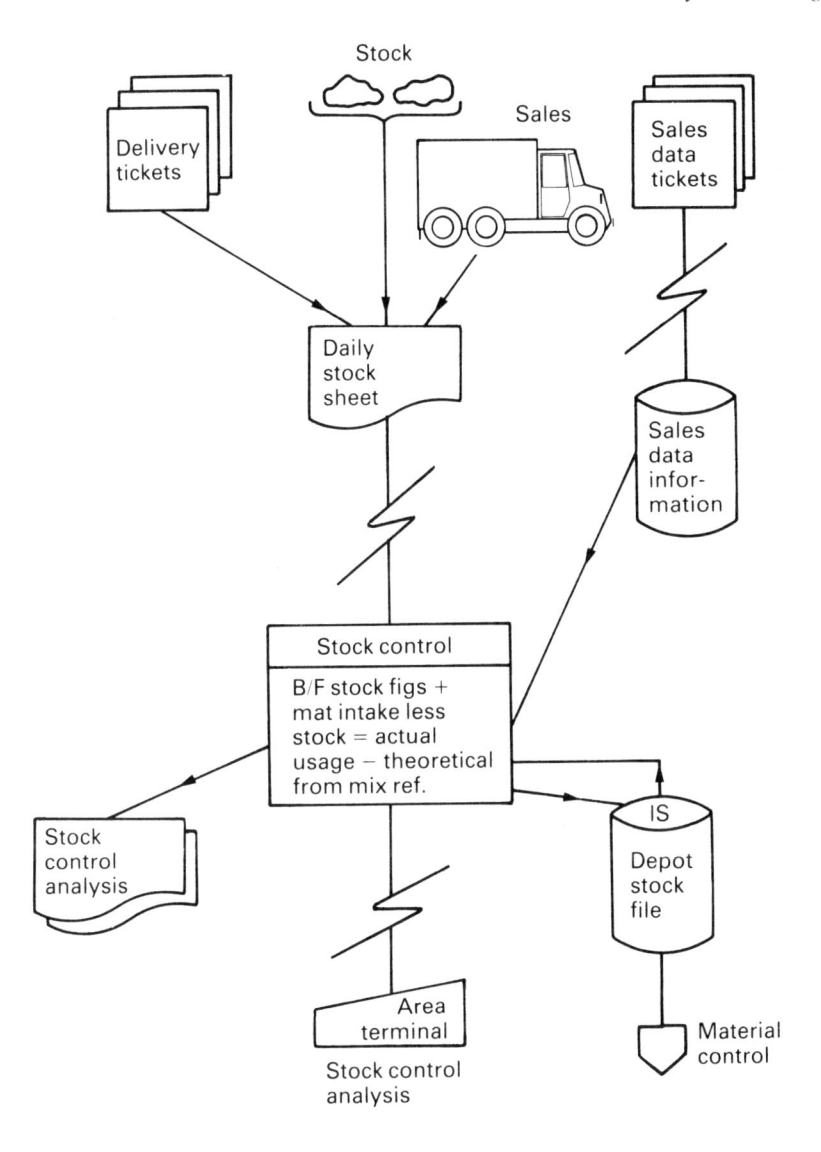

Figure 5.3 *Overview flowchart*

In Figure 5.3 note the analyst's use of pictorial work to make the flowchart more representative. This form of flair and creativity is welcomed in most systems design departments.

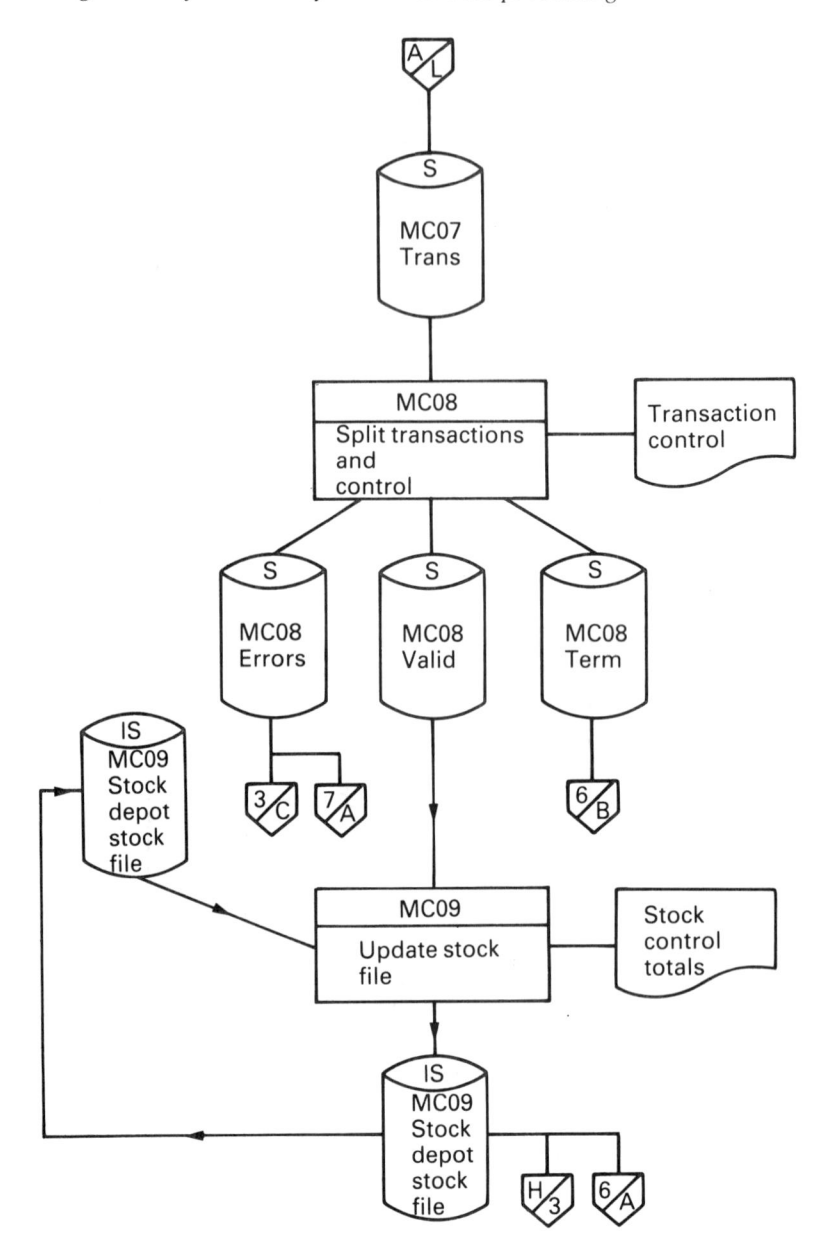

46 — *Management information systems and data processing*

Figure 5.4 *Detailed systems flowchart*

The more detailed system flowchart, Figure 5.4, shows only one part of the overall system and indicates each step of the procedure, together with the actual file names. Links with other systems are indicated by the use of 'off-page' connectors.

In both these examples the charts have been drawn vertically, with the flow from top to bottom. It is also possible and quite common to draw charts with a horizontal flow, moving from left to right. In the case of horizontal charts the 'off-page' connections are drawn in the more appropriate position, i.e.

Programming Flowcharts

Program flowcharts (see Figure 5.5) are yet a further step of detail, taking each particular program step indicated on the system flowchart by one symbol and showing exactly how the program works. Two additional symbols are used:

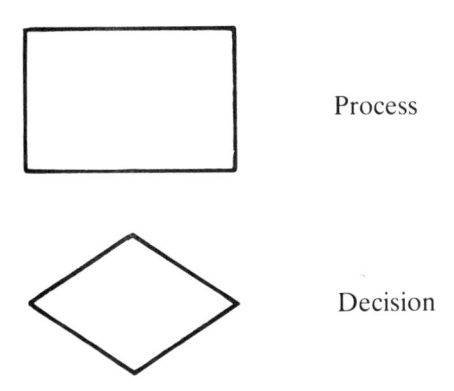

Process

Decision

A program is an element of the system chosen because of the ability to take a defined input and process it to achieve a given result, specified in the systems specification. The program should, therefore, have no loose ends. Data should enter and leave the program in a known and controlled way. This is clearly shown on the flowchart.

Flowcharts are an invaluable aid to good systems analysis and programming. People who attempt to write programs without first having drawn the flowcharts risk making many errors, which are normally solved only by additional programming, leading to long, inefficient programs.

The use of flowcharts and the approach of the analyst will depend to a large extent on whether the system designer has decided to design a batch processing system or an interactive system.

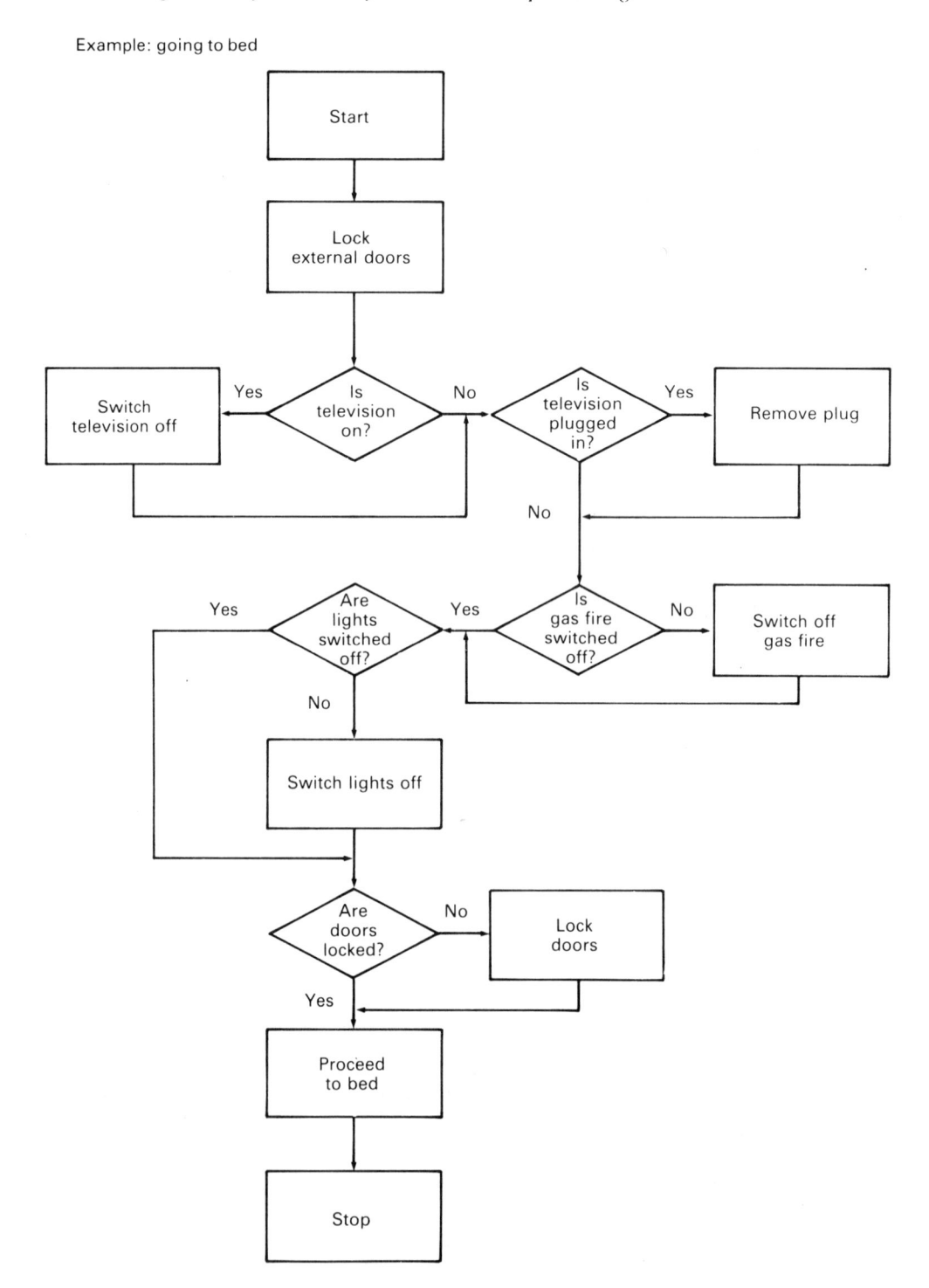

48 — *Management information systems and data processing*

Example: going to bed

Figure 5.5 *Program flowchart*

5.7 BATCH AND INTERACTIVE PROCESSING

There are basically two ways that data can be processed by the computer: (a) in batches; or (b) in individual transactions. Batch processing is a straightforward approach which copies the manual systems replaced by the machine. Processing data in batches means that the programs and files required to handle and store the data are used once for each batch. The batch is recognized by a label at the front which tells the computer what it is and how to deal with it.

Files are updated and controls changed once for each batch. If a number of batches of the same data are processed together this is run as a job on the computer. Batch processing is similar to the way accounting machines are used. One of the problems of this approach is that the files being used are not available to anyone else. Another problem is that if certain transactions miss a run they have to wait for the next. Some systems require data to be processed continuously; this approach is generally referred to as transaction processing.

The difference between batch processing and transaction or interactive processing can be likened to the difference between a lift and an escalator. The lift carries groups of people together in stages, i.e. batches, whereas the escalator is a continuous system dealing with each person as he or she arrives.

In transaction processing there are a number of points the computer requires programs to decide:

1. What is this transaction?
2. Can I accept it?
3. What do I have to do with it? This will include such questions as:
   (a) What files do I need?
   (b) What programs must I use to do the processing?
   (c) In what order should I do it?
   (d) What controls do I have to bring in?
4. How do I do these tasks? (The programmers tell it this.)
5. What parts of the machine do I need? (Job control programs.)

This procedure must be followed for every single transaction. In batch processing the questions can be asked for the whole batch of data, but for transaction processing (needed for most modern data base systems using visual display units) the questions must be asked for every record.

The system designer must take great care in deciding which approach to follow. Batch processing is a very practical, economic and simple way to process data. With developments of much cheaper memories and more powerful computers, interactive processing systems have become more attractive, if not more glamorous, but sometimes there is just no need to use this more complicated approach.

No accountant worth the name would give an accounts clerk a set of documents including purchase invoices, sales invoices, requisitions, orders, cheques, remittances, statements, etc., and expect the clerk to go through them one by one entering them into the system, using different records, and changing the controls every time; and then expect to balance his books. But this is exactly what transaction processing means. Extend this to, say, 50 clerks all trying to get at the procedures, files and machines at the same time and it would be chaos.

To make it possible for several users to access the computer for different systems, it is necessary to have a machine powerful enough and with enough storage capacity to allow program and file sharing. Designing interactive systems is also more complicated and it is more difficult to get them to work satisfactorily.

Some years ago, after completing a long and hazardous rock climb in the Lake District, the climbers overheard a small boy ask his father, 'Daddy, why did those men come up that way?'. His father gave them an embarrassed smile and said, 'I think it's because they find it more exciting than doing it the easy way.'

There are some systems where there are large benefits to be obtained from the speed of processing available using interactive methods. These are usually designed as a single system with a limited number of transactions, equipment which is not used for any other system, and a clearly defined set of operating rules. Airline reservations and holiday bookings systems fall into this category.

There are many more systems, though, which simply do not need interactive processing. In these systems data are input in batches, files are updated in batches and regular reports produced. The updated files are then available by using direct access methods.

The advantages and disadvantages of the various methods of approaching systems design are dealt with in the next chapter.

5.8 SUMMARY AND REVISION NOTES

Systems design is the overall term used to describe all the separate activities from the definition of system objectives through to successful implementation. Good systems design produces a system which is flexible, reliable, economic, simple and helpful.

Every systems project follows a life cycle in four main stages: birth, development, implementation and completion. During the life of the project enthusiasm rises, then falls, and effort is concentrated towards the end of the project. There are 12 stages in systems design:

1. Initial review.
2. Systems proposal.
3. Detailed survey and preliminary design.
4. Design report.
5. Detailed design.
6. Systems specification.
7. Construction.
8. Test report.
9. Implementation.
10. Operation.
11. Evaluation report.
12. Support and maintenance.

The management and control of systems projects depend on management skill and the operation of three key activities:

1. Planning.
2. Resource scheduling.
3. Control.

Systems analysis is the central element of systems design and is concerned with breaking down the designer's solution into the specific elements for the construction of the system. The main output of the systems analyst is the systems specification.

Flowcharts are a vital part of the designer's and analyst's tool kit. They ensure that logic is followed, indicate missing steps and duplication, and simplify the description of the system.

Batch and interactive processing are two different approaches to processing data. Batch processing deals with data in batches, running each batch through the system. Interactive processing deals with each transaction separately, regardless of the system to which the transaction relates.

QUESTIONS

1. 'Systems design is a creative activity; you cannot control it in the same way as you would a production department. The designer must be given free rein unfettered by constraints.' Discuss.
2. You have just been to a meeting with the data processing manager, who has been very critical of the system you have designed, with particular emphasis on the ease of operation on the computer. He does not deny that the objectives are achieved and the user satisfied, but he thinks it is at too high an operational cost. In the place of a systems analyst, what would you do?
3. Explain how a flowchart should be used by a systems analyst, indicating the main benefits he or she will obtain from using it. (IMS)
4. Construct a flowchart to represent the following situation. A department store is to have its weekly sales represented in the following way:

    (a) Total value of sales on account.
    (b) Average value of cash sales.
    (c) Value of largest cheque accepted.

    1 = cash, 2 = cheque, 3 = account. The following checks are to be reported:

    (a) Items not coded 1, 2 or 3.
    (b) Credits.
    (c) Individual sales exceeding £10 000.
    (IMS)

5. A computer salesman has visited your managing director and has suggested that your present batch processing systems are out of date and that you should use interactive processing. Your managing director has asked you for your comments.

CASE STUDY EXERCISE

The managing director has decided to go ahead with the development of a management information system and he has asked you to write a report setting out what is involved, the stages of the project, the project time scale and the skills needed by the project team – in other words, to produce a systems proposal.

6
Systems Selection

6.1 THE RIGHT APPROACH

The design report provides an excellent basis for deciding on the best approach to the achievement of the system objectives. It is important that the objectives are defined and agreed before the system designer proceeds to examine how he or she will achieve them.

There is a wide variety of ways in which systems can be developed. For clarity it is useful to examine systems selection in two distinct sections:

1. Hardware.
2. Software.

Hardware

The provision of computer facilities can be done in four ways:

1. Purchase.
2. Bureaux.
3. Turn-key.
4. Facilities management.

Purchase. Purchasing a computer and running it 'in house' calls for considerable knowledge and expertise. This is true for small as well as for large computers; however, the staffing levels to manage a large computer system are much higher. When making a decision to buy, the purchaser is faced with a number of problems, including:

1. What size and type to buy.

2. Who to buy it from.
3. The contractual arrangements.
4. Service and maintenance.

The size and type to buy will depend on the definition of systems objectives. Who to buy it from depends on reputation, suitability and price. When the machine is bought it may be rented or leased, but this is only a way of financing the deal.

The contractual arrangements are rather special (see Section 6.3).

Service and maintenance are crucial, and efforts must be made to obtain guarantees.

The cost of buying a computer is not simply the purchase price, but also includes staff costs for managing it, maintenance, etc., and all these costs should be carefully evaluated (see Section 6.7).

Bureaux. A computer bureau is a company that offers a service to companies who do not own their own computer. They normally offer general facilities such as payroll, purchase ledger and sales ledger, or more specialist services such as systems modelling. The bureau charges according to the amount of work they do for their clients, with a minimum charge for every job.

They will take information in its raw form from documents or from computer input media such as punched cards and magnetic tape produced by the client. The output can take many forms, including printed documents and reports, magnetic tapes and microfilm.

Bureaux are successful for two main reasons:

1. They provide a local service to small and medium-sized companies who do not want to face the cost of selecting, installing and running their own computer.
2. They provide a specialist service based on some particular system they have developed which can be used by many clients who would not want to incur the high systems-development costs involved.

With the advent of modern communications it is possible for clients to use computers many kilometres away – even at the other side of the world. This is done using a terminal and the telephone system, and is a special kind of bureau service known as 'time sharing'. These computers are very large and have very sophisticated systems available for clients. When clients join the bureau they are given a special code which the computer uses to recognize them and to calculate the charges, which are based on the time the clients use.

Time sharing is a growing form of computer use, as it is relatively inexpensive and puts the power of very large computers within reach of even the smallest companies.

It has always been felt that the advent of small, cheap mini-computers would threaten the existence of the computer bureaux, but this is not happening. Their charges are reasonable and in most cases their service is excellent, in addition to which the client does not have to worry about breakdowns or other problems.

Many large companies who have their own computers use bureaux as well, particularly for services such as payroll.

As the client puts more and more work on the bureau, the cost grows, as well as a certain amount of inconvenience through not being able to change systems easily to meet the company's needs. When this happens companies start to think of acquiring their own computer, and one way they can do this is to go to a turn-key company.

Turn-key companies. A turn-key company offers a comprehensive service, from examining the client's computer needs through to the installation of a working system. This involves the following:

1. Review business problem and specify requirements.
2. Select the hardware.
3. Select the software (often written by the turn-key company).
4. Installation of the hardware and software.
5. Systems testing.
6. Operational hand-over.

This is an expensive way to obtain a computer but it has the distinct advantage that the client can be sure that the computer selected will be put to work effectively before it is accepted and paid for.

The service the turn-key company offers is partly consultancy, partly technical and partly the role normally played by the computer supplier. For a company that has no knowledge of computing the service offered is very attractive. There is, however, the disadvantage that turn-key companies are normally linked in some way to a computer manufacturer. This is perfectly understandable, as it seems unreasonable for such a company to employ analysts and programmers capable of working in any language or on any machine. Apart from this limited disadvantage, turn-key companies offer an important service, especially to first-time users.

As client companies grow they can develop their own computer systems. In fact many turn-key companies actually recommend this and assist in the recruitment and training of the personnel. If clients do not want the problems associated with managing their own computer they can obtain such a service from specialist companies.

Facilities management. Facilities management is a form of consultancy which offers a company a unique service which is provided in one of two ways:

1. The client owns its own computer and employs the staff on its payroll, while the facilities company provides the manager and supervisory staff.
2. The client owns the computer, but all the staff work for the facilities company.

With either approach the client is relying on the professional expertise of the facilities company, for which he is paying. If the facilities company fails to meet its obligations, then they would be liable by law for substantial damages, so the client is protected. On the other hand, it is a difficult decision to place the management of a crucial asset, on which the company may be dependent, in the hands of an 'outside' organization.

Software

Software is becoming a very expensive element of the computer system. As hardware costs are falling relative to the power and storage capacity, software costs are rising.

Deciding on the best approach is very difficult. There are many alternatives to any problem. There are, however, three ways in which the systems can be produced:

1. By developing a systems department within the company (in house).
2. By obtaining the services of a specialist company known as a software house.
3. By using standard programs (called packages) offered by the computer manufacturer or software houses.

The formation of an in-house systems development team has the distinct advantages of dealing specifically with the company's needs and reacting quickly to changing requirements, though these advantages are affected to some extent by the need to recruit and train the necessary staff. However, once this has been done the service, if managed properly, is usually excellent (see Section 6.4).

For the small company buying a computer for the first time it may not be economical to set up an in-house team, in which case the company can ask a software house to design and program the systems required. Software houses offer an excellent service but they have the distinct disadvantage of not knowing the company or fully understanding its needs. This can lead to inappropriate systems. The response to requests for changes is not always as quick as it should be, and software houses prefer to design and implement systems rather than maintain them. There is also the problem, as with facilities management, of being in the hands of an outside organization (Section 6.4).

A common and growing alternative to having systems specifically designed is to use standard packages. The main advantage of this approach is that they can be guaranteed to work. A second advantage is that they are relatively inexpensive. There is, however, one major disadvantage, and that is that they may not meet the company's needs, so the company will have to bend its requirements to fit the package. In some cases this may eliminate the advantage of using a computer. There are several areas where packages are extremely effective, and payroll is one such area. It is very rare indeed to find any company, large or small, actually designing and programming a payroll system. Standard accounting packages are also quite effective, but again the company must fit itself to the system, which can limit the value of the output (Section 6.5).

The software referred to here is generally called application software. The other form of software is operating software, usually provided with the machine (Chapter 10).

6.2 DEALING WITH MANUFACTURERS AND SUPPLIERS

One of the major problems encountered by organizations making the selection decision is the level of computer knowledge in the organization. The manufacturers and suppliers will, of course, be well versed in their own equipment and in computers in general, and without an equivalent level of knowledge the organization will be at a disadvantage.

The manufacturers and suppliers are trying to sell as much equipment as they can, though to maintain their reputation most computer companies do genuinely attempt to meet the needs expressed by their customers. This is another reason why such needs have to be clearly defined.

There is, however, one well known ploy which the majority of computer companies use, though they might not admit it, and this is known as 'undersell'. The computer company will examine the organization's needs and then propose the smallest possible computer system which will just meet those needs. When the system is subsequently installed and developed, additional equipment is required, so the cost rises considerably above the initial order. This particular approach is met much more often where small computer systems are being sold to first-time users, who generally have limited knowledge of computers. Salesmen are salesmen the world over, and any customer who has limited knowledge of the product is likely to be swayed by their persuasive arguments.

When a decision is made to purchase a computer system, the buyer is faced not with a simple order form, but with a rather complex contract which has been prepared to protect the computer company, not the customer.

6.3 CONTRACTS

It helps to remember that the contract has been written to protect the supplier. This may mean that clauses are inserted which reduce liability for a wide range of eventualities.

The best approach is to obtain legal advice and to make sure that the contract is reasonable. Most contracts will be in several sections. The first will deal with the general conditions of sale, the second with the hardware that is to be supplied, the third will deal with the software which is invariably only leased to the customer, and the final section will deal with payment terms and conditions, including maintenance, etc. The sections will not necessarily be in that order.

The principal item that the computer company is concerned to protect is their liability for the unsuccessful operation of the system. To do this they include terms relating to the operation of the equipment in a 'suitable' environment and the use of software for 'suitable' purposes. It is necessary to spell out what is generally believed to be suitable.

There are good reasons for the supplier to limit their liability. The main one is that the success of the system is dependent, to a large extent, on the way it is used within the company. If the system objectives were ill defined, then failure cannot be blamed on the equipment supplier.

The same is true of software suppliers, but this differs, depending on whether it is tailor-made or package software.

6.4 TAILOR-MADE SOFTWARE

Software can be specially produced 'in house' or by an external software house. The advantages of tailor-made software are:

1. The systems objectives can be more closely catered for in the detailed design phase.
2. Requirements peculiar to the company can be built into the system.
3. Emphasis can be placed on those aspects of the system considered by the company to be critical.
4. The software can be simpler and more compact. (This is, however, not always the case.)
5. Changes can be more easily handled.

The disadvantages are:

1. Time. The writing of the programs can be time-consuming, usually counted in man-years of effort.
2. They can be expensive, because of the time taken and the cost of the people.
3. Software projects are not easy to control and invariably over-run the predicted deadlines.
4. Staff continuity is not always guaranteed and this can lead to delays.

When using an external software house the advantages are scaled down and the disadvantages increased. The reason for using the external resource would be because the skilled staff were simply not available, and this is often the case with mini-computer installations. The answer to the disadvantages lies in the use of packages.

6.5 PACKAGES

Though a software package will overcome most of the disadvantages of tailor-made software, it cannot provide any of the advantages unless:

1. The systems requirements are fully met by the package.
2. The basis of the needs are standard within the industry, or even within the country.

This means that when a package solution is selected it is because it provides the most cost-effective solution, even if there is some compromise to be made.

With the installation of more and more small computers, and with the rising cost of programmers, the package market is growing rapidly. The key to selecting the right package is to find a close match with needs and then to check the reliability and performance of the package. This is done by testing.

6.6 BENCHMARK TESTS

There is a lot of controversy in the computer world about testing systems and computers, especially for selection purposes. The use of benchmark tests, by which a certain set of programs are run on all the machines being examined so that the speed and efficiency of the machines can be measured, is not always welcomed by suppliers.

The reasons for this are twofold: first, the amount of work necessary to set up and run the tests, and second, the interpretation of the results. Regardless of these attitudes, effective tests should be carried out, or visits made to existing customers who are using the equipment and software being evaluated.

It is far better to test the equipment and software before selecting than to discover its limitations after it has been installed. Perhaps the most important question to be answered is: 'Can the supplier demonstrate how the company's needs can be met with the equipment and software proposed?'. The word 'demonstrate' is used here quite specifically. It is not sufficient for this to be done theoretically; it must be a live demonstration of the relevant equipment and software, preferably in a customer location. The second vital question is: 'How many of these machines working with this software have been installed in the UK?'. If the answer is fewer than ten, then it is probable that the company will be pioneering new developments – not a bad thing to do, but fraught with more problems than obtaining an existing, widely used system. Of course, in the latter case it is possible that the equipment will be overtaken by technical developments, but there is always an argument in favour of the old system that works rather than the new system that does not.

The testing of packages is a vital task and no contract should be signed until the package has been seen to run on the equipment on which it will be used, or until the supplier offers a guarantee to get it working before payment is made.

6.7 EVALUATION AND RANKING

Benchmark tests are one way of comparing different equipment and software, but the problem remains that it is rare to find any two pieces of equipment or software that are directly comparable. Each will have certain features that are attractive and others that are not.

The answer to this problem lies in the evaluation of each alterntive against a predefined schedule of selection criteria. This schedule will be formulated from the design report and will have been prepared on the basis of achieving the system objectives.

The elements which are crucial to the business are highlighted by a scoring system which ranks the criteria in order of importance. Each alternative is then scored against each criterion. The alternative with the highest score becomes the front runner, and probably the final choice.

An example of a schedule of selection criteria is included at the end of this chapter.

The company is out to obtain the best possible system to meet its needs. This requires time and effort in the selection process so that the right decision is made. At present the choice of possible equipment and systems is very wide, and the differences between the approaches will be minimal. To ensure that an effective selection is made, the company concerned should make sure that:

1. They have the knowledge necessary to make a judgement.
2. They know exactly what they want.
3. They are prepared to put the effort into the selection.
4. They are prepared to pay for independent advice if necessary.
5. They are prepared to accept the disruption caused by the change to a new system.

6.8 SUMMARY AND REVISION NOTES

Selection of the best system is dependent on having defined the systems objectives correctly.

When this has been done the system can be selected, looking at both hardware and software. Hardware facilities can be obtained in four main ways:

1. Purchase.
2. Bureaux.
3. Turn-key.
4. Facilities management.

Software can be selected or produced in three main ways:

1. In house. ⎫
2. Software houses. ⎬ Tailor-made
3. Packages.

When dealing with manufacturers and suppliers, considerable knowledge is required to understand and to question the proposals. Manufacturers and suppliers are concerned primarily with selling their products, not with meeting the buyer's real needs, although sometimes the two are synonymous.

Contracts written to protect the sellers of hardware and software must be critically examined, preferably by a legal adviser.

Tailor-made software has the primary advantage of being produced to meet the specific needs of the company, but takes a long time to produce and is expensive.

Packages usually require a compromise on systems objectives but are economical and readily available.

Testing both hardware and software by using benchmark tests is not always mentioned by suppliers, but it must be carried out before a selection is made.

The evaluation of different proposals is possible only if a schedule of selection criteria is produced and ranked according to the importance to the company of each element. To make an effective selection the company must:

1. know what it wants to do;
2. have adequate knowledge of computers, or be prepared to pay for independent advice;
3. spend time over the selection.

QUESTIONS

1. 'The advent of the mini-computer represents a threat to both the business of computer bureaux and the sales of full-scale computers.' Discuss this statement and compare the relative advantages and disadvantages for the smaller business of owning a mini-computer or of using a computer bureau. (ICMA)

2. Because of ever-increasing development costs many companies are using packages for routine applications.

    (a) What are application packages?
    (b) What are their advantages and disadvantages?
    (c) What major factors should be examined when considering the use of a package?
    (ICMA)

3. What are the key factors to examine when selecting a computer-based system?

4. Show what is meant by selection criteria and produce an example for a company that you know, giving a thumb nail sketch of the company.

5. Numerous support facilities and services can be bought by organizations with data-processing requirements. Typical of the services available to them are the following:

    (a) Generalized software systems.
    (b) Specific software support.
    (c) Bureaux services.
    (d) Turn-key services.

    Describe for each of the above categories the nature of the service offered, stating an example of where an organization could find its use advantageous. (ICMA)

CASE STUDY EXERCISE

The systems proposal has been accepted and you have now been asked to proceed to produce a design report, indicating the possible alternative approaches that might be followed to achieve the systems objectives.

CRITICAL CRITERIA FOR ASSESSING COMPUTER SYSTEMS PROPOSALS

The selection criteria are presented in four sections:

1. Hardware
2. Software
3. General
4. Costs

Hardware

1. The hardware must provide sufficient facilities to allow the full operation of system requirements with an additional capacity of 50 per cent.

2. Limits of expandability of both main memory and disc store must be stated in the proposal.

3. The environment required by the machine, i.e. air conditioning, must be stated and priced.

4. Back-up facilities should be available from either the supplier or local installations.

5. The remote location equipment must:
    (a) be easy to operate;
    (b) have operator-proof operating system;
    (c) not require professional DP staff;
    (d) not require a special air-conditioning environment or specialized electrical circuitry;
    (e) easily achieve redistribution of work (re-organization);
    (f) be capable of being connected to central computer (dial up, private circuits, unattended and attended transmissions);
    (g) be capable of running and receiving compiled programs from the mainframe.

6. Terminal equipment must have, or be capable of having:

    (a) adequate screen size;
    (b) adequate speed of operation;
    (c) alphanumeric keyboard;
    (d) off-line capabilities;
    (e) communications on-line or off-line;
    (f) store facilities as required by the system.

7. The output devices, particularly printers, must meet the system requirements for size, content and speed.

8. All the equipment proposed must be capable of being demonstrated at an existing user's site.

Software

1. A proven data base management system must be available from the supplier or the supplier must guarantee the provision of such a system, at zero or a known cost level.

2. The operating system must have the following capabilities:

    (a) The ability to run up to seven job slots concurrently.
    (b) Dynamic or virtual store.
    (c) On-line program development and job entry procedures.
    (d) The ability to develop and test remote site programs and load the programs down the line to the sites.
    (e) The ability to support a simple 'end user' language.
    (f) The ability to allocate and change priorities to batch as well as communications jobs.
    (g) Device substitution (e.g. discs and tapes).
    (h) Dynamic device allocation.
    (i) Automatic file size handling (both for excess and for redundant space).
    (j) Operator intervention for hardware and software errors.
    (k) Disc read after write checks.
    (l) Engineering diagnostic tests running concurrently with live work (batch or communications).

3. The supplier must guarantee continuing development and support for the proposed operating system for at least ten years.

4. If a single machine or a tightly coupled machine is proposed, communications work (including systems development) must not affect batch work and vice versa.

5. The equipment proposed must be capable of being upgraded to a larger, more powerful facility without further conversion of programs.

6. The supplier must provide a full schedule of software packages together with prices.

7. The programming language should conform to international standards.

8. The supplier must be capable of demonstrating the software in an existing customer site.

General Criteria

1. An effective engineering service must be available which will guarantee a fault response in less than one hour for mainframes and two hours for remote sites.

2. The suppliers must prove their ability to deliver the hardware and software in accordance with the implementation programme and prove their ability to do this by demonstrating systems working on customers' sites.

3. The proposed equipment must not require additional staff resources in either computer operations or systems development. Note: the supplier's recommendation on optimum staffing levels would be welcomed.

4. The supplier must guarantee to supply training when, where and in the form requested, including in-house training.

5. The supplier must guarantee to protect the company from obsolescence due to technological development by offering new equipment in place of the present equipment at no additional cost.

6. The suppliers must prove their ability to provide continuing support by providing evidence of financial stability and market reports on equipment effectiveness.

Costs

1. Costs should be stated in three sections as detailed below.
    (a) *Capital costs*: mainframe and peripherals; terminals; software – operating systems, utilities, packages.
    (b) *Starting-up costs*: conversion costs from present system to the new system; training; general technical support; costs arising in the company (staff time, etc.).

(c) *Annual costs*: maintenance – mainframe, terminals; operating systems; other software utilities, packages.

2. Wherever possible the probable cost to the company of failure of the computer system facility should be calculated and the supplier asked to indemnify the user to this extent.

7

Systems Installation

7.1 JUSTIFICATION

When a system is selected it should mean that the proposed solution has been justified. Such justification should be quantified, preferably in financial terms. This will mean examining three factors:

1. Costs.
2. Benefits.
3. Time scale.

The justification should, therefore, state what the solution will cost, the benefits it will produce and when both will take place.

For systems development and installation the pattern will appear as in Figure 7.1. This pattern occurs quite naturally and the key part of the justification is to prove that the benefits will outweigh the costs, allowing for the time scale. This is not easy, for though costs can be predicted fairly accurately, benefits can not.

Costs

The costs involved fall into four categories:

1. Hardware.
2. Software.
3. Installation.
4. Maintenance.

Hardware. Hardware costs are those associated with the purchase of the equipment and ancillary supplies. A disc drive unit is no use without discs.

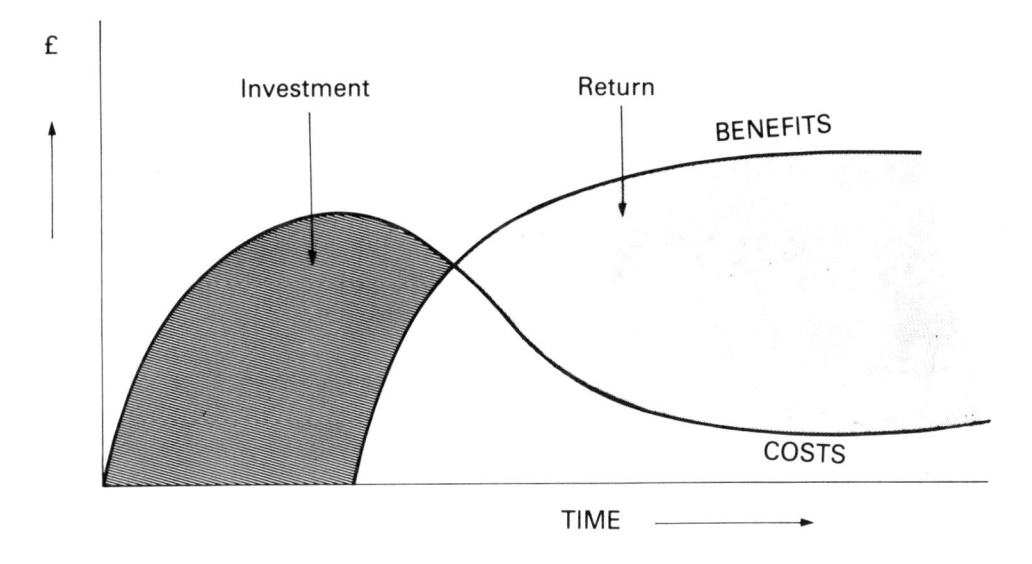

Figure 7.1 *Costs and benefit patterns*

Software. Software costs are separated into two sections: the software to run the machine, purchased or leased from the supplier, and the preparation or purchase of application software. Quite often hardware and software costs are related, e.g. to run certain software more hardware may be required.

Installation. Installation costs cover changes in stationery, the cost of training and the cost of disruption of present systems.

Maintenance. Maintenance covers both hardware and software and runs at approximately 10 per cent per annum of the original capital costs, increased broadly in line with inflation.

Benefits

Benefits fall into two broad categories:

1. Quantifiable.
2. Unquantifiable.

Quantifiable benefits are those which show a direct increase in profits emanating from the project and which, if the project did not occur, would not take place.

Unquantifiable benefits are general improvements and advantages which cannot be directly associated with an increase in profits.

68 — *Management information systems and data processing*

In a major computer-based systems development, benefits were summarized as follows:

1. Reducton in interest paid by a reduction in debtors of £750 000, which at 15 per cent is equal to £112 500 p.a.

2. Reduction in existing staff levels equivalent to 15 grade 3 clerks, which is equal to £60 000 p.a.

3. Increase in sales income of £400 000 by reducing delivery period by one week, which is equivalent to a contribution of £200 000 p.a. to profit.

Total quantifiable benefits £372 500 p.a.

4. Improvement in information on stocks and sales.

5. Better information for production planning.

In the above example the last two benefits, though no less real, cannot be quantified in financial terms.

Time Scale

A very important consideration in the justification is how long it will take for the benefits to be realized. It is not uncommon for the benefits of computer-based systems improvements to take several years to appear. Costs, however, start to appear as soon as time is spent examining the project.

If possible, systems projects should be subdivided so that management do not have to wait too long before benefits appear (Figure 7.2).

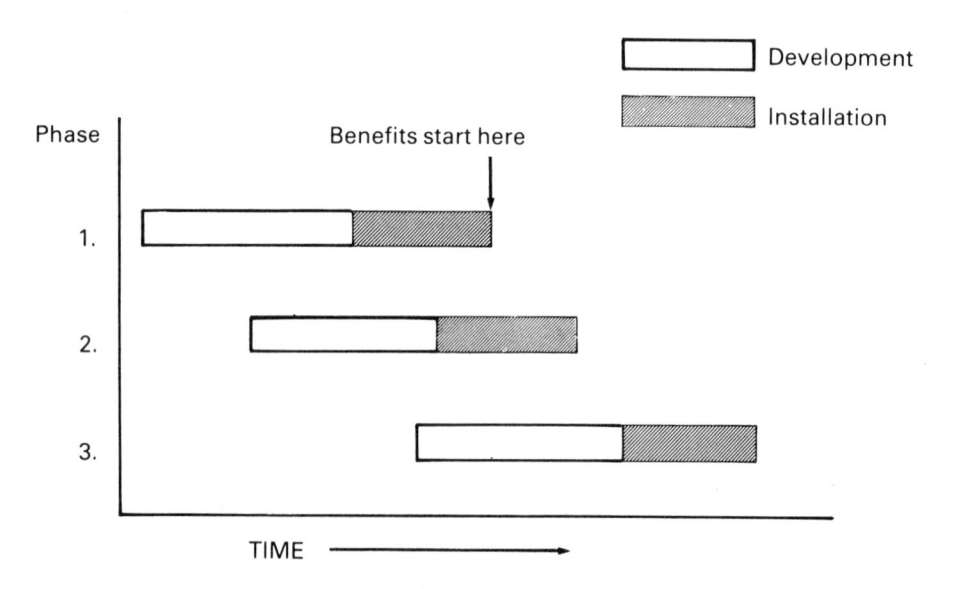

Figure 7.2 *Systems planning*

One of the main problems with time scale is that actual performance begins to lag behind the plan, so though costs are being incurred, benefits become harder and harder to produce. Every project, therefore, should clearly state the cost of failure.

Cost of Failure

There are three levels at which costs of failure occur:

1. Failure to develop the system within the cost levels agreed. So, though benefits are created, they are inadequate.
2. Failure to produce the benefits predicted.
3. Failure to produce a working system.

The first situation is quite normal. Costs escalate to a point where, had the level been predicted, the project would not have been approved.

The second situation is also fairly common, with the actual benefits falling far short of the predicted levels.

The third case, though less common, still occurs, and has on occasion caused the failure of the company.

It is important, therefore, that the justification includes a section on the cost of failure, with an indication of the effects on the business of each type of failure.

7.2 MANAGEMENT AGREEMENT

No system should be designed and installed unless it has been fully justified and agreed by management. In Figure 5.2 the stages of systems design are shown together with the appropriate points at which management approval is required. This approval is important, as management must:

1. share the responsibility for failure;
2. be fully committed to the new system;
3. take full responsibility for the success of the implementation.

The system is intended to serve management and the business, and no system can be successfully implemented unless supported by management. Support does not mean backing success; it means sharing the possibility of failure. Support also means taking responsibility.

In reality it is very difficult, if not impossible, to install a system without the full agreement and support of the management concerned. Agreement is more easily obtained if the managers are involved in all the stages of systems design and if the proposals are effectively sold.

Change is rarely welcomed, so obtaining agreement is a form of salesmanship or persuasion. This is done in several ways:

1. Discussion.
2. Demonstration.
3. Explanation.

Discussion can be both formal and informal. Formal discussions take place at meetings, specially arranged and with a predetermined objective and an agenda. Informal discussions consist of ad hoc meetings, telephone communications, and so on. It is important during discussions that the managers are given the opportunity of expressing their ideas and opinions. For the system designer the discussion is an opportunity to listen and learn.

Demonstration is carried out either formally or informally and, if the demonstration goes well, it is an excellent way to persuade people. However, if the demonstration goes badly it is an equally powerful dissuader.

Explanation is carried out both during discussion and, perhaps more usually, through the medium of the written report.

7.3 REPORT WRITING

Report writing is a skill which can be learned. Persuasive reports are a rather special kind of report written in a special way. The objective of the report is to persuade the reader to accept the recommendations. This will not be achieved unless care is taken to control the way the report is read. A persuasive report should be written in the following sequence:

1. Title page.
2. Introduction.
3. Summary of recommendations.
4. Present position.
5. Scope of survey.
6. Observations on recommendations.
7. Concluson.
8. Appendices.

All reports should have a meaningful title, be dated and carry the author's name. This should be followed by the introduction, which states the reason for the report and what the report covers.

In the summary of recommendations each recommendation should be written briefly (one sentence) and clearly, so there is no doubt in the reader's mind of what the author means. The aim of summarizing recommendations is to ensure that the reader reads the rest of the report looking for evidence to support them. When most people receive a persuasive report the first thing they want to know is the recommendations, and there is no way they can be stopped from reading them first, even if they are on the last page.

Next, the report writer should explain that he or she understands the present position. This convinces the reader that the author knows his or her starting point.

After this the author indicates the work he or she has done to arrive at the recommendations.

The main selling point of the report is the section dealing in detail with the recommendations. Here each recommendation is dealt with separately, giving full weight to the arguments for the recommendations. Any disadvantages should be discussed and overcome.

The report is concluded, preferably with an action plan for the next stage of the development.

Appendices are used to remove detail from the body of the report and to contain supportive statistics, etc. which do not need to be in the body. If they were, they would spoil the smooth flow for the reader. Interest and readability are the keys. Just because a report is technical there is no reason why it should be badly written and boring. If properly written, persuasive reports are excellent for obtaining management's agreement and can also be used in user education and training.

7.4 USER EDUCATION AND TRAINING

One of the vital, if not the most vital, elements of successful system installation is the education and training of the users. Good system design considers the training aspects at an early stage so that the system can include design features which make the operation easier, and consequently reduce the training problem. Training is concerned with two factors:

1. Knowledge.
2. Skill.

Knowledge is knowing what to do, and skill is being able to do it. The training programme must be planned to cover both these factors, and this is achieved by a process which does three things:

1. Explains.
2. Demonstrates.
3. Provides practice.

The explanation is best done formally, using audio-visual aids and supported by detailed training manuals.

Demonstration is important, as it shows that the system works and that someone, the trainer, can operate the system.

Practice is the opportunity for the users to gain the skills necessary and to consolidate the knowledge they need to operate the system.

Unfortunately, training is often overlooked or underestimated, and this has significant implications for successful installation, no matter how well the system has been designed and built.

If care has been taken in the design of the training programme, then major difficulties should be avoided. The following rules are essential for successful training.

1. Training should be carried out by local management with project team assistance. This gives confidence to the staff, who can see that their own supervisors are fully aware of all the implications of the system.
2. User manuals must be available during training both as a guide to the trainee and as a morale booster to show that a comprehensive written document is available as support.
3. The training should be phased, with the final session taking place immediately before the live date.

If these three basic rules are observed it is likely that the training will be successful. If they are not observed, it is almost certain that the training will fail to achieve the desired results.

The phasing of the training should be done at three distinct levels:

1. General overview of the system.
2. Specific procedures and activities, including use of forms, etc.
3. Controls, error procedures and recovery procedures.

The general overview is aimed at showing what the system is designed to do, why it has to be done and how it is going to be done.

The specific procedures and forms are explained step by step following the overview. The trainees should be provided with sample forms and asked to complete them and to question the design and purpose of each form and each activity.

The final stage in the training should be concerned primarily with what can go wrong and how to put it right. This should be carried out as near the live date as possible.

The phasing of training in this way is done for the following reasons:

1. Staff involvement.
2. Staff comment and suggestions.
3. Staff confidence.
4. Staff readiness.

Phases one and two will usually be carried out before the systems test, so that user staff can partake in the systems test as a further training step. Phase three should follow the systems test when the bulk of possible errors should have been established and correction procedures designed.

7.5 SYSTEMS TESTING

Testing must be thorough and exhaustive at each of the three testing levels, namely:

1. Program testing.
2. Run testing.
3. Systems testing.

Program Testing

Each program is tested when written, and corrected until the test is satisfactory. With modern computer software there are many aids for the programmer to use when writing and testing programs.

Run Testing

Several programs working together form a run, and this is tested as and when the programs making up the run have all been tested individually. Apart from ensuring that the programs all work together to achieve the objective of the run, it is important to check that the run time and use of the computer agree with the planned requirements.

Systems Testing

Program and run testing are carried out within the systems development department and do not directly involve the user. The systems test, however, must be carried out with the user and the computer section playing their respective roles. Systems test data should be produced by user staff, the system should be run by computer personnel and the results should be checked by systems development and the user.

It is important to prepare a schedule of expected results and to ensure that all features of the system are tested. This is done at two levels:

1. Contrived systems test.
2. Real systems test.

The contrived systems test contains deliberate faults and errors aimed at testing the validation and control procedures. Every conceivable variation of data should be included: numeric fields should be alpha and vice versa, batch balances should be wrong; impossible codes, dates and values should be used. The test should also contain correct data.

Following the contrived test, when errors have been detected and corrected, the real test is run. This comprises a test using a representative period of real data, perhaps the preceding month, for which actual results are available on the old system. This real test may throw up additional problems caused by the volume of data and errors not previously discovered.

The full systems testing procedure is also a form of training for all concerned, and this aspect should not be overlooked.

The satisfactory completion of testing is a vital requirement before the system is implemented. Errors will occur after implementation but these should not materially affect the operation of the system. Any short cuts in the testing procedures will almost certainly result in some degree of systems failure.

The members of the project team should be well aware of the changes which have taken place in the system since the design report was written. The managers

'GO' – 'NO GO'

| SYSTEM | | DATE ISSUED | |

QUESTIONS	YES	NO
PROJECT LEADER		
1. Have all tests been completed satisfactorily		
2. Are all Manuals complete : Systems		
Operations		
Control		
Procedure		
3. Is all stationery available		
4. Have all staff been trained		
5. Have all files been converted		
6. Has all equipment been installed and is working		
7. Has the system changeover been planned		
8. Has all Program Documentation been completed		
9. Is Systems Documentation complete		
10. When will you be ready to GO LIVE	:	:
COMPUTER SERVICES MANAGER		
11. Have all operating procedures been agreed: Computer		
Terminal		
Data Prep.		
12. Have control procedures been agreed		
13. Have operations and control staff been trained		
14. Has the systems timetable been agreed		
15. Have other system interfaces been tested		
16. Has a satisfactory and complete system test been processed		
17. Has computer stationery been ordered and delivered		
18. When will you be ready to GO LIVE.	:	:
USER		
19. Have all staff been trained.		
20. Is the procedure manual complete.		
21. Is the operator manual complete.		
22. Is all stationery complete.		
23. Are all requirements met by the tested system.		
24. Is adequate standby available.		
25. When will you be ready to GO LIVE.	:	:

AGREED LIVE DATE : :

O & M328

AGREED BY	SIGNATURE	DATE
PROJECT LEADER		
D P MANAGER		
USER		
O & M MANAGER		

Figure 7.3 *Go–no go statement*

concerned will not be aware of the detail. The test report is intended to provide management with a clear picture of the existing situation and of the detailed implementation plans. This will be their last chance to abort the project. The report will contain:

1. Changes. Any changes of a significant nature should be commented on. This should cover:

    (a) the nature of the change;
    (b) the effects on the system;
    (c) the reasons for the change.

2. Operating requirements. Due to changes or experience during the real test, operating requirements may need amending. Whether or not this is the case the operating requirements should be reiterated and agreed.
3. Summary of tests. Nothing gives greater confidence than evidence that the system works. By summarizing the tests carried out and providing examples of the documentation and reports created by the system, the systems designer is virtually assuring approval.
4. Monitoring. No system can be designed without certain aspects being more critical than others. Such sections of the system should be identified and listed for close monitoring during implementation. This is important not only from the system designer's point of view but also from that of the user, who will then pay more attention to these aspects of the system.
5. Go–no go. This statement (Figure 7.3) should be completed, signed and included in the report. It is used for two purposes:

    (a) As a discipline to ensure that each section has been carefully examined.
    (b) As written confirmation that the user and computer operators are ready and willing to proceed.

    The systems designer would be foolhardy to proceed without the completed statement.
6. Implementation. The detailed steps to be taken to implement the system should be set out. This will cover the activities and the dates. There should always be a period for monitoring between the initial implementation and the phased introduction of the system into other areas, regions and divisions.

The importance of thorough testing cannot be overemphasized. Short cuts sometimes save time, but more often than not they cause you to lose your way. Implementation should not go ahead until everyone is ready. It is far better to delay implementation than to produce a faulty system.

Software Packages

The development of 'tailor-made' software is gradually being superseded by the use of application packages. This is particularly true for microcomputers and minicomputers. For small computers inexpensive packages are widely available but they suffer from the problem that they cannot be amended to suit the business needs. This means that it is important to evaluate and select the package against carefully defined needs.

For larger machines it is possible to persuade suppliers to amend their package or to allow the buyer to do so. Modern packages are being developed which have built in a degree of adaptability which provides the user with an opportunity to more closely fit the packages to his or her needs.

7.6 CHANGEOVER

When a new system is being installed it is usually replacing an existing system. This means that existing documentation and procedures have to be changed over to the new system. Changeover can be carried out in four main ways:

1. Pilot.
2. Parallel.
3. Phased.
4. Direct.

Pilot schemes are smaller versions of the new system and may operate for one section of the company, or a selected number of customers, etc. When the pilot scheme is proved to be effective it is extended to the whole company.

Parallel changeover, as its name implies, means running the new system alongside the old system until the operation is satisfactory. This does mean extra work but it is an effective and safe method of changeover.

Phased changeover means bringing the system into operation in stages. Each stage is introduced on either a parallel or a direct changeover.

Direct changeover is when the old system ceases one day and the new system starts the next day. This is the most difficult way to change over, but there are situations where the work involved in running parallel is either too much or simply impossible.

It is not uncommon for a major system to be implemented in a combination of these ways.

A large building society introducing a new computer-based system for counter transactions planned and implemented the system in:

1. phases;
2. branch by branch;
3. direct change from old to new.

The phases were different elements of the system and branch by branch was a form of pilot scheme operation, but at each branch it was essential to change over directly.

Prior to the changeover, files have to be converted or created and new documentation has to be introduced, as well as the installation of the equipment. These, added to training and the inevitable errors which arise, make this stage of systems installation a difficult and traumatic experience.

7.7 DATA CONVERSION

Data conversion is one of those factors which can create a considerable amount of work, depending on circumstances.

A mail-order company was planning to change from manual agents' records to computer-based records. This meant converting tens of thousands of handwritten documents onto the computer files. The problems were:

1. How was it to be done?
2. Should just the balances be converted or a history?
3. If a history, for how long?
4. What would happen to movements in the accounts during the changeover?

All these questions had to be resolved before the changeover could be contemplated.

Not only does data conversion have to be carried out, but the new files have to be verified with the old files, and anomalies removed. One advantage of data conversion is that it does provide an opportunity to 'clean' the records and make a fresh start.

Unfortunately, no matter how successful the conversion, it is usually necessary to retain the old records for dealing with queries which arise, and in some cases for statutory requirements.

7.8 MANUALS

Prior to the installation the changes should be fully documented in three types of manual:

1. Training.
2. Procedure.
3. Operating.

Training manuals have already been mentioned and should be produced in advance of the training and provide a supporting document to the training programme.

Procedure manuals should set out the new procedures simply and clearly step by step, preferably with each page of the manual dealing with a particular step of the system. When forms or screen formats are involved, these should be placed on the facing page (Figure 7.4).

Operating manuals cover the actual operation of equipment (which keys to press to provide which reaction) and would include the procedures to follow for breakdown and recovery, including a maintenance log.

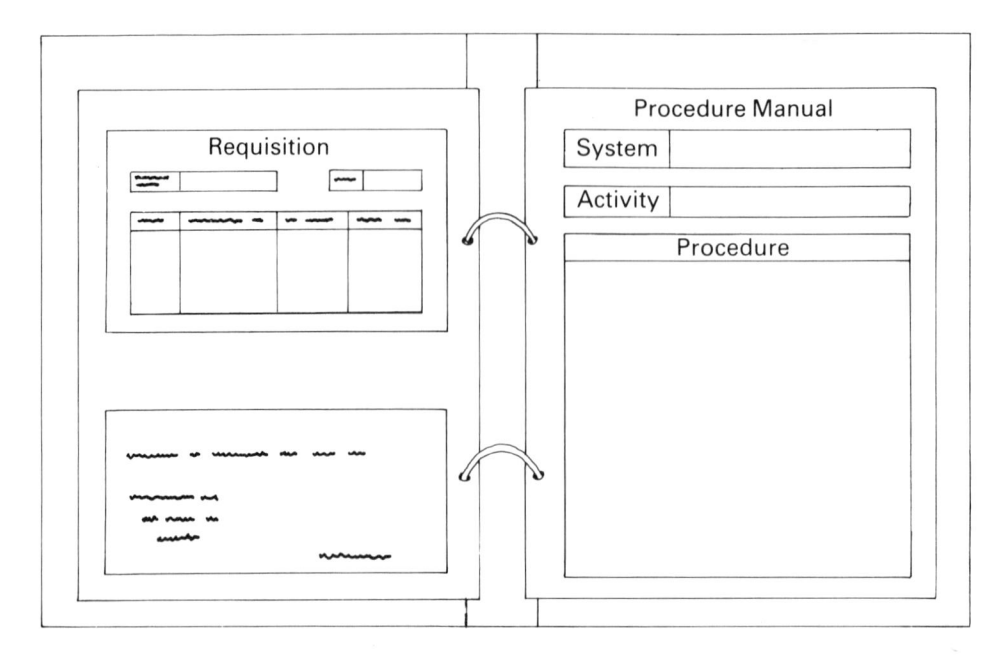

Figure 7.4 *Procedure manual*

7.9 IMPLICATIONS OF CHANGE

People do not naturally welcome change. There is an instinctive reaction against it. People find comfort and security in the known and the understood. Change, therefore, generates fear in people's minds and fear makes people defensive. If these natural effects are appreciated, then change can be planned and defences overcome.

The two main forms of change are:

1. Physical.
2. Psychological.

The physical changes cover new equipment, new furniture, new office layout, etc. Though these may cause disruption and be a nuisance, resistance to them is fairly easily overcome.

The psychological problems are more difficult, as these are largely hidden in the minds of individuals, who do not necessarily voice their fears. Resistance to such change is best overcome through effective training and involvement. The emphasis should be on generating confidence in their own abilities, so that the fears of 'not being able to cope' or of 'making mistakes' can be dispelled.

Whenever a new sytem is being designed the likely problems of change should be carefully predicted and plans made to overcome them. This might have an effect on the design of the system, so that change is minimized.

If individuals believe that their present knowledge and skills will not be completely wasted, and that they will be able to learn the new ones, then the battle is half won. The rest comes from generating confidence before, during and after the installation of the system.

7.10 SUMMARY AND REVISION NOTES

Systems projects have to be cost justified and quantified. If expenditure is to take place, benefits must be generated to make an adequate return on the expenditure.

The cost of failure should be assessed, as this will determine the amount of effort and money which is expended to prevent failure.

Management agreement to the proposals is essential before the installation, and this is obtained by:

1. Discussion.
2. Demonstration.
3. Explanation.

Report writing is an important factor in obtaining approval. Persuasive reports need to guide the reader so that he or she agrees with and accepts the recommendations.

User education and training is one of the most important factors in the successful installation of information and control systems. The users have to acquire the knowledge and skill to operate the new system. The training is carried out in phases, dealing with:

1. General overview.
2. Specific procedures.
3. Errors and recovery procedures.

An element of training can take place during systems testing, which needs to prove that the system works. There are two main systems tests:

1. Contrived – to try to beat the system.
2. Real – to simulate the real situation.

The test report is the final stage of testing and needs to show that the system works and achieves the objectives set out in the design report, or in the case of packages the supplier's claims.

The actual changeover from the old to the new can be done in four ways, or a combination of the four. These are:

1. Pilot scheme.
2. Parallel.
3. Phased.
4. Direct.

Data conversion is an important factor which can create a considerable amount of work and which must be carefully planned and organized.

Documentation, particularly user manuals, is crucial to successful installation. Users will need three manuals:

1. Training.
2. Procedure.
3. Operating.

With good training and comprehensive manuals the fears of impending change will be lessened and the people involved in the new system will quickly overcome any minor problems.

The implications of change for people have to be considered and planned, and every effort made to overcome doubts and generate confidence.

QUESTIONS

1. A production planning and control system is being investigated with a view to computerization. The systems investigators have been asked to include a financial justification for the new system in their report. What would such a justification include and how might the financial effects of the system be monitored after installation? (ICMA)

2. You have been working on the design of a new information system for improving production control. Explain how you would go about obtaining management agreement to your proposals.

3. You are reaching the end of the system design cycle and have to produce an implementation plan. What will the plan cover and what aspects will be emphasized?

4. It is not uncommon for system designers involved in the introduction of computer-based data processing to encounter resentment and opposition from existing employees. For what reasons may employees react in this manner? What steps can the system designer take to reduce this resistance? (ICMA)

5. 'The key part of systems installation is the testing of the system. Once the system is seen to work the rest is simple.' Discuss.

CASE STUDY EXERCISE

The design report you prepared previously has been approved and you have been asked to prepare a report for management to obtain their agreement to the programme for building and installing the system.

PART TWO
Data Processing

8

The Role of Computers

8.1 COMPUTERS IN BUSINESS

Computers are now used in every walk of life and if society is not already largely dependent on computers, it soon will be. Government, energy services, transportation, communication and health services all use computers extensively. The degree of dependence can be clearly seen when computer staff strike for more pay.

In business, computers are used for a wide variety of tasks. These can be divided into six broad categories:

1. Administration.
2. Communication.
3. Production.
4. Design.
5. Control.
6. Information services.

Administration

In administration there is a wide variety of basic systems for receiving and processing the customer's order, accounting for purchases and sales, preparing the payroll, maintaining basic records and feeding data into the information system.

Communication

Communication services, in the past largely dependent on the use of telephones and the post, are now being replaced by the transfer of information via a computer network linked with word processors for the creation of the message in a readable form.

Production

Production, already highly mechanized, is increasingly being automated with the use of computers. In some cases these are linked to robots operating an unmanned production line. This kind of automation is growing, and most new factories are highly automated.

Design

In the design field, computer aided design (CAD) is not only speeding up the design process, but is also providing designers with the opportunity of creating a wide range of possible models and testing their performance, all within the computer, saving expenditure of time and money in building abortive prototypes. This is particularly relevant to the design of products such as engines, where the working parts cannot be seen when the engine is built.

Control

Control is obviously a vital factor in business and the computer can be used to monitor what is happening and to compare the actual performance levels with a predetermined standard. As variations are detected the computer can initiate a warning signal or act directly to correct the deviation. This improves the level of control, increases the quality of the products and prevents serious breakdowns.

Information Services

In medium-sized and large companies, information services are mainly computer based. These systems start with basic management accounting systems and end with extensive modelling facilities. In between these two extremes is a wide range of analytical systems feeding information to management for a wide range of decision-making needs.

8.2 COMPUTER CATEGORIES

The computers in use fall into three main categories, as detailed below, plus word processors, which are a rather special development of computer potential.

1. Mainframe computers.
2. Minicomputers.
3. Microcomputers.
4. Word processors.

There is a variety of opinion about what constitutes each type of computer. By looking at the main characteristics of each, it is possible to see why the different descriptions exist. There are, however, many grey areas and there is a good deal of overlap between the categories (Figure 8.1). Word processors are somewhat different devices, but word processing facilities are now available on most mainframes and minicomputers, and on a number of microcomputers, as well as on special machines.

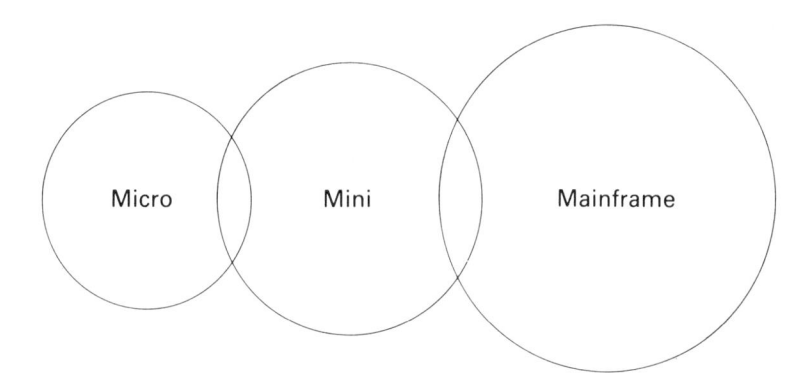

Figure 8.1 *Computer categories*

Mainframe Computers

Mainframe computers have been with us for 30 years and most people have a good idea of what constitutes a mainframe. The term came into being to distinguish the large central computers from the small or minicomputers which started to appear about 15 years ago. The main features which distinguish a mainframe from a mini are:

1. They are multi-purpose machines.
2. They are sold by the manufacturer with full support for both software and maintenance.
3. Programming is normally done by the user's staff.
4. They require a special air-conditioned environment.
5. They require specially trained operators.
6. They are almost certainly multi-program machines and can handle batch processing and on-line at the same time.
7. They can handle large numbers of peripheral devices such as discs, tapes, printers and terminals.
8. The mainframe can be the controlling computer in a distributed network of terminals and minicomputers.

Minicomputers

Minicomputers have been developed primarily from small, special-purpose scientific machines. Facilities were gradually added until they became almost a small-scale equivalent of the mainframe. There are, however, still some differences:

1. They are usually sold by companies who assemble components from other equipment manufacturers, known as OEM suppliers.
2. They are usually sold to small, first-time users who do not have systems development staff and so the supplier or, more usually, a software house writes the programs.
3. It is much cheaper, because of the programming difficulties, to buy the supplier's packages.
4. Programming languages vary almost machine by machine.
5. Though relatively small, as they have been developed from scientific and process-control fields, they are very good on-line but not so good on batch.
6. They are often used for a single purpose, i.e. stock control or production control.
7. They are not as expandable as mainframes, usually having a limit on store size, number of terminals, peripherals, etc.
8. They are not usually able to control high-speed printers.

A number of these limitations are changing as new machines are developed, and it is almost certain that within the next couple of years machines with the capabilities of medium-sized mainframes will be available in a computer no bigger than a desk, for a price of around £15 000.

Microcomputers

There is now a wide range of microcomputers with relatively large storage capacities and many application packages. These microcomputers come in a variety of forms, the smaller ones being single-user machines, but the larger ones being capable of supporting several users. Portable microcomputers are also growing in popularity with lift-up, flat screens and very useful software including 'specialists', database and word processing. The term PC stands for 'personal computer' or 'professional computer', and is widely used to describe desk-top single-user microcomputers.

Microprocessors

Microprocessors, about which there has been a great deal of publicity, have been the basis of the minicomputer for some years. They came into being with the development of large-scale integrated circuits which can be photo-etched onto slivers of silicon called chips. Each microprocessor looks like a thick postage stamp with about 40 gold legs or pins and, when mounted on a 'board' together with some form of memory, power connections and input/output controls, forms a microcomputer in its own right.

The microprocessor is like the central processor unit (CPU) of the mainframe computer, but now the whole board is being replaced by a chip which combines the memory and input/output controls, and this will soon be available for a few pounds. The normal programming language is BASIC, but some of the very cheap versions have to be machine programmed for specific tasks. However, the low price means that it is cheaper to get one for each task than to build a multipurpose device.

Word Processors

Word processors have developed from two main bases (see Figure 8.2):

1. The typewriter.
2. The computer.

The first hesitant steps towards the modern word processor began when IBM attached a paper device to one of their electric typewriters so that information punched into the tape could be transferred to the printing head of the typewriter. This produced the automatic typewriter, which was capable of taking punched paper tape from the computer.

In 1964 IBM launched a magnetic tape electric typewriter and this development was followed over the next ten years by a variety of developments, including the use of magnetic cards and the introduction of screens for text editing.

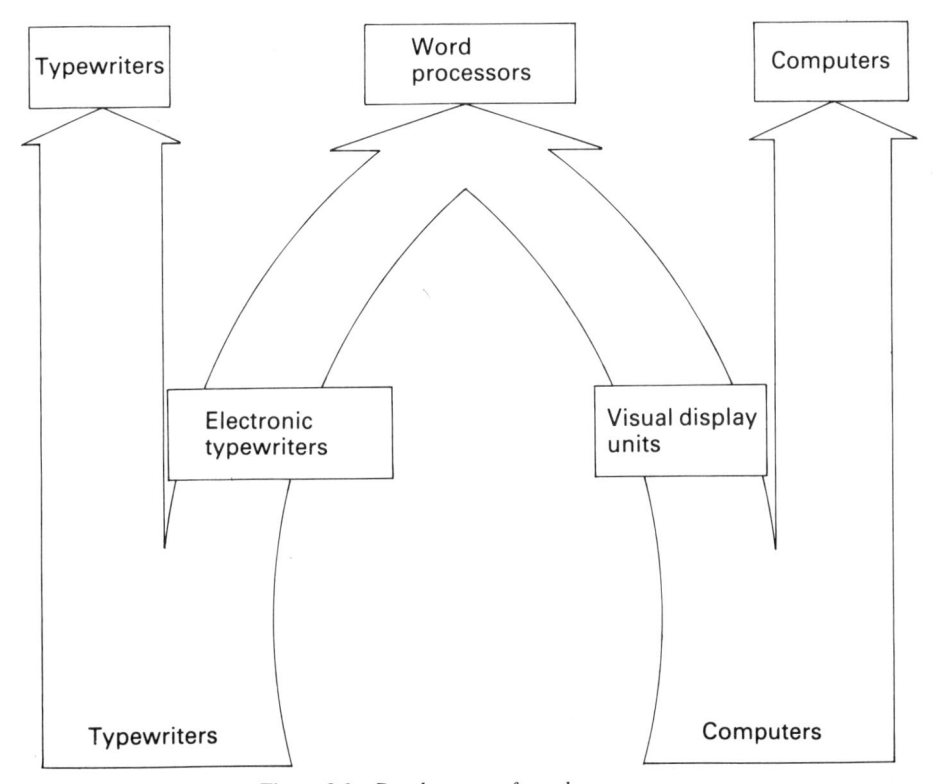

Figure 8.2 *Development of word processors*

At this point the computer companies, who already had screens used for data processing, realized the potential of this device and entered the word processing arena. As the 1970s proceeded, the range of word-processing facilities multiplied. It is now possible to purchase a wide range, from a modest electronic typewriter to the most sophisticated machine, namely a multi-purpose office computer offering word as well as data processing.

If we add to all these developments the link with the telecommunication system we have the basis of the electronic office. This is often referred to as 'converging technology' and provides a basis for linking together all the separate activities which make up office work. Unfortunately, the range of equipment widely classified as word processors has led to considerable misunderstanding and confusion. The three levels of machine are:

1. The electronic typewriter.
2. Single-screen processor.
3. Multi-screen processor.

The electronic typewriter, as its name implies, is like a normal typewriter to which electronics have been added in the shape of programs and storage facilities. These extend the work range of the typewriter far beyond the standard electric variety. The machine looks like a typewriter with a keyboard and platens for feeding the paper on which the 'processed' words are printed.

The single-screen processor is a departure from the typewriter. It looks different and it works in a manner not easily associated with typing. There is a keyboard, a screen and a printer, together with some form of storage medium. This machine resembles a computer more than a typewriter.

The multi-screen processor resembles a computer even more than the single-screen version does. Several screens 'share' the processor, which is housed in a separate box. A printer may be 'shared' in the same way. It is not unusual for the processor and the printer to be housed in separate rooms, thus removing it even further in appearance from the standard typewriter.

It is not surprising that there is confusion if you contemplate the range of machines in each of these three categories, especially when some systems can be built up from the basic electronic typewriter to the multi-screen system.

8.3 COMPUTER STRENGTHS

The wide use of computers indicates that they offer valuable facilities which would be difficult to simulate in any other way. These facilities can be seen as strengths, and fall into four sections:

1. Speed.
2. Storage capacity.
3. Reliability.
4. Flexibility.

Speed

The first of the computer's strengths is speed. Data can be manipulated within the computer at speeds which defy recognition. A millionth of a second is a measure of speed which we just cannot visualize. What it means in reality is the number of tasks the computer can carry out in short time scales. It also enables the machine to respond very quickly to requests for information, access to files, etc.

Storage Capacity

The scope of the files which can be held on the computer is the second strength. Today it is possible to hold files containing hundreds of millions of records, automatically available on the computer to users with facilities to access the files. Development of new types of file storage is continuing and in the near future the scope for storage of information will for all real purposes be unlimited.

Reliability

In spite of many tales of errors made by the computer, the machines are extremely reliable. There are very few moving parts and the electronic devices have a very low wear rate. The items which are most likely to fail are input and output and the disc storage devices, which do have moving parts subject to wear and tear. The errors which occur are mostly concerned with data input errors or programming errors, both of which are caused by human beings.

Flexibility

The fourth strength of the computer is the degree of flexibility available to the user. The computer is a data manipulation tool. The way the tool is used is entirely dependent on the way the user programs the machine. The comment often heard in computer departments that 'we can do anything' is largely true, but is, of course, dependent on the ability of the people to create a system which meets its objectives, and this is more difficult than it might seem.

8.4 COMPUTER WEAKNESSES

Of course computers, like any tool, have a number of weaknesses which present certain constraints on the way they can be used. The weaknesses of computers fall into two main categories:
1. Physical weaknesses.
2. Operational weaknesses.

Physical Weaknesses

Physical weaknesses are associated with the machinery itself; as has been stated, the machines are very reliable, but they do break down. This can affect the operation of the system, the accuracy of the data held on file and the quality of output. If the business is dependent on the computer for processing orders, taking bookings or controlling production, it is vital that some back-up is available.

The machines are also affected by interruptions in the supply of power. This can be a fluctuation of current or a complete power cut. When this occurs the system in operation has to be checked and re-run, as when power fails it affects the data held in the system.

Physical weaknesses also exist in the medium used for input and output. Records held on magnetic tape and magnetic disc can be damaged if they are not handled properly. Great care is needed in the way these files are used, since they are not as robust as their appearance might suggest.

The environment in which the computer operates can have an effect. Noise, vibration, temperature, humidity, dust, magnetism and static can affect the machines, and this is particularly true in production areas, where care has to be taken to produce robust machines housed in special protective boxes.

Operational Weaknesses

Operational weaknesses are not really the fault of the machine, but of the way it is used. Operators are responsible for running the right systems at the right time with the right files. Though this sounds simple, in a large computer department it requires a high degree of planning and control. These weaknesses can be overcome if proper operational procedures are followed (see Chapter 13).

Computer-based systems do, therefore, have to cater for the weaknesses and optimize the strengths if they are to be considered good systems.

8.5 COMPUTER-BASED SYSTEMS

Computer-based systems can be examined in four elements, each of which is closely related to the others. These are:

1. Data collection.
2. Data processing.
3. File maintenance.
4. Data output.

Data collection covers the collection of data from outside the machine, the input of the data into the machine and the validation of the data to ensure it is acceptable to the system. There are a number of rules to follow when designing good data collection systems, and these are dealt with fully in Chapter 12. It is important to appreciate that the data collection system is a separate system with the objective of providing the main system with the right data at the right time.

Data processing deals with the way the data are manipulated within the machine and includes the transfer of data, calculations, file creation and the operation of the computer. All these aspects are considered in detail in Chapter 13.

File maintenance deals with the way the files held in the system are updated, checked, controlled and deleted. The link between files and the creation of data bases is a crucial element of the file maintenance section of systems design (see Chapter 11).

Data output is in effect the result of the system, the primary reason for the system. Whether the output is in control signals, electrical pulses, printed information or a display on a screen, it is this element for which the system has been designed. Designing a good output system involves knowledge of the facilities available and a careful selection of the method most appropriate to the needs of the user. This is dealt with at length at Chapter 14.

These four elements of computer-based systems can be depicted as part of a systems framework (Figure 8.3). In the framework the elements are shown in the order in which the system is designed, starting with the objectives, the output, moving on to file maintenance, then to processing and finally to data collection.

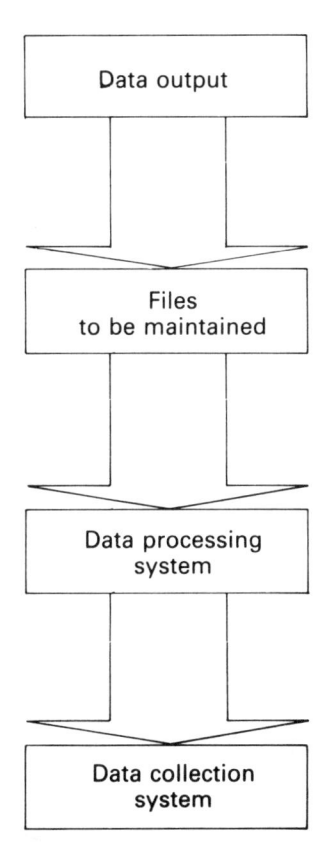

Figure 8.3 *Elements of computer-based systems*

The system is, of course, operated in the opposite direction to the way it is designed, but, as has been stated several times, the design is aimed at meeting system objectives, so this is the point where the design process starts. The aim is to meet the user's needs.

8.6 DISTRIBUTED PROCESSING

As computers have been developed it has become possible to locate the data processing power closer to the sources of data and to the users who will receive the output. This applies not only to businesses which are geographically scattered, but also to large single sites where different parts of the factory can operate their own system linked to the main system.

This approach to spreading data processing power around the organization is called distributed processing. The advantages are that data travel less distance, the local system can be designed for local needs, local management are more closely involved in systems design, and the system can cope with one-off local requirements that might be quite special.

The disadvantages are the lack of central control, fragmentation of systems effort, and reduced quality of systems design and management. These disadvantages will certainly arise if the distributed processing approach is not carefully designed and related to the needs of the business.

The choice of central processing or distributed processing depends primarily on the way the organization is structured and the management style in operation. Distributed processing is particularly relevant where the organization is structured in a decentralized way with a high level of local management autonomy, probably controlled on the basis of profit responsibility.

Where this management style is followed centralized data processing creates frustration and limits the local management's freedom to operate the way they want to.

Where management control is centralized it makes sense to operate a centralized data processing service. When the organization structure changes, it is also sensible to examine the appropriate data processing service that is required.

8.7 NETWORKS

Distributed processing systems depend on the network of communication lines that link the various elements together. Communications between parts of the system depend on the telephone system available. In the UK British Telecom offers several services based on:

1. The hire of private lines.
2. The use of the public network.

Private lines are leased from British Telecom on an annual basis and the rental is based on the distance and type of line installed. Private lines provide a high quality of service, which is dedicated to the company concerned.

The public network can be used and is paid for in the normal way of so much per minute or unit. The choice of private line or public network depends on the use to be made of the line, i.e. the amount of data traffic, the cost and the speed of line required.

Whichever type of line is used it is necessary to have a piece of equipment between the computer and the line. This is called a modem, which is a shortened version of *modulator demodulator*. The machine converts the signal from the computer – an electrical pulse – into a soundwave to travel along the line. At the other end the modem converts the soundwave back to an electrical pulse.

The links between computers and the telephone facilities are being developed and, with the introduction of computerized exchanges and satellites, will provide vastly improved services.

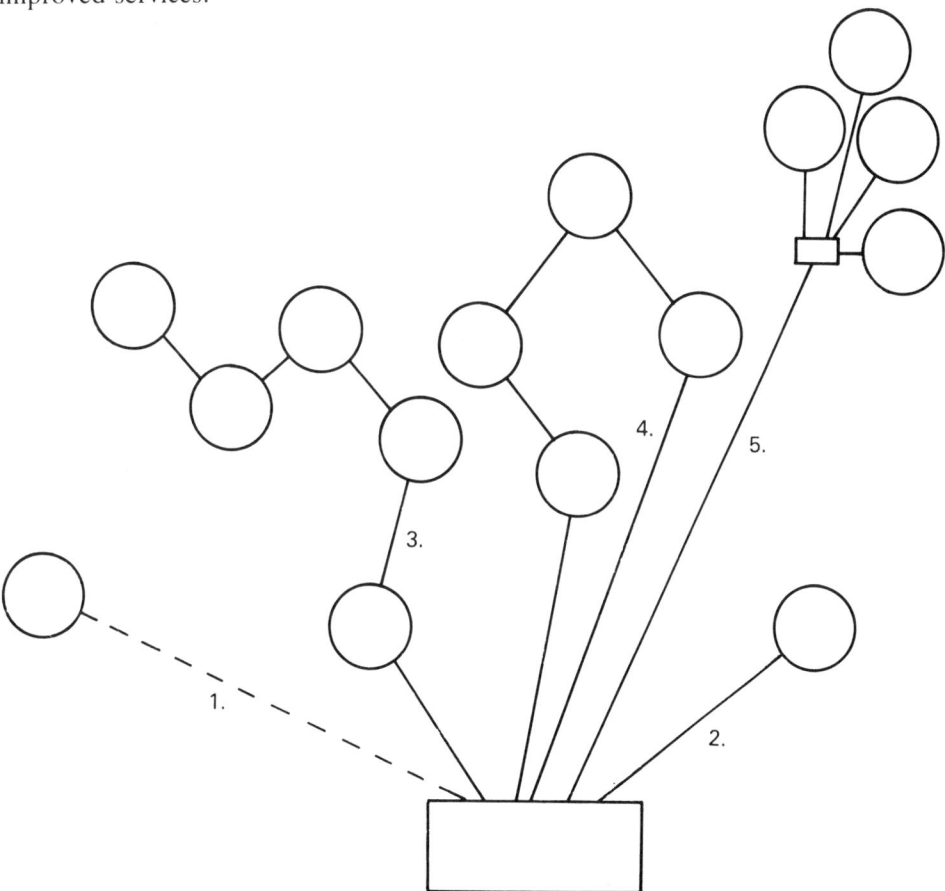

Figure 8.4 *Networks. 1. dialled line; 2. point to point private line; 3. multi-drop line; 4. loop line; 5. star configuration (concentrator)*

The design of a network is a very technical task and, if the most cost-effective network is to be designed, a specialist should be involved. Network design services are available from British Telecom, communication equipment manufacturers and consultants. The equipment available allows a variety of lines to be used and linked in ways which provide the most cost-effective solution. The three main types of network are:

1. Point to point.
2. Multi-drop.
3. Star.

The point to point, as it name implies, is a direct connection between two points.

Multi-drop is a network using one main line to which a number of sites are linked using suitably located concentrators.

The star network is where a numer of sites are linked into one centre, which itself is linked point to point to another centre.

These three methods are depicted in Figure 8.4. The choice depends on the needs of the system and the cost effectiveness of the result.

No matter how the network is constructed, it has to meet the needs of the distributed processing system, which in turn has to meet the needs of the organization and the individual managers.

Local Area Networks (LAN's)

The desire to link computers together within the same location has created the need for 'local area networks'. These are systems of cabling within a building which link computers to each other and allow them to share common devices such as printers, as well as communicate with each other.

These networks are usually of two kinds, narrow band and wide band. Narrow-band networks only allow for transmission of digital data whilst wide-band networks allow the transmission of digital, voice, pictorial (video) and viewdata. Some of these networks will allow any computers to be connected; others are more restrictive.

8.8 SUMMARY AND REVISION NOTES

Computers are used in industry in six main areas:

1. Administration.
2. Communication.
3. Production.
4. Design.
5. Control.
6. Information services.

The computers used fall into three main categories, plus word processors. These categories are:

1. Mainframe computers.
2. Minicomputers.
3. Microcomputers.
4. Word processors.

The computer has both strengths and weaknesses. The strengths are concerned with:

1. Speed.
2. Storage capacity.
3. Reliability.
4. Flexibility.

Computer weaknesses are twofold:

1. Physical.
2. Operational.

Computer-based systems have to be designed in four main elements:

1. Data collection.
2. Data processing.
3. File maintenance.
4. Data output.

The design process starts with data output, the objective of the system, and moves to the final design phase of data collection. The system does, of course, operate in the opposite direction.

Distributed processing is a term used to describe the method of spreading the data processing system through the organization to match the needs of the business.

Distributed processing needs a communication network to link the various parts of the system. Such networks can be designed in three main ways, depending on which is the most cost-effective solution.

1. Point to point.
2. Multi-drop.
3. Star.

It must not be forgotten that the design of the system and the choice of approach are aimed at meeting users' needs in the most cost-effective way.

QUESTIONS

1. 'The computer is a versatile management tool which can be used to solve any problem.' Discuss.

2. List the strengths of the computer and give an example of an application of each of the computer's strengths.

3. 'Modern hardware developments are causing a movement away from centralized data processing systems to dispersed systems operating at or close to actual business activities.' Describe the hardware developments referred to in this quotation. What are the advantages and disadvantages of this movement? (ICMA)

4. Explain what 'distributed processing' is and why it is being implemented by many large and medium-sized companies.

5. Distributed processing requires the building of a network. Explain what a network is and explain the three main types of network that can be constructed.

CASE STUDY EXERCISE

Set out the approach you will take to the application of computers as a part of the system you have designed. Explain the role the computer will play and give the reasoning for your approach, indicating whether it is centralized or distributed. Your approach should be based on utilizing the strengths of the computer.

9

Computer Hardware

9.1 ELEMENTS OF THE COMPUTER

The computer is not flattered by its name, which implies that it is a device for carrying out computations. This is in fact only one of the computer's many capabilities. The computer can be more correctly described as a device for manipulating and storing data.

The computer consists of two distinct but inseparable parts – hardware and software. The hardware is in physical apparatus, the pots and pans of computing. Software refers to the programs, the instructions which control the computer's operations. The hardware consists of five main elements (Figure 9.1):

1. Input devices.
2. Central processing unit.
3. Storage.
4. Output devices.
5. Communication channels.

Whichever type of computer is referred to, these elements must all exist, although they do so in different forms in different computers. This is due to the way the computers are built, referred to as the architecture of the computer.

The architecture is the way the physical parts of the computer are constructed and linked together, and this in turn affects the way in which the computer is programmed.

The computer referred to here is the digital computer.

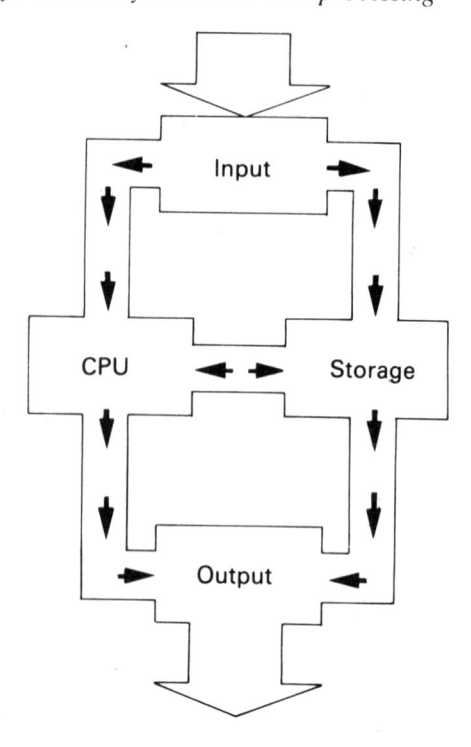

Figure 9.1 *Elements of the computer*

9.2 DIGITAL AND ANALOG COMPUTERS

It is important to distinguish between these primary types of computers.

A digital computer is a machine capable of performing operations on data represented in digital or number form; i.e. the data is represented as a series of discrete elements arranged in a coded form to represent numbers.

This definition from *A Dictionary of Computers* (1975, Harmondsworth: Penguin) goes on to explain how this coding is carried out by using binary notation using 0 and 1, which is extremely convenient for computers.

Binary notation is convenient because the circuits and storage devices can hold data in the form of zeros, or non-energized circuits, or ones, in the form of energized circuits. This simple principle of on/off is the basis of the operation of most digital computers.

Analog computers differ from digital computers in that the data manipulated are represented by physical units rather than a digital code. These physical units could be electrical voltages or, in mechanical machines, could be the physical measurements of the parts of the model.

Analog computers are used in scientific, design and production environments. Each one has to be constructed to do a specific job and will respond very quickly to changes in the measurements input.

Digital computers are used widely in administration and control systems and in the production of management information. By using digital to analog converters it is possible to link both kinds of computer to provide comprehensive information and control systems.

9.3 OPERATING FUNCTIONS

Within the computer hardware there are a number of particular functions which have to take place to perform the various processes required. These functions are controlled by the software, which is entered into the machine before the processing takes place. The functions can be described as a series of steps:

1. Discover where the data are.
2. Go to get the data in the file.
3. Move them to where they are needed.
4. Use the data.
5. Return them to the file.

These steps are very much the same as the procedure you would have to follow if you wanted to obtain a book from a library.

1. You would refer to the assistant or the index to discover where the book was located (its address).
2. You would go to that location and find the book.
3. You would remove the book from the location and the assistant would record where it had gone.
4. You would take the book away and use it.
5. When you had finished with the book you would return it to the library.

The procedure in the computer is basically the same and follows the same steps. This is depicted in Figure 9.2. The word 'bus' is used to indicate a route along which data flow. There are normally two 'buses', a data bus and an address bus. As the names imply, data flow along the former and the address it is to be returned to flows along the latter.

When data are input they are given an address in memory. When the program, held in the instruction unit, requires those data, it asks for them by address and the data are transferred to the arithmetic unit to be processed. When the processing is complete the results are addressed and sent to the memory, or to be output, and the original data are returned to the file.

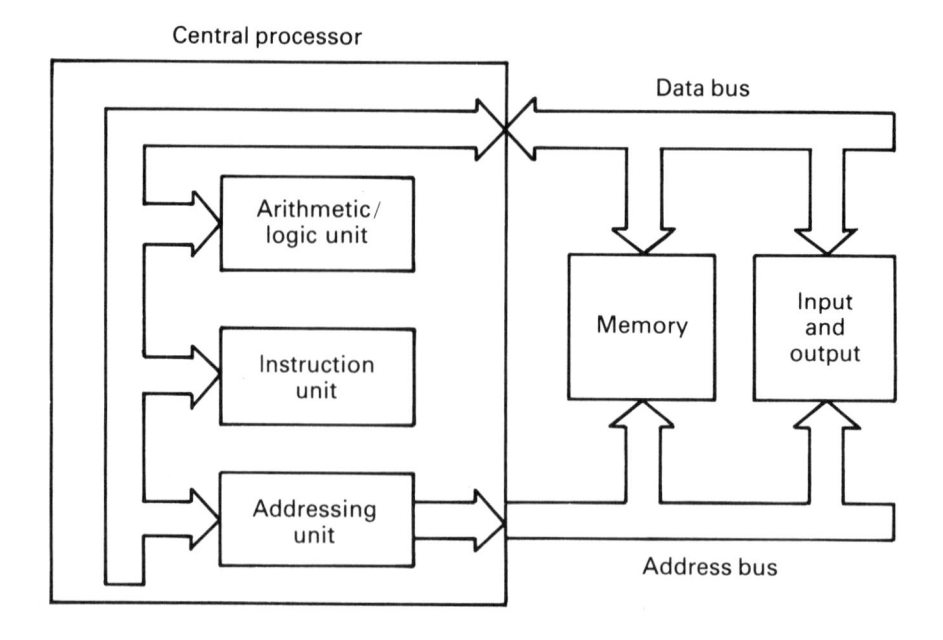

Figure 9.2 *Operating functions*

The central processor contains three separate elements:
1. Arithmetic unit.
2. Instruction unit.
3. Addressing unit.

The arithmetic unit carries out the tasks allotted to it by the program held in the instruction unit. These tasks cover such things as sorting, merging, comparing, calculating, selecting, etc.

The instruction unit holds the program and controls the functioning of the arithmetic unit, the addressing unit and the buses.

The addressing unit decides where the data have to go when the arithmetic unit has finished.

The speed at which these various operations take place is counted today in millionths of a second. It is this speed, and the complexity of data movements within the computer, that give it an aura of magic.

9.4 INPUT DEVICES

The computer is useless without data to process. The input of data is the first step in data processing operations and requires the conversion of facts and figures in alphabetical and numerical form into a form the computer can use. This, as we saw earlier, means converting all data into the binary digits 1 and 0, which can be represented by electrical impulses. Fortunately, modern computers can accept data from a variety of different media, all of which are created by a machine which is used by an operator who enters numerical or alphabetical data, or which reads signals on input documents. The methods used are:

1. Punched cards.
2. Punched paper-tape.
3. Magnetic tape.
4. Magnetic discs.
5. Teletype.
6. Visual display unit.
7. Magnetic ink character recognition(MICR).
8. Optical mark reading (OMR).
9. Optical character recognition (OCR).
10. Bar coding.
11. Voice recognition.

Punched Cards and Punched Paper-tape

Punched cards and punched paper-tape work on the principle that a hole in card or paper will allow a photoelectric light cell to send a signal to the computer. Where a hole is punched a positive digit is read; no hole is a negative digit. Hence for every position on the card or tape a code is read. The program in the computer interprets the code according to the predetermined layout of the card or tape. The holes are punched by an operator using a numeric keyboard on a special machine. One of the problems is the accuracy of keying, and so the cards or tape are check keyed through a second machine called a verifier, or through the same machine switched to verify status. The same data are keyed in and, where an error occurs, the machine indicates it.

Once the cards or tape are verified they are read by a special device connected to the computer. On modern computers the data are usually transferred onto magnetic tape or disc held on the computer. This is done because the card and tape readers are relatively slow and would slow the computer down. Punched cards and punched paper tape have virtually disappeared from modern use.

Magnetic Tape and Discs

Magnetic tape and discs are produced in a similar way to cards and paper-tape. The systems are generally referred to as key-to-disc. These methods have now more or less replaced punched card and paper-tape. They are more accurate for the simple reason that the data are checked as they are keyed and the operation is stopped if there is an error.

Magnetic tape and disc are easier to handle, can be read much more quickly and can be keyed more easily; thus operators should be able to process more data more accurately. Like cards and paper-tape, the data entered are placed on the magnetic tape in a coded form which once again is integrated by the program held in the computer.

Teletype and Visual Display Units

Teletype machines input data by transmitting the data entered on the keyboard via a telephone line directly into the computer. On the machine the characters typed are printed onto paper as in a typewriter, and at the same time are transmitted to the computer. It also works in reverse, receiving signals and transferring them onto paper. They are, therefore, both input and output devices.

Visual display units operate in a similar way to teletype machines, replacing the paper with a screen on which the keyed data appear.

These two types of machine transmit data in one of two ways:

1. Synchronous, which means a block of data is transmitted at once and is held in the terminal in a buffer until ready for transmission.
2. Asynchronous, which means each character is transmitted as it is keyed.

In synchronous terminals errors can be corrected by returning to the place on the screen and changing the character. With asynchronous devices additional data have to be entered to replace the incorrect data.

It is important when designing a data collection system to distinguish between the two terminal types, selecting the one most suitable for the application. Generally speaking, the synchronous type is more expensive, and this must be taken into account.

Character Recognition and Mark Recognition

Apart from these methods of input from keyboards, a number of alternative methods have been developed for inputting data, all of which use marks on original documents. The idea is simple and in certain situations the use of such marks eliminates the need for input via a keyboard. The machines are separated into two categories:

1. Character recognition.
2. Mark recognition.

There are two kinds of character recognition, magnetic and optical. Magnetic characters are specially printed in magnetic-based ink which, when fed through a special machine, can be read by the computer. The best example is the coding used on cheques.

Optical characters are read on the basis of the shape of the character conforming to a pattern held in the machine through which the document is fed. The problem is making sure the characters are printed or written correctly.

Mark recognition falls into two categories – optical mark reading and bar coding. Optical mark reading depends on a mark being placed in an appropriate position on a predetermined layout on a form. The machine senses a mark by light reflection and the program interprets the information.

Bar coding is a special system where data are represented by a series of bars in a block of a certain size. A light source is passed across the block and by reflection a signal is transmitted and the data read. Examples of bar coding systems can be seen on library cards and grocery packages.

Mark recognition systems are both accurate and efficient when the marks can be specially printed on the primary documents or containers. This is quite suitable when the documents can be returned for reading after they have been used, like cheques, or when the bar codes can be read at the point of sale, as with grocery packages.

Voice Recognition

Perhaps the most important current development in the inputting of data is voice recognition. At the present time the voice recognition systems available rely on a limited number of words or phrases, usually spoken in a pre-defined way. The day is not far away when voice recognition will replace several methods of input, particularly those using keyboards.

Direct Input

There is one further way for data to enter the computer and this is via direct monitoring of physical activities via an analog converter. This is done by using a transducer to measure temperature, pressure, etc.; analog signals are passed to the computer, converted to digital signals and used in the computer system. Such direct input is a growing method, particularly in the automation of production processes.

When designing systems the method of input has to be carefully considered to ensure that the best method is chosen for speed, convenience, accuracy and cost. (See Chapter 12.)

9.5 STORAGE FACILITIES

The modern computer uses three main forms of storage:

1. Magnetic tape.
2. Magnetic discs.
3. Silicon chip memory.

Magnetic Tape

Magnetic tape has been used for many years and is still the main method of storing data outside the computer. In recent years fast tape drives have been developed so that data can be transferred from discs at high speed and stored outside the computer.

The reasons for doing this are security, convenience and cost. It is essential to ensure that copies of files on the computer are available if the data are corrupted on the machine. In addition, much data do not need to be available to the computer all the time, so storing them on high-speed discs would be wasteful and expensive.

The main problem with data held on tapes is that they can be accessed only sequentially, by running the tape from beginning to end until the data are found. Tapes are rarely used in this way today and normally they are used only for copying and for permanent storage rather than being a part of data processing. Quite often one of the first steps in a computer job is to transfer data from tape to disc.

Magnetic Discs

Magnetic discs are used both as storage off the computer and as a part of the normal data processing procedure. Magnetic discs come in a variety of sizes and types, which can be categorized as:

1. Fixed discs.
2. Cartridges or disc packs.
3. Diskettes or floppy discs.

All these have the facility of a moving read/write head which moves across the disc in a fixed position from centre to rim. As the disc spins, any part can be read very fast indeed.

Fixed discs. Fixed discs, as the name implies, cannot be removed, and they are used as an adjunct to the main memory of the computer, usually holding the programs until they are required.

Cartridges or disc packs. Cartridges and disc packs can be removed from the disc controller and stored. In some installations they are replacing tape for current data, hence saving the job of transferring from tape to disc.

Diskettes or floppy discs. Diskettes or floppy discs are similar in appearance to 45 r.p.m. records held in a special pack. They are flexible (hence the name 'floppy'), small and contain a limited amount of data. They are used mainly in mini and microcomputers and are both convenient and inexpensive, so there is little need to use magnetic tape for permanent storage on the smaller systems.

Silicon Chip Memory

Computer memory, that is the memory within the computer itself, is mostly in the form of silicon chip memory. Each transistor on the chip holds one digit of binary data (bit), and chips are currently being made which hold 256 000 bits of data, or 256 K as it is usually called. Developments will lead to larger and larger chip memories and technicians are talking of the 1 megabyte chip, or a chip that will hold 1 million bits of data. Chip memories come in several forms:

1. Random Access Memory (RAM).
2. Read Only Memory (ROM).
3. Programmable Read Only Memory (PROM).
4. Erasable Programmable Read Only Memory (EPROM).

Random Access Memory. RAM memory is used for the processing of data and could contain programs being used, data calculations, etc. This memory is volatile and will hold data only while the power is on. Therefore during power cuts or voltage fluctuations it is possible for data to be corrupted. RAM memory is the working memory of the computer.

Read Only Memory. ROM memory is not volatile and is used to hold the instructions which form the control software of the computer. It is inconvenient if these instructions have to be loaded every time the machine is switched on and there is always the danger of malfunction. ROM memory, as the name implies, can only be read and so cannot be changed.

Programmable Read Only Memory. PROM memory is the same as ROM except for the fact that the ROM is empty until programmed using special development equipment. Again, once loaded the memory remains and cannot be changed.

Erasable Programmable Read Only Memory. EPROM has the additional feature of allowing the ROM to be erased and a new program entered.

A combination of RAM and ROM chips provides the memory of virtually all computers, and older, more expensive types of memory, such as magnetic drum and ferrite core memories, can be considered obsolete.

New Developments

Modern developments are leading to a number of new forms of memory which promise larger capacity in smaller space at less cost. These are video discs and bubble memory.

Video discs, although they can be written only once, have a capacity so great and a cost so low that they will almost certainly provide a replacement for tape and magnetic discs in the future.

Bubble memory is a special form of chip which, instead of holding data in transistors, holds them in the form of a magnetized area or domain in a thin film of material, hence the name 'bubble'. They are non-volatile, have no moving parts, and are robust and reliable. They are available now, but are very expensive.

Developments will, of course, continue, and there is no doubt that we shall see chip memories with very large capacity at low cost gradually replacing the other forms currently in use.

9.6 COMMUNICATIONS

The transmission of data in digital form along telephone lines and via satellite has led to the development of world-wide computer systems. The speed of transfer of data is very fast and the levels of accuracy are very high.

The concept of communication networks was dealt with in the preceding chapter. As far as computer hardware is concerned, the device which links the modems with the computer is a communications controller. In terminals, microcomputers and minicomputers this takes the form of a board containing suitably programmed chips. In the mainframe computer it is usually looked after by a separate device (small computer) called a communication handler or front end processor.

The reason for the larger device on the mainframe is to sort out the number of lines coming into the computer, and to ensure that the response goes back to the correct user.

When a signal is received the communications device sorts out the type of signal and relays it to the CPU, where it is processed and returned to the communications device to be sorted out and returned to the user.

In large networks with many lines coming into the centre it is also advisable to have a network controller. This is a machine which monitors the performance of lines and helps to diagnose problems with both lines and modems.

Developments in the telecommunication field are many and varied, but perhaps the most important is the use of computerized telephone exchanges which will bring about great changes in the way we use the telephone system. With a computerized exchange you can, for example, dial ten calls one after the other. The computer will store your calls and get them one by one. It will also be possible to send a package of data instead of a string of bits.

Packet switching, as it is called, provides speed and efficiency and is a major factor in the development of an electronic mailing system. Electronic mail will allow data to be transferred from one computer or word processor to another via the telephone line. At the receiving end the individual will key in his or her reference number and the machine will display on the screen or type out all the mail held on the recipient's file. It is believed that this will considerably reduce paperwork in the office.

9.7 OUTPUT

The primary objective of the computer system is to produce information for administrative planning and control. The bulk of this information has to be read by people.

There are several ways in which information can be retrieved from the computer. Some of these cannot be read directly by human beings and some can. The unreadable forms usually appear in two ways:

1. Punched cards and paper tape.
2. Magnetic tapes, discs and cassettes.

Both of these forms of output are intended for further use on computers or on computer terminals, and really constitute the input for a further stage in the data processing procedures.

The readable form of information appears as a display or some form of printed report.

The visual display unit (VDU) allows the user to look at a limited amount of data on the file. The limit is determined either by the size of the screen or by the file and the access programs. The screen size is, however, the usual limitation. VDUs are used either as a 'read only' device or as an 'interactive' device allowing the user to change the information on the screen and then return the amended information to the computer file. This means that many systems can use VDUs in place of printout which has to be scanned for information, then amended manually and re-input to the system. This considerable increase in efficiency is bought at the expense of sophisticated security and control procedures, but when used in the right way VDUs provide an excellent form of output.

If information is required for regular and wide distribution to people not directly using terminals, it has to be printed onto paper. Printed information is produced by a variety of different types of printers. The main problem facing the system designer is to find a method which can work at high speed and yet produce the quality of printing desired by management. Printers come in two main forms:

1. Line printers.
2. Serial printers.

Line Printers

Line printers, as their name implies, print a whole line at once. This is achieved by the use of a print chain, bar, roller or barrel on which the characters are held and which rotate continuously. As each character required comes into the print position the program instructs a hammer to be fired electrically. The paper and the ribbon lie between the hammer and the print. In this way a whole line of between 60 and 160 characters is printed at speeds of from 150 to 2500 lines a minute. These speeds are rarely achieved because of the need for spacing (moving the paper up one line) and skipping (moving up multiple spaces).

Serial Printers

Serial printers print one character at a time across the page, with the printer head usually moving across the paper. The best known serial printer is the electric golfball typewriter. Serial printers, though slower, usually produce a much better quality than line printers. The appearance of the print depends on the method used. Recent developments of thimble and daisy wheel printers work in a similar way to golfball printers and produce excellent quality. The names 'golfball', 'thimble' and 'daisy wheel' refer to the appearance of the printhead.

There are two main kinds of serial printers – impact and non-impact. Impact printers are mostly of the matrix type in which a group of wires in a 9 × 7 block are pushed forward to form a character. This is then transferred to the paper through an ink ribbon. Up to six copies can be produced. The characters are very clear but it is always possible to see the way the character is formed of dots.

Non-impact printers use one of three methods to place a character onto the paper; these are electrostatic, electrothermal and ink jet. The first of these methods places a charge on special paper, the second burns the character on special paper and the third squirts ink in the shape of the character on to the plain paper. Non-impact printers cannot produce copies.

Block, Roll and Laser Printers

There are several other types of printers which are not as common as line and serial printers. These are block printers, roll printers and laser printers.

Block printers are a mixture of line and serial. They use a rotating drum with about nine characters which moves across the page printing characters in blocks.

Roll printers, like adding machines, have a tally roll on which up to 20 characters can be printed.

Laser printers (IBM 3800) (ICL LPS14) use the xerographic process to print a set of characters on to a photo-conductive surface which is then printed using a laser and an electric charge. These printers are very fast, printing 13 000 lines a minute, and print additional copies by repeat runs.

The type of printer attached to the computer will certainly limit the way in which information is presented, but these technical limitations hardly affect the flexibility and scope with which printers can be used.

What really matters in presenting information effectively is good form design, linked to an understanding of the limitations of computer output. This is dealt with fully in Chapter 14.

9.8 SUMMARY AND REVISION NOTES

There are five main elements in computer hardware:

1. Input devices.
2. Central processing unit.
3. Storage.
4. Output devices.
5. Communication channels.

Digital computers operate by representing data in number form coded in binary, using two states, 1 and 0, represented by the presence or lack of an electrical charge.

Analog computers represent data in physical units such as voltage levels or mechanical switches.

Computer operating functions work in five stages.

1. Discover where the data are.
2. Go to get the data.
3. Move data to where they are needed.
4. Use the data.
5. Return them to the file.

The central processing unit, CPU, contains three elements:

1. Arithmetic unit.
2. Instruction unit.
3. Addressing unit.

Input devices fall into five groups:

1. Punched card and paper-tape.
2. Magnetic tape and discs.
3. Terminals.
4. Character and mark recognition.
5. Voice recognition.

Whichever device is used the key to successful input is accuracy and speed related to the needs of the system.

Storage facilities fall into three categories:

1. Magnetic tape.
2. Magnetic disc.
3. Silicon chip memory.

These are used in a variety of ways. Tape storage is normally used for long-term storing outside the computer. Magnetic discs are used as part of the processing procedure, transferring data and programs to the main memory of the CPU, which is made up of silicon chips.

Communication facilities handle the receipt of data from the telephone lines, organize it and ensure that the response goes back to the correct terminal.

New communication developments could lead to less paper in the office as electronic mail systems replace the use of paper.

Output from the computer falls into two main types:

1. Machine readable.
2. Human readable.

Machine readable output is in the form of punched card, tape and magnetic media. Human readable output is either displayed or printed. Displays are on screens and printing is usually on paper.

Printers are produced in a wide range, but are usually either line or serial printers, the latter being either impact or non-impact.

New developments are increasing the quality and speed of printing, but this does not necessarily increase the quality of the presentation of the information.

QUESTIONS

1. Because of rising labour costs and a high staff turnover you are investigating the replacement of your existing punched card input procedures by an alternative non-key-punching method.

    (a) Describe three non-key-punching methods and state for each its advantages and disadvantages.
    (b) In what circumstances is the use of non-key-punching methods most appropriate?
    (ICMA)

2. Describe the operating functions that can take place in the central processing unit (CPU) during a routine data processing job.

3. Although in the earlier days of computerization the majority of files were held on magnetic tape, nowadays magnetic discs are more common. Describe the characteristics of the two storage media given above and discuss some of the problems of storing and accessing records on tapes and on discs. (ICMA)

4. Describe five computer output devices. Discuss the advantages and disadvantages of each. (IMS)

5. A computer system consists of a mixture of hardware devices assembled into a configuration to meet the system's needs. Describe the essential parts of such a configuration.

CASE STUDY EXERCISE

Put forward outline proposals for the computer configuration, indicating your reasons for the various elements.

10
Software

10.1 WHAT IS SOFTWARE?

Software is in concept quite simple; it consists of the instructions which the computer follows to carry out the required tasks. Hardware, as we have seen, functions under the control of the software fed into the computer.

In modern computers some software is held permanently in ROM (Read Only Memory), and this form of software is being referred to as 'firmware' to distinguish it from the software that has to be fed to the computer when it is used. With the development of the microchip, this form of control software will increase, and additional control facilities will be added by using additional microchips.

These developments are moving at an increasing rate and it will not be long before all the control software in even the largest computers will be held on microchip. This brings advantages in reliability and speed but can lead to rigidity and make changes expensive. No matter which software we are concerned with, it has to be held in the computer.

10.2 STORED INSTRUCTIONS AND LANGUAGES

The major breakthrough in the early days of the computer was undoubtedly the ability to store instructions which would control the processes carried out by the machine. These instructions were stored in binary in the central memory and, as each one was executed, the machine returned to the next one, and so on until the list of instructions came to an end.

In the early days the instructions were fed in in binary form called machine code, which was both time-consuming and tedious, and errors were easy to make. The people producing the sets of instructions or programs became known as programmers.

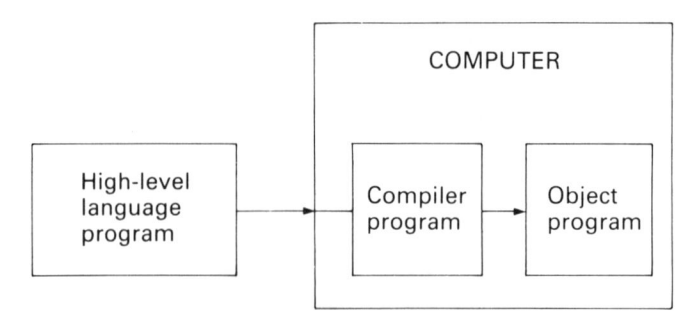

```
┌─────────────────────────────────────────────┐
│                  COMPUTER                    │
│                                              │
│  ┌──────────┐    ┌──────────┐   ┌─────────┐ │
│  │High-level│    │ Compiler │   │ Object  │ │
│  │ language │───▶│ program  │──▶│ program │ │
│  │ program  │    │          │   │         │ │
│  └──────────┘    └──────────┘   └─────────┘ │
│                                              │
└─────────────────────────────────────────────┘
```

Figure 10.1 *Compiling programs*

Gradually the methods of inputting the instructions changed from machine code to a high level of code called a language, which the computer converted to machine code via the use of a special compiler program.

A computer language, no matter what it is called, is really a coding system with rules of grammar and syntax similar to a spoken language such as English. Languages have been developed to make the programming job easier. They have been possible only because of the software built into the computer which converts the language to the machine code called the object program. The method used is depicted in Figure 9.1.

In the modern computer there are several factors which affect the form of software and the way it is stored. These are:

1. The architecture of the hardware.
2. The control instructions built into the ROMs.
3. Computer-operating software, including language interpreters.
4. The size of the computer storage available.
5. The work the computer is going to do.

Before programming a particular computer the programmer has to examine these factors and establish the best way to program. There are many similarities between different computers, but it is rare to find two different computers which use exactly the same programming systems, even if the language is the same. The COBOL (Common Business Oriented Language) used on IBM is not the same as the ICL or HONEYWELL COBOL. This does not make the programmer's life easy, but fortunately, as we shall see later, the coding element of programming is by far the easiest stage.

10.3 LEVELS OF SOFTWARE

Software can be subdivided into three main levels:

1. Operating software.
2. Software facilities.
3. Application software.

Operating Software

This is the software designed by the computer manufacturer and is the control software for the computer. It determines:

1. The manipulation of data within the machine.
2. Management of the computer devices.
3. The languages used, interpretation, etc.
4. Operating procedures.
5. Console messages to operators.

Operating systems determine, to a large extent, the efficiency of the computer system. The way the operating system manages the central memory is a good example. Two methods available are called partitioning and dynamic allocation. (Other methods are discussed in Chapter 13.) In partitioning the memory is separated into several partitions, each of a size requested by the user (Figure 10.2 (a)). When one program finishes

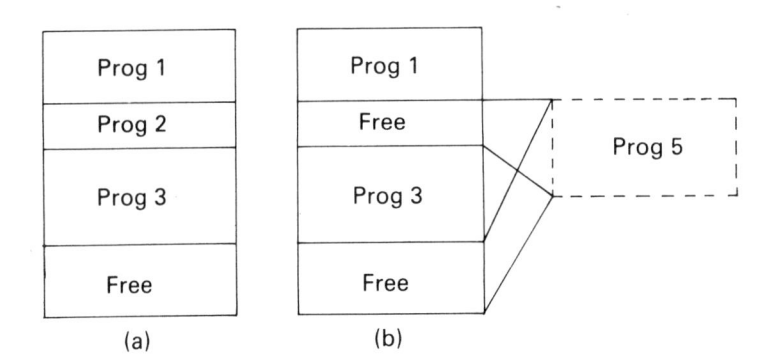

Figure 10.2 *Memory allocation*

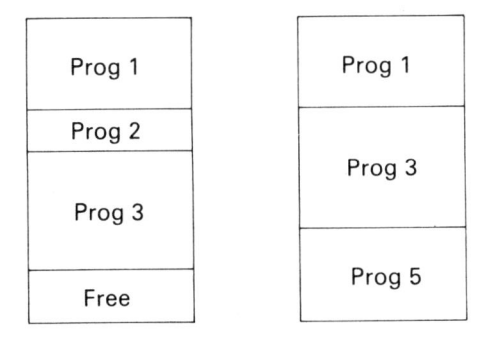

Figure 10.3 *Dynamic allocation*

it releases a partition of a fixed size. If this is too small for the next program, it won't fit and must wait (Figure 10.2 (b)).

In the dynamic allocation system the memory starts off in a similar way to partitioning, but when the program moves out the memory is re-aligned to make all the necessary space available for the next program (Figure 10.3).

There is a vast range of features such as these which are built into the operating system.

Software Facilities

Further aids are available to programmers in modern computers. These take the form of optional facilities which are provided as software packages. These may be for providing ready-made programs for generating reports, for producing financial models, for file management and for many other tasks.

Application Software

Application software consists of special programs written to meet the specific needs of the user. They are usually written in a high-level language, within the limits of the operating software, and where necessary using special facilities.

Application programs can be specially written or purchased in the form of pre-written packages. The majority of programming that is done outside the computer manufacturers is application programming. A wide range of languages are used, including the following:

1. COBOL: COmmon Business Oriented Language.
2. ALGOL: ALGOrithmic Language.
3. FORTRAN: FORmula TRANslation.
4. PL/1: Programming Language 1.
5. BASIC: Beginners All-purpose Symbolic Instruction Code.
6. PASCAL: A new language with the advantages of COBOL and ALGOL.
7. RPG: Report Program Generator.
8. ASSEMBLER: Machine code language.

COBOL. COBOL is written in four sections:

1. Identification, containing descriptions of the program.
2. Environment, which deals with the specification of the computer, including such items as size of memory, number of peripheral devices, tape decks, printers, etc.
3. Data, the section which is used to give names to the units of data on which operations are to be performed; input and output files are defined, as are records and fields used.
4. Procedure, the section which gives the step-by-step instructions necessary to solve the problem. The instructions are written in a form of English.

ALGOL. ALGOL programs consist of:

1. Data items.
2. Statements.
3. Declarations.

Data items are the variables which are to be manipulated by the operations represented by the statements, with the declarations stating the quantities and sizes of variables. ALGOL is normally used for mathematical and scientific use.

FORTRAN. FORTRAN is another high-level language used mainly for mathematical and scientific problem-solving. The program is made up of:

1. Data.
2. Executable and non-executable statements.

The program is built in segments, one of which is a master segment and the others optional segments and sub-routines.

PL/1. This language was developed to combine features of languages such as COBOL and ALGOL. The reason for doing this was to bring the data-handling facilities of commercial languages such as COBOL together with the problem-solving strengths of the scientific language, making a more useful language.

BASIC. BASIC is a simple, easy-to-use program which is usually used in programming microcomputers. It is written in a form of English and works in the following way:

1. Define program name.
2. List data.
3. List instructions.
4. Produce results.
5. End.

It is like saying:

> These are the data and this is where they are.
> This is what I want to do with them.
> This is where I wish the result to go.

It is an excellent language for beginners.

PASCAL. PASCAL is a modern language developed as the modern answer to commercial programming. It has advantages over COBOL and ALGOL, is relatively easy to learn and easily replaces PL/1, which has never gained wide acceptance.

RPG. RPG, though it started out as a very high-level language for generating reports, has gradually been extended and is now quite powerful.

ASSEMBLER. ASSEMBLER is a machine code language which is used by professional programmers to gain the speed and efficiency that can be obtained by writing directly in machine code. It is possible and sometimes of significant advantage to write ASSEMBLER sub-routines linked to COBOL programs.

All these languages and other, less popular ones are methods of instructing the computer to carry out certain tasks. They all have to be converted to object code and this creates a pattern of software depicted in Figure 10.4.

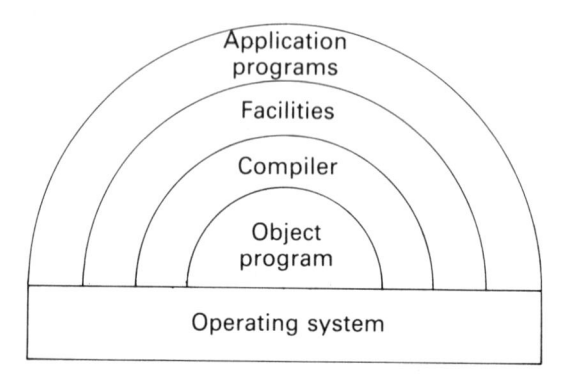

Figure 10.4 *Software pattern*

10.4 PRINCIPLES OF PROGRAMMING

Good programming demands crystal-clear thinking, the application of logic, and care and thoroughness in writing the program. Regardless of the language used, the programmer has to carry out seven steps from conception to birth of a working program. These are:

1. Define the problem.
2. Analyse the problem.
3. Decide how to arrive at the solution.
4. Write the program.
5. Test the program.
6. Correct the program.
7. Run the program.

Defining the Problem

Most programmers make the fatal mistake of jumping in with both feet at step 4 of the programming process, without first having correctly defined the problem. The problem can be defined by setting out the objectives that are to be achieved at two levels:

1. Primary objectives.
2. Secondary objectives.

A primary objective might be to update a file with certain transactions. Secondary objectives might be to produce a report of what has been done and to calculate new control totals.

Analysing the Problem

Once the objectives have been defined, it is possible to analyse the problem by asking a series of questions, such as: Which file to update? Where do the data come from? What volumes are involved? What are the sizes of the data fields? Where are the control totals filed? What should be reported? And so on.

When all the pertinent questions have been asked and answered, it is possible to decide how to arrive at the solution.

Deciding how to Arrive at a Solution

There are usually many ways of achieving the objectives that have been defined. Deciding on the best path is where the skill and flair of the programmer come into play. This requires a deep knowledge of the particular language, as well as a clear view of the logic involved.

It is at this stage that programming flowcharts are of greatest value. A simple flowchart is shown in Figure 10.5. Once the flowchart is complete it is possible to write the program.

Writing the Program

The program may be written on coding sheets or direct via the keyboard. In some ways it is preferable to use coding sheets because this allows a further process of analysis before the program is keyed in. No matter which method is used the key is to ensure that the requirements of the language are met and that the syntax is correct.

It is very important to make sure that instructions are entered in the correct logical sequence. If this is not done then the program will malfunction. If logic fails, then the program will also fail. It is interesting to note that the logical requirements of programming are very similar to the grammatical requirements of learning the English language. If the words are used in the wrong way, or if presentation and spacing are incorrect, then it will not be understood.

Testing the Program

When the program has been written it has to be compiled and tested. Modern computers will check the program for syntax errors during the compilation and report

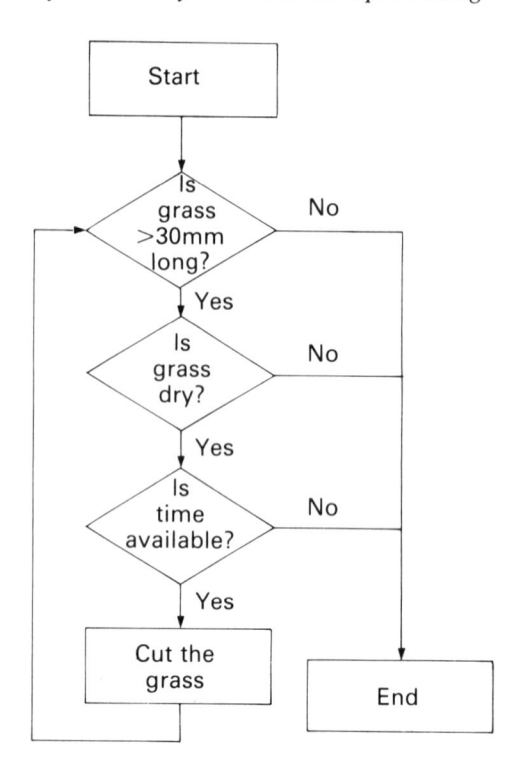

118 — *Management information systems and data processing*

Figure 10.5 *Program flowchart (grass)*

to the programmer, either on paper or on the screen. The program is then checked and corrected, re-compiled and tested again.

Some programmers seem to think that this process of compilation and testing is the way to program. They put very poor programs into the computer and use the computer to spot mistakes, which they then correct. This ad hoc, lazy way to program produces long, inefficient programs.

Correcting the Program

Programs, because of the immense detail usually involved, are unlikely to work first time. They may malfunction for various reasons, including:

1. Syntax error, e.g. using a full stop instead of a comma.
2. Logic error. For example in Figure 10.5 if the instruction to loop back after 'cut the grass' was missing, the program would not reach 'end'.
3. Missing instructions, coding error.
4. Missing data definitions.
5. Missing field definitions.

Before the program can be corrected the reason for the error must be found. Without clear thinking and a properly documented analysis this can be, and often is, a very time-consuming process.

Running the Program

When it is known that the program works it can be run with real data, checking that the anticipated results occur, and when each program in the system has been tested, they can all be tested together.

Very often in large data processing departments the programming activity is reduced to the very menial task of writing coding sheets from detailed flowcharts and instructions produced by systems analysts. This approach removes the problem-solving element from the programmer's job and so degrades it. It also leads to major problems in getting programs to work. In this type of environment, programmers want to move on to the more interesting job of analysis, and so programming is done by the most inexperienced staff.

The good analyst is not necessarily a good programmer and vice versa. It is quite realistic and very effective for analysts and programmers to work side by side at all levels. The alternatives are depicted in Figure 10.6.

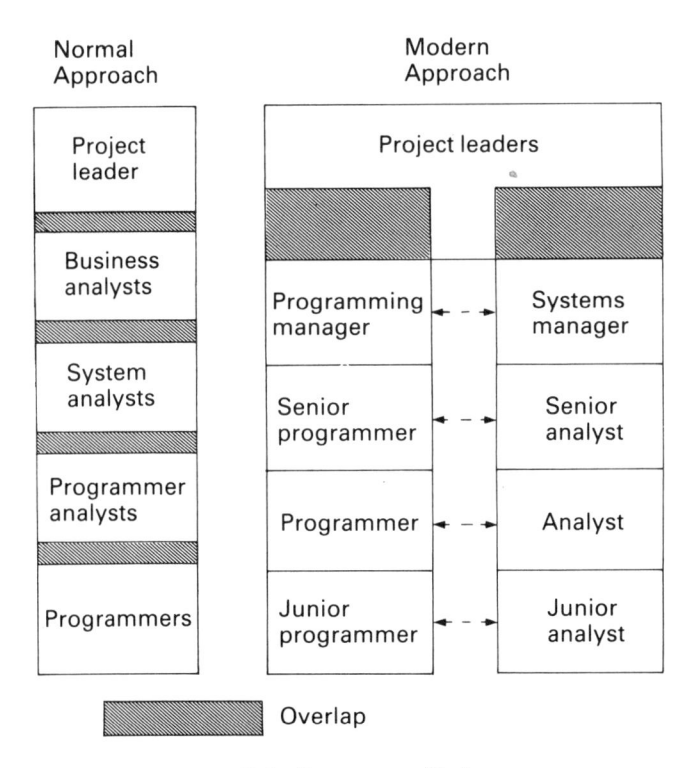

Figure 10.6 *Programmer effectiveness*

10.5 MODULAR AND STRUCTURED PROGRAMS

The names 'modular' and 'structured' programming relate to the approach to programming which demands careful analysis of what the program is trying to achieve. From this point the program is divided into elements, each of which has an input point and an output point within the logic of the program. From this division it is possible to devise the most efficient logic flow with the minimum of loops. This leads to simpler, smaller programs where each module fits neatly into the structure of the program.

The advantages of these techniques of programming are:

1. The logic in programs is vastly improved.
2. Programming is simplified.
3. Smaller programs can be produced.
4. Overall program design is improved.

In addition to these advantages, structured programming is very important in the design of interactive and data base systems. This raises the question of differences in software associated with the type of data processing.

10.6 BATCH PROCESSING PROGRAMS

In Chapter 5 the differences between batch and transaction processing were described. These differences affect the approach to programming.

In batch processing the programs are dealing with a large volume of transactions in groups organized and identified in the most appropriate way for the program. The data are processed in batches from beginning to end of the set of programs. The programs are therefore usually written to do as much as possible with the data while they are being manipulated by the program. They are, therefore, usually large programs doing a good deal of sorting, merging and calculation.

For many years COBOL has been the main language used for programming batch processing systems, and it is only as more and more interactive processing is being done that COBOL is being replaced by other, more appropriate languages.

10.7 INTERACTIVE SOFTWARE

Interactive systems, processing transactions one by one as they are received, have to be written in a different way so that they function very quickly. They are therefore written in modules, usually quite small, doing one or two steps with the data and responding directly with the input device.

Programmers who move from writing batch processing programs to writing interactive programs find that the change is quite a big one. One of the main differences is the way in which they have to link their program with the computer's transaction processing (TP) facilities software. This is, of course, becoming more commonplace with the development of more interactive systems with mini and microcomputers.

10.8 DATA BASE SOFTWARE

In its simplest form a data base is a file holding data in a predetermined sequence which can be accessed by one or more keys held in each record.

If several files are grouped together to create larger data bases, then the problem of updating the data base and subsequently accessing it is made more complicated.

The operation of data base systems is dealt with in more detail in Chapter 11, but from the software point of view the programmer has to be very careful to ensure that data are properly defined and that calculations are carried through to all the appropriate files.

In modern computers it is usual for data base software facilities to be available to the programmer, who then has to write the application program so that it passes data to, and receives data from, the appropriate element of the software. This does, of course, simplify the programming.

The decision to use data base software means a high cost in terms of the memory needed to hold the facility. Data base management systems are of necessity complex and bulky programs to manipulate the files and the data transfer. They also need special controls to avoid the creation of rubbish data through incorrectly accumulating the same data held in more than one file.

As systems have grown, and as more and more memory has become available, so software has increased in complexity. Programmers today have numerous aids which can assist them to produce efficient and adequate programs. But even with all these tools, if their basic thinking is not crystal clear, they will still produce inadequate programs.

10.9 SUMMARY AND REVISION NOTES

Software is the name given to the instructions which control the computer's operations.

These stored instructions are fed to the computer by the programmer, using a coding system called a language.

The language used by the programmer has to be converted (compiled) into a coding system understood by the machine. This becomes the object program.

There are three main levels of software:

1. Operating software.
2. Software facilities.
3. Application software.

Programming consists of seven main steps:

1. Defining the problem.
2. Analysing the problem.
3. Deciding on the solution.
4. Writing the program.
5. Testing the program.
6. Correcting the program.
7. Running the program.

Modular and structured programming are approaches to programming which first demand a careful analysis of the underlying logic before developing the program.

Batch processing programs are written in such a way that a great deal of processing is done with a batch of like data.

Interactive programs are created to do a small amount of processing with each transaction as it is received.

Data base software exists in modern computers as a facility to aid the programmer who is writing application programs which need to access related data files.

QUESTIONS

1. Programming has become less machine oriented and more problem oriented. Define these terms and explain how changes in programming languages have made this possible. (ICMA)

2. 'A modern computer covering both batched operations on conventional peripherals and terminal based demand processing is as much dependent on software as it is on hardware. Ideally it has only minimal dependence on the human being.' Discuss the roles of operational software and the human element in the context of this quotation. (ICMA)

3. Describe, with the aid of examples:

    (a) programming logic;
    (b) software;
    (c) application packages.
    (IMS)

4. Programming involves a number of distinct tasks. State what these tasks are and indicate the order and priority you would give to each one.

5. A wide range of computer languages is available. Explain what is meant by a language and give two examples of languages currently available, describing each one.

CASE STUDY EXERCISE

Bearing in mind the computer configuration you have suggested, prepare a schedule of software requirements, with some indication of whether the main approach will be for batch or for interactive software.

11

Data Generation and Processing

11.1 DATA: A DEFINITION

'Data' is a word used to describe collections of facts and figures, i.e. names, numbers, etc. Grammatically the word 'data' is the plural of 'datum'; however, in general use the word 'data' is treated as a collective noun. Saying 'data are' is awkward and not common usage, so in data processing it is normal to say 'data is'.

Data processing is concerned with the manipulation of the facts and figures of the business. These consist of names, descriptions, numbers, values, etc., all in some meaningful relationship. When these data are processed they are sorted, merged, calculated, stored and output in the form needed by management, which we call information.

Data are, therefore, the raw material of information. The resulting information produced by the system is only as good as the quality of the data of which it is constructed. The old saying 'Garbage in, garbage out' is still true today. If we want information systems which are reliable then we must concentrate on good design and good data collection.

11.2 FORMS OF DATA

Within the computer system data are manipulated on several levels:

1. Characters.
2. Fields.
3. Records.
4. Blocks.

Characters

Characters may be in several forms:

1. Integers: numerical codes, dates, etc.
2. Alphabetic: names, descriptions, etc.
3. Alphabetical/numerical: mixed codes.
4. Real numbers: values, often to several decimal places, for quantities, money, etc.

Within the machine each character is converted into a binary number and is manipulated in this way throughout the machine.

Fields

Fields are made up of a number of characters. The field is the number of characters needed to make up a meaningful piece of data. If we take a name, e.g. JOHN SMITH, each alphabetical letter is a character, and the whole name forms the field. Such a field may be set as two fields in the computer to allow for first names and surnames of different length, e.g.

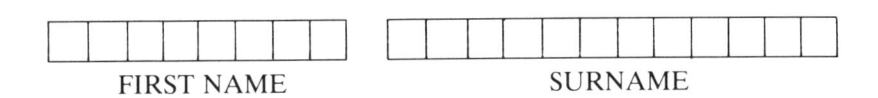

```
┌─┬─┬─┬─┬─┬─┬─┬─┐    ┌─┬─┬─┬─┬─┬─┬─┬─┬─┬─┬─┬─┐
│ │ │ │ │ │ │ │ │    │ │ │ │ │ │ │ │ │ │ │ │ │
└─┴─┴─┴─┴─┴─┴─┴─┘    └─┴─┴─┴─┴─┴─┴─┴─┴─┴─┴─┴─┘
     FIRST NAME                SURNAME
```

In this example it can be seen that fields are described as FIRST NAME 8 Alpha characters, and the second field as SURNAME 12 Alpha characters. When the name JOHN SMITH is entered there are a number of spaces, e.g.

```
┌─┬─┬─┬─┬─┬─┬─┬─┐    ┌─┬─┬─┬─┬─┬─┬─┬─┬─┬─┬─┬─┐
│J│O│H│N│ │ │ │ │    │S│M│I│T│H│ │ │ │ │ │ │ │
└─┴─┴─┴─┴─┴─┴─┴─┘    └─┴─┴─┴─┴─┴─┴─┴─┴─┴─┴─┴─┘
```

Records

Records are meaningful groups of fields strung together to create a successful piece of information. In the above example the fields for names might be part of a record which contains additional fields, e.g. the employee record on the opposite page.

If the record is seen as a simple, long string of fields each will be separated by spaces when input, so the record size might be 99 + 11 spaces = 110 characters. Within the computer there are software facilities which remove the spaces on input and replace them on output. This is called packing and is done to reduce the space needed in memory, in the central program and on the files.

	Field Size	Definition
Record type	(2)	Numerical (N)
Name – First	(8)	Alphabetic (A)
– Second	(12)	Alphabetic (A)
Address	(12)	Alpha-numerical (A/N)
	(12)	
	(12)	
	(12)	
Start date	(6)	(N)
Length of service	(4)	(N)
Sex	(1)	(A)
Date of birth	(6)	(N)
Department	(12)	(A)
	(<u>99</u>)	

Blocks

Blocks of data consist of groups of records which take up a certain amount of space on the files or in the memory. In the above example a block could be 20 employee records.

The definition of data into these elements is important for the checking and control of the accuracy of the data input. Data validation is very important and is dealt with at length in Chapter 12.

11.3 DATA HIERARCHIES AND NETWORKS

Within the established records and fields there is a relationship between the various parts of the record. In the employee record example the employee's name will probably be the key piece of data for finding the record, amending it or deleting it from the system. Because people can have the same name it might be necessary to give each employee a number. In this case the employee number becomes the more accurate key.

Once the key is identified then, by using the key, we can access the data available. This will consist of all the data held as part of the employee record. There may also be another record using the employee number, and this might be held on the payroll system. So not only do we have to know the key to unlock the data, we also need to know which lock to insert the key into.

Within the different information systems operating on the computer there will be many pieces of data which appear to be the same. Dates, names and values may appear in many places and it is only by knowing the relationship between data elements, the systems in which they exist and the appropriate files that mistakes are avoided.

Finding data in the system is rather like finding certain products in a large supermarket. First of all you look for the general area, which is indicated by large signs. When you reach the area you look for the appropriate shelf and then the appropriate product. In addition the product has to be properly defined. If you went shopping for peas you could find them in three areas: greens, tinned goods and frozen foods. It all depends on which kind of peas you want.

In data processing the programmer must know exactly what data are required and where they are. This is a very important aspect of programming and, as in the supermarket, the approach the programmer takes is to label and address data so that he or she knows where they are.

11.4 FILE STRUCTURES

All data that are processed in the computer are held in some form of storage, either temporarily or permanently. Temporary files consist of transaction files which contain new input and which are being processed and moved into permanent files.

The permanent files exist in a structured form within which some data are constantly changing. Imagine an employee file which contains records of the employee's name and pay details. The name will remain constant, but the details of pay, tax, etc. will change weekly. In addition the control totals on the file will change every time the file is updated.

There are a variety of ways in which files can be structured, but the main ways normally used are:

1. Simple structure.
2. Multiple level.
3. Related files.

Simple file structures consist of a number of like records held under a main key, with a file identification record and control totals. The records will usually be of the same length. An employee file could be made up of records like the one illustrated under

'Records' in section 11.2, all held under the name key in alphabetical order.

Multiple-level files consist of several levels of records, each with its key. In the example of the employee file it could be structured as a multiple file as follows:

> Employee file
> Department   (First level)
> Section   (Second level)
> Sex   (Third level)
> Employee   (Fourth level)

The department record could hold details of name, location, number of employees and total labour cost. The section record could hold details of the name of the section, number of employees, production hours and labour cost. 'Sex' could hold, for each sex, number of employees, age and length of service. Finally, we come to the details of individual employees.

Related files are another way of handling large amounts of data. Each file is usually structured as a simple file, but the record of the main file holds keys to other files. This structure is depicted in Figure 11.1.

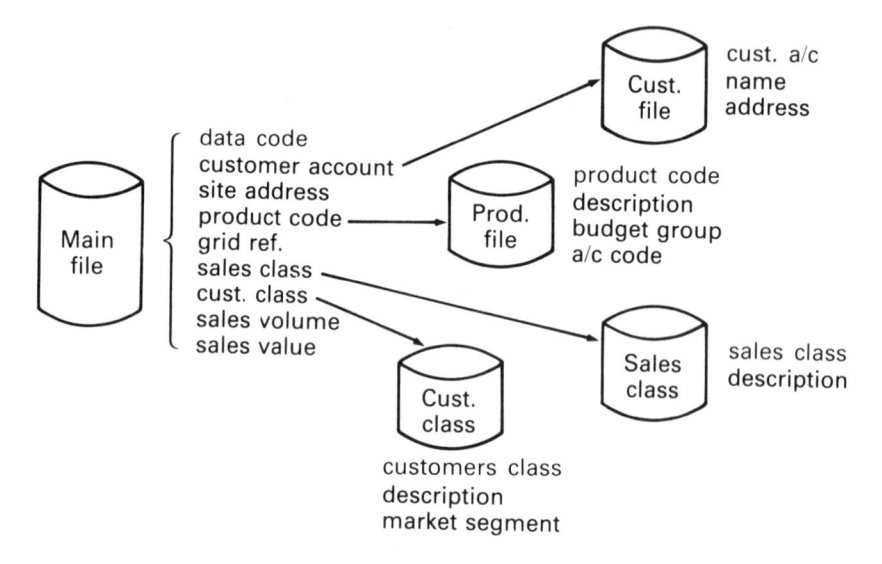

Figure 11.1 *Related file structure*

The reason for these various file structures is to enable files to be kept as small and as relevant as possible, to make updating and access as fast as possible. In the case of the related file structure shown in Figure 11.1, the four secondary files carry data which are more constant than the main file, which is updated regularly. The multiple-level file allows access to summary information where only that level is required, but enables direct access to the detail if needed by using the appropriate key. Of course, to get at an employee in the multiple file it is faster to give all keys. If only the employee key is given, it could take a long time to search the file.

Files are, therefore, structured as necessary to satisfy the needs of the system. This calls for efficient file organization.

11.5 FILE ORGANIZATION

When data are held in a computer-based file they have to be accessed for use within the system, and to be used in reports for management. The efficiency of data processing depends to a large extent on the speed with which data can be recovered from files. The speed itself is dependent on the way the data are organized within the file. There are four main ways in which this is done:

1. Sequential.
2. Indexed.
3. Indexed sequential.
4. Random addressing.

Sequential Organization

Sequential organization, as the name implies, holds all records in the direct sequence of the key. To find a particular record it is necessary to examine every record from the first until the required record is found. This could, of course, mean reading the file from beginning to end. When files are held on magnetic tape there is little choice but to hold them sequentially because the tape has to be read from the start until the required record is reached.

Indexed Organization

Indexed organization is used where there are a lot of data and holding them sequentially would mean time-consuming file searches. With the advent of discs data can be accessed on any part of the file providing the read head can be directed to the correct address on the file. As in a book, an index is used to direct the reader to the correct part of the file.

The index is created quite simply. If there are 500 records held on a file numbered from 100 to 599, we can index where each record is held by using an algorithm:

$$\text{Record Key} - 99 = \text{index number}$$

The index number states where the record can be found. Key codes which have not been allocated are given the position 0 in the file.

If key 100 is not used, then index 1, i.e. 100 − 99, will show 0. Key no. 275 will be index code 176. If key 275 was the first used it would be held as record 1, so the index would appear as shown below:

INDEX	
NUMBER	RECORD NO.
176	1

Key 319 is the next number used. This will be index 220, which will be record 2. If number 101 is used as the 90th record, it will be indexed as 2. So we have:

INDEX	
NUMBER	RECORD NO.
1	0
2	90
176	1
220	2

By calculating the index position the program can then go to the appropriate record position.

Insertions and deletions are straightforward. Inserts are made where there is a 0, and this record number is replaced with a 0 when it is deleted.

The index file is limited by size because the index has to be held in the main memory of the computer when the file is being accessed. Where this does not occur the index can be held as a file, but this slows the process down.

Indexed Sequential Organization

This method of organization uses a similar indexing approach, but all the records are held in sequence in the main file. They are indexed in blocks, with the index holding two pieces of information — the highest record key of the block and the record number. Looking for the key in the index above the one required leads to the block of records, which are then searched sequentially. So we have a combination of an index and then a short sequential search. This is excellent for large files but creates a few problems with insertions and deletions, as the records have to be fitted into the correct sequence. One way of doing this is to leave spaces in the sequence for future records. These spaces are referred to as overflow. When full, the file has to be re-organized.

Random Addressing

Random addressing is a form of organization which does not require an index, but calculates the record position by an algorithm used with the key code. An example of such an algorithm is shown below:

Record key ÷ Planned file size, then take remainder + 1
1096 ÷ 500 96 + 1 = 97
∴ record 1096 will be found in file position 97

This method will create the same pattern for different records; for example, record 1596 would also go to position 97. This is called a collision, and is overcome by taking the next available position. When retrieving records this collision problem leads to a short sequential search until the record is found.

File organization is, therefore, related to the size of file, the storage medium, the speed of accessing required and the problems of insertion and deletion. Selecting the correct method of organization is very important.

11.6 DATA MANIPULATION

Within the computer system, data are manipulated in a number of ways. These can be summarized as follows:

1. Sorting.
2. Calculating.
3. Comparing.
4. Merging.
5. Inserting.
6. Selecting.
7. Transferring.
8. Deleting.

Sorting is particularly important when preparing information for processing in batch processing and in preparing data for access or input to a sequential file. It is obvious that data can be processed quickly if they are in the same sequence as the file to which they relate. Sorting is also an important processing step when preparing data to be printed. In batch processing there is a good deal of sorting of data, and this is greatly assisted by batching information in transaction types prior to input. When data are held on indexed files sorting usually takes place after the data have been selected and before they are printed. Sorting may also be necessary if data are transferred from an indexed file to a sequential file.

Calculation of data is the processing step which most people associate with computing. It is, however, surprising that relatively little calculating is done in commercial data processing. Data do, however, have to be added, subtracted, multiplied and divided in many of the systems which form the basis of the information system. Most control records held in the computer demand calculating what happens to data, e.g. record counts, control totals.

Comparing data is a primary processing step, particularly in validation programs, when the content of data fields is being checked. Comparing is also done when files are copied and merged. In addition to these processes, comparing is done as a key part of the programming sequence, e.g.

If Record 4 is > record 5, move to instruction 103. This is not written in a programming language, but shows how the comparison is done between 4 and 5 linked to a calculation.

Merging of data takes place when, for example, this month's data are merged with the brought forward file to create the carry forward file. Merging usually involves calculation and comparison. This is seen in Figure 11.2.

Existing File

Record	Value
137	197.50
140	382.10
141	111.90
150	813.20
170	900.10
180	1100.00
	3504.80

New Data

Record	Value
137	88.90
139	210.20
150	50.10
160	100.10
	449.30

New File

Record	Value
137	286.40
139	210.20
140	382.10
141	111.90
150	863.30
160	100.10
170	900.10
180	1100.00
	3954.10

Figure 11.2 *Data merge*

In the example in Figure 11.2 the control totals would be input with the new data and the program would calculate the new file control total, then add the old file and the new data control, and then compare the two figures. This shows how a particular program step can include several methods of data manipulation.

Inserting is the process by which additional records are inserted into the appropriate place in the file, depending on the way in which the file is organized. This could also involve sorting and selecting. Inserting usually means looking for the space nearest to the one where the record should be. In an indexed sequential file, if the overflows are inadequate, then the file has to be re-organized.

Selecting is really a combination of a search and comparison. The keys required are given to the program and it goes to the file and searches it for the records required. These are then selected and transferred from the file to a temporary file. Before they are printed the records may have to be sorted. This processing step is a crucial step in interactive data processing, where each transaction is dealt with separately. In this case the record selected is transferred to the communications line and out to the terminal.

Transferring data from input to file, from file to file, and from file to output is going on constantly in the data processing procedure. The operating software in the computer controls the way in which all data are handled and is particularly relevant for transferring. When data are transferred they need to be preceded by special codes saying what the data are, the address to which they are going, and where they have come from. The end of the data being transferred is signalled by another code.

Normally data are transferred in blocks, and the block size is determined by a combination of the record size, the operating software and the hardware.

Deleting data from files is similar to a transfer except that not only is the file read and the record transferred, but the fields are filled with zeros. This is also referred to as 'zeroizing' or resetting the field. Normally when records are deleted they are transferred to a temporary file and printed out and probably stored on magnetic tape.

Within all the data processing steps discussed the computer will be doing one of three things with the data on the file:

1. Read only.
2. Write only.
3. Read/write.

The read only task is appropriate for file searches and selections, or when the person accessing the file for data is not allowed to change the data on the file. You will recall that ROM memory can only be read.

Write only is normally done when files are generated and when files are copied. The danger with write only instructions is that they may over-write valid records, thus corrupting the file.

Read and write is more time consuming, but a safer method of handling data. Modern hardware and operating software make the time difference so small that it does not really matter.

The operating power and speed of a computer are usually measured by two factors, both of which relate to the speed with which data are handled. These are:

1. Cycle time.
2. Transfer rates.

Cycle time refers to the time it takes for a single piece of data to go into, be processed in, and come out of the central processing unit.

Transfer rates are measured, usually in bits per second (BPS), and refer to transfers from file to file and from CPU to file, and include transfers to discs.

The hardware affects the way data are processed and, for example, if the machine used only magnetic tapes, all processing would have to be batch processing and files would be sequential. However, this is rare today, as most computer systems use magnetic discs with tape for back-up. With magnetic discs, data can be processed in any of the ways mentioned here and files organized in the most suitable form, providing the operating software is available.

The way in which data are processed and what can be done at one and the same time depend on the size of computer memory, the number of data channels and the peripherals, discs, printers, etc. The programmer has to bear these factors in mind when producing a program and when designing the file structures.

These physical limitations are becoming less important as new technology increases the size and speed of memories, etc. However, the well designed data processing system is the one which balances these factors and allows the efficient operation of the whole system (Chapter 13).

11.7 DATA BASE DESIGN PRINCIPLES

Files of data are the life-blood of information systems. The handling of primary data and the creation and maintenance of files are fundamental tasks in data processing. As more and more systems find their way onto the computer, so more and more files are created. Many of these files contain the same or similar data, possibly under different keys and probably used in different ways.

In any organization there is only a limited amount of data and, in theory, if all these data are held on one immense file, they should answer the needs of all the systems. This, it is suggested, will provide three advantages:

1. Space used up by duplicated files will be reduced.
2. Computer procedures for updating and maintaining files could be simplified and processing time reduced.
3. Data would be consistent for all users.

To achieve these advantages it is necessary to construct a data base. A data base can be defined as:

> a method of storing data so that they are shared by all the systems with which the data are associated.

This means that the design of the data base and the software that is necessary for managing the data base have to be developed in the full knowledge of the demands that will be made on the data base. This means that the selection of data base is very important. It can also be expensive in terms of development cost, additional hardware and the cost of maintaining and re-organizing data.

Two approaches have been tried to provide the advantages of data base technology:

1. Systems data base.
2. Total data base.

A systems data base serves a particular system. It is really a common data file for the system. This is a limited form of data base and, though it is a very effective way of handling the data that serve a particular system, it does not really meet the objectives of a data base and does not have the advantages listed above.

If the advantages are to be achieved it will be from the operation of a total data base. This is very far-reaching in its implications. It means that all the data needed by the information system are held on a common structured file system. It cannot simply be called a file.

To operate a data base it is necessary to use a piece of software called a data base

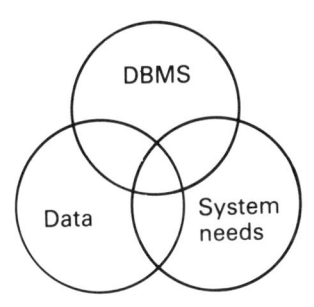

Figure 11.3 *Data base factors*

management system or DBMS. This software determines how the data elements and their relationships are defined and consequently how the data base is structured. The system designer has to understand the DBMS thoroughly and, more importantly, exactly how the data are going to be used by all the systems. There are, therefore, three factors, all of which have to be considered by the designer (see Figure 11.3).

With a total data base this places an enormous burden on the system designer. The effects on system design and development are so far-reaching that the decision to use a DBMS should be made at the highest level.

Once the decision has been made the DBMS has to be selected, and this means choosing a system which is not only the most appropriate, but which is also one that matches the hardware.

There are a number of different makes of software available, all of which vary in the way the data base works. Apart from these differences, there are two main ways in which the data base system may be designed:

1. Relational.
2. Hierarchical.

Relational data bases work in a similar way to related files mentioned earlier. They are not, strictly speaking, data bases but file management systems which operate by relating the data held in a number of files. It is possible to find data by being directed from the primary file to secondary files, and so on, for several levels of files. Data are given a file address, and this is where the data are held for any system need, depending on their relation to other data elements.

Hierarchical data bases work by linking all data elements in a hierarchy which starts with the highest keys and works down to the smallest elements of data. The data elements are designated owners and members, and data are grouped in sets. Members of one set could be owners of a lower sub-set and so the hierarchy grows (see Figure 11.4).

In this form of data base every data element is coded with its level and the level of which it is both owner and member. In this way every element of data can be traced, provided it is correctly related to other elements by the system designer.

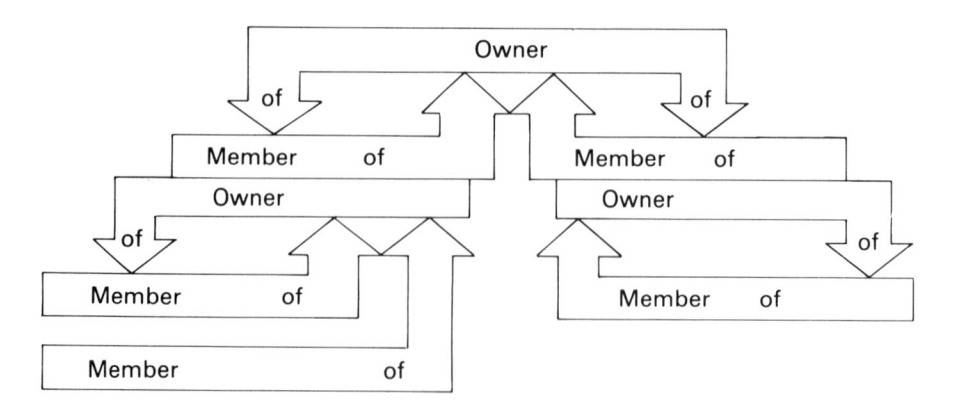

Figure 11.4 *Hierarchy data base*

The success of the data base system depends almost entirely on the efficiency with which this design task is carried out. Therefore the designer needs to use a data dictionary so that he or she can both keep up to date with the current appearance of the data base and add additional data elements. The data dictionary lists all data with records used and gives their relative place in the data base, together with the systems and programs that use the data. Without a data dictionary the generation of a DBMS is virtually impossible.

11.8 DATA ADMINISTRATION

Perhaps the most significant implication of data base systems is the need for careful control of data. It is normal where a DBMS is in operation to appoint a data administrator whose job it is to maintain the data dictionary.

This calls for considerable knowledge and understanding of data flows within the organization and of the way data are used. The data administrator must know:

1. What data flow through the organization.
2. The relationship of all data elements to each other.
3. The way data are used by the systems.
4. The potential for corruption of data by unauthorized access.

When data are held on a data base there must be stringent controls of who is allowed to change the data, since any change affects all the systems using the data. The advantage of consistency becomes a major disadvantage if the data are incorrect, however, as they will be wrong in every system. Data administration is no easy task and, as the quality of the data in the data base controls the quality of the output, it is a key factor.

Data generation and processing — 137

11.9 SUMMARY AND REVISION NOTES

Data are the life-blood of the system and describe the facts and figures that are manipulated by the programs.

Data are made up of characters that can consist of integers, alphabetic, alpha numerical or real numbers. These characters are manipulated in fields, records and blocks (see Figure 11.5).

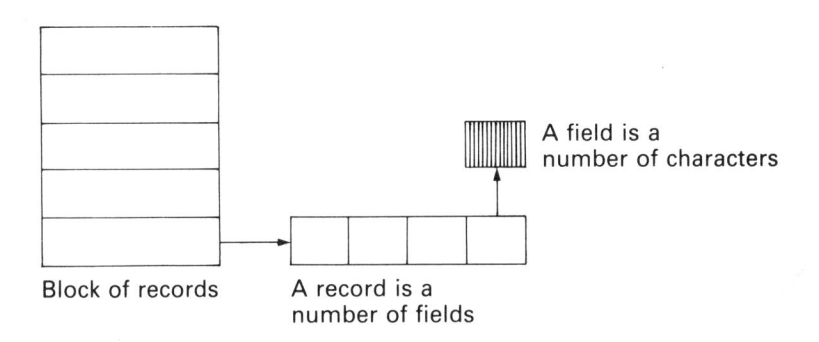

Figure 11.5 *Data format*

Data are controlled in hierarchies and networks which link fields, records and blocks in a meaningful relationship. This enables data to be traced, updated and controlled.

Data are held in files which are structured in three ways:

1. Simple files of records held under one key.
2. Multiple-level files, where different records are kept within groups of master records.
3. Related files, where one master file leads on to other files.

Files are organized in one of four ways, depending on the needs of the system, the volume of data and the hardware and software facilities available. They are:

1. Sequential.
2. Indexed.
3. Indexed sequential.
4. Random addressing.

Data are manipulated in a variety of ways, and program instructions may require several of these methods to carry out a task. The methods are:

1. Sorting.
2. Calculating.
3. Comparing.
4. Merging.
5. Inserting.

6. Selecting.
7. Transferring.
8. Deleting.

When moving data into and out of files the computer will be doing one of three things, depending on the program needs:

1. Read only.
2. Write only.
3. Read and write.

Data base design principles cover the use of data as a common resource within the computer to be used by all systems.

Data bases can be for systems or for the total environment. The systems data base is of limited value, but the total data base is difficult to build and use.

To operate a data base a data base management system (DBMS) is needed. This is a piece of software that provides a framework for data to be inserted and managed.

There are two main kinds of data base:

1. Relational.
2. Hierarchical.

To maintain all data bases it is essential to have a data dictionary and for this to be controlled by a data administrator.

The quality of all systems depends on the quality of the data contained in the data base, so great care has to be exercised to maintain the highest quality possible.

QUESTIONS

1. An increasing number of organizations are contemplating installing, or have installed, systems involving a data base. What factors have led to these developments and what are the characteristics of an efficient data base? (ICMA)

2. Taking a typical sales invoicing system as your subject matter:

    (a) Illustrate the application of the system design formula: Output data − Input data = File data + Calculated data.
    (b) State how you would then determine the contents of the file or files required by the system producing the invoices.
    (ICMA)

3. Describe the main ways of organizing data in files, giving the advantages of each method and an example of a typical use of each method of organization.

4. Define each of the following data processing steps, saying how each is used and giving an example of each in use:

(a) Sorting.
(b) Transferring.
(c) Deletion.
(d) Merging.

5. There are three main ways of structuring files. State what these are and describe the advantages of each, illustrating the advantages with examples.

CASE STUDY EXERCISE

From the previous studies you should now be in a position to specify the main files to be held in the system, to state how these files will be used, the processing steps involved, the structure of the files and the way in which they will be organized.

12

Data Collection and Communication

12.1 DATA COLLECTION: THE FOUNDATION

It is a simple fact that if the foundations of a building are not constructed properly the building, no matter how well designed, will eventually fall down. The same is true of data collection. No matter how elegant an information system may be, if the data collection stage is not given the appropriate attention, the system will fail. In any organization data are used and collected to:

1. Get things done.
2. Control by providing information.

These tasks can be depicted as a pyramid with the largest and most important part being the data collection stage, which is the foundation of all that follows (Figure 12.1).

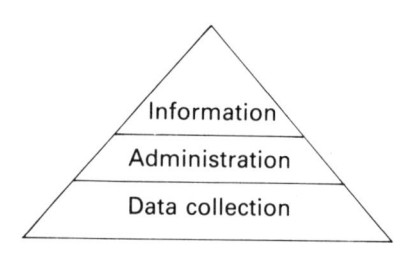

Figure 12.1 *Data collection pyramid*

Recognition of the importance of data collection leads to the thorough analysis of the need for data and the best way of collecting the data to meet the needs of the system.

Data are created in a wide variety of ways, but all as a result of a transaction carried out for a specific purpose. Data can have, and most do have, more than one use; e.g. hours worked by an employee are used for payment purposes, for measuring performance and for costing. When combined with other data the information created has further use for management and control.

It is vital, therefore, that the methods used to capture data are relevant to the data's subsequent use.

12.2 METHODS OF DATA COLLECTION

When deciding which method of data collection is the most appropriate it is essential to answer the following questions:

1. What data have to be collected?
2. Which is the most appropriate source?
3. What are the time constraints?
4. What are the quality constraints?

With the answers to these questions it is possible to examine the best way to capture the data. There are, of course, many different attitudes and approaches that might be followed.

Take, for example, the collection of data for sales used in two different department stores. Both need to collect the data to control cash and determine re-order quantities, and for sales and marketing information.

In the first store the attitude is to collect the data as every sale takes place. This is known as point-of-sale data capture. To do it they use a small punched card tag on every product sold. When the sale takes place the tag, which contains details of the item, its price, etc., is fed into a small terminal which reads it and stores the data.

The second store does not collect the data at point of sale, but by recording all the items delivered to the store. This information is needed for checking invoices. Then, once a month, they deduct the stock remaining in the store. The difference between the two figures represents the sales data.

These two examples show how differently the collection of data can be viewed, particularly with regard to the timing and accuracy of the data, which is dealt with later.

The methods that can be used can be subdivided into:

1. Indirect.
2. Direct.

Indirect Methods

Indirect methods of data collection are those which use existing sources of data as a means of collection. This form of data collection is widespread and has the following advantages:

1. There is no need to create special data collection paperwork or systems.
2. It means the collection of one set of primary data which is used for several purposes.
3. It is less costly.

Unfortunately, this form of data collection suffers from a major problem. Since the data are collected as a spin-off, they do not always meet the timing and accuracy constraints.

Direct Methods

Direct methods of data collection are those which have been designed specifically for that purpose. This does, of course, have the major advantage that the data collected are what is wanted by the system. It is usually more expensive, but will produce more accurate data when they are needed.

Data, both indirect and direct, are collected in a number of ways:

1. Paperwork.
2. Pre-coded documents.
3. Keyed input.
4. Direct transfer.

Paperwork

Paperwork has always been of vital importance in the process of data collection. It is still of considerable importance, and a vast amount of data are collected from documents such as invoices, orders, time sheets, delivery notes, etc. The problem with paperwork, whether designed for direct collection or as indirect spin-off, is that the data have to be transferred into the computer. This transfer process creates problems of time, control and errors.

Pre-coded Documents

Pre-coded documents overcome the problem of transfer, but can be used only where the system ensures the return of the document. Examples are cheques and price tags. Though they have to be specially designed and initially can be expensive, the advantages in overcoming problems of data transfer are considered worth while.

Keyed Input

Keyed input, as its name implies, is data that are keyed into the system via a keyboard, often with a screen. This form of input covers an enormous range of possible applications and is a growing form of data collection. The system is still open to errors, but with built-in checks these can be reduced.

In a quarry weighbridge, keyed input is being used to collect data on deliveries of materials. The system also produces the delivery ticket, which is no longer used as a basis for input as it was previously.

In a factory the operatives key their starting time into the machine they operate. The time the machine is working is recorded by the machine and so, by a combination of keyed input and direct transfer, the time sheet is eliminated.

Direct Transfer

Direct transfer of data is perhaps the fastest-growing form of data collection. It is not new: methods of direct transfer have been available for many years. Magnetic strips on cards such as Cashpoint cards have been available for well over ten years, and bar-marked cards have been used in libraries for a similar period. Bar marking is now being used on grocery packaging for point-of-sale data collection in supermarkets.

New methods of direct transfer include the use of microprocessors to record time, temperature, volumes, numbers of items, etc., and feed these data directly into the computer system. One recent example of this kind of data collection is the tachograph used in commercial vehicles. The tachograph records data such as time operating, miles travelled, speed, etc. These data are recorded on magnetic tape or on a memory chip. The data can later be transferred into the computer system. Because of its accuracy the tachograph has been resisted by the drivers' unions and has been called 'the spy in the cab'.

12.3 CODING

When data are collected there has to be a means of signalling where the data have to go. This is done using a system of coding.

It is amazing how a piece of information can travel from one end of the world to the other simply by placing it inside a folded piece of paper (an envelope) and addressing it. The word 'address' is used to denote the place where the information has to go. The word is now used in computing to show where data are held on file.

If we examine a typical address we can see how simple the process is:

    JOHN SMITH   the person in the house
    127 EVERY STREET   the house in the street
                         the street in the town

ANYTOWN   the town in the area
WEST COUNTRY   the area in the country
ENGLAND   the country

It is typical of the human mind that we write down the address in the most logical manner – logical, that is, when we are writing it down; it is the wrong way round for the reading and sorting process which follows.

The classification and coding system will enable data to be sorted, processed and stored in a way which will make them useful to management for control and planning purposes. Information which is going to be used by managers when they are making decisions must be timely, accurate and related to the decision. Its relevance will depend on the classification and coding system; its timeliness and accuracy will depend entirely on the data-collection system. As with any product, the value of information is dependent on its being available at the right time, in the right place, in the right form, and at the right price. It must also, of course, contain the right data. The final output is only as good as the original input. In the computer world this is referred to as GIGO – 'garbage in, garbage out'.

The first step is to consider what data are required. This will stem from the information required, the form in which it will be presented, and the timing of the presentation. These factors all control the methods of data collection to be employed.

Much of this sophistication is unnecessary if the need for the data is examined before the collection system is designed. The steps in efficient data collection are:

1. Know what data are required.
2. Discover the most appropriate source.
3. Establish the time constraints.
4. Establish the quality constraints.
5. Design the collection system.

Rules to follow are:

1. Don't collect unnecessary data.
2. Collect them at the correct level of detail.
3. Ensure a smooth data flow.
4. Ensure a minimum of data handling.

Coding should be structured in levels so that it can be summarized or broken down by moving from one level to the next.

If, for example, we take a small organization which has five locations and up to 20 departments at each location, we might have a structure such as the one that follows:

Company code	0–9
Location code	0–9
Departmental code	0–99
Account code	0–999
Made up of (a) A/c type	0–9
(b) Expense code	0–99
Analysis code	0–9999

This allows any item of expense or income to be subdivided to a detailed level which might be required by the company.

Figure 12.2 is an example of a coding system devised for a company in the construction industry.

12.4 INPUT DEVICES

The actual equipment (hardware) used for input is dealt with in Chapter 9. In this section the importance of the input device in the data collection system is discussed.

When designing the data collection system the most important consideration is the data to be collected, and the timing and quality of the data. The question of how the data are to be collected is important, but secondary. The input device forms the interface between the creators of data, usually people, and the machine. Its selection, therefore, is very important, as it must meet the needs of the data collection system and be easy to use, preferably not requiring specialist skills.

The selection also depends, to some extent, on the kind of processing being done. If batch processing is in operation the data will need to be collected and accumulated in batches ready for input, and this will probably be done off line. If the system is an interactive system then the data will be collected and input on line. In the batch environment a wide range of input devices are possible, but in the on-line environment the input is almost certain to be keyed or by direct transfer. Some examples will serve to illustrate the use of various input devices.

In the first example a building society changed from using paperwork for collecting data in a batch environment to a keyboard for collecting data in an on-line environment. In the first case, as payments and withdrawals were made, they were entered onto a transaction pad. At the end of the day this was balanced and sent to head office, where it was punched by operators and input to the computer. The accounts were then updated in batches. The system was changed so that when customers paid money in or withdrew it, the transactions were input via the keyboard and updated the accounts on the head office computer immediately. In this example the input devices were dictated by the system design and selected to meet the needs of the system.

The second example concerns a large food-manufacturing company which sells via telesales staff. The original system consisted of using optical mark reading order forms held in a special frame. These were coded as the telesales representative received the orders over the telephone. The sheets were then input to the computer in batches on a daily basis. Stocks were updated daily and the telesales reps were given stock levels each morning. The system was changed to an on-line system using keyboards and screens. The order sheet now appears on the screen and orders are entered via the keyboard when the rep is on the phone to the customer. When the order is complete the data are transferred into the computer for action. Stock is updated as each order is processed and the reps are warned of low stocks as they occur.

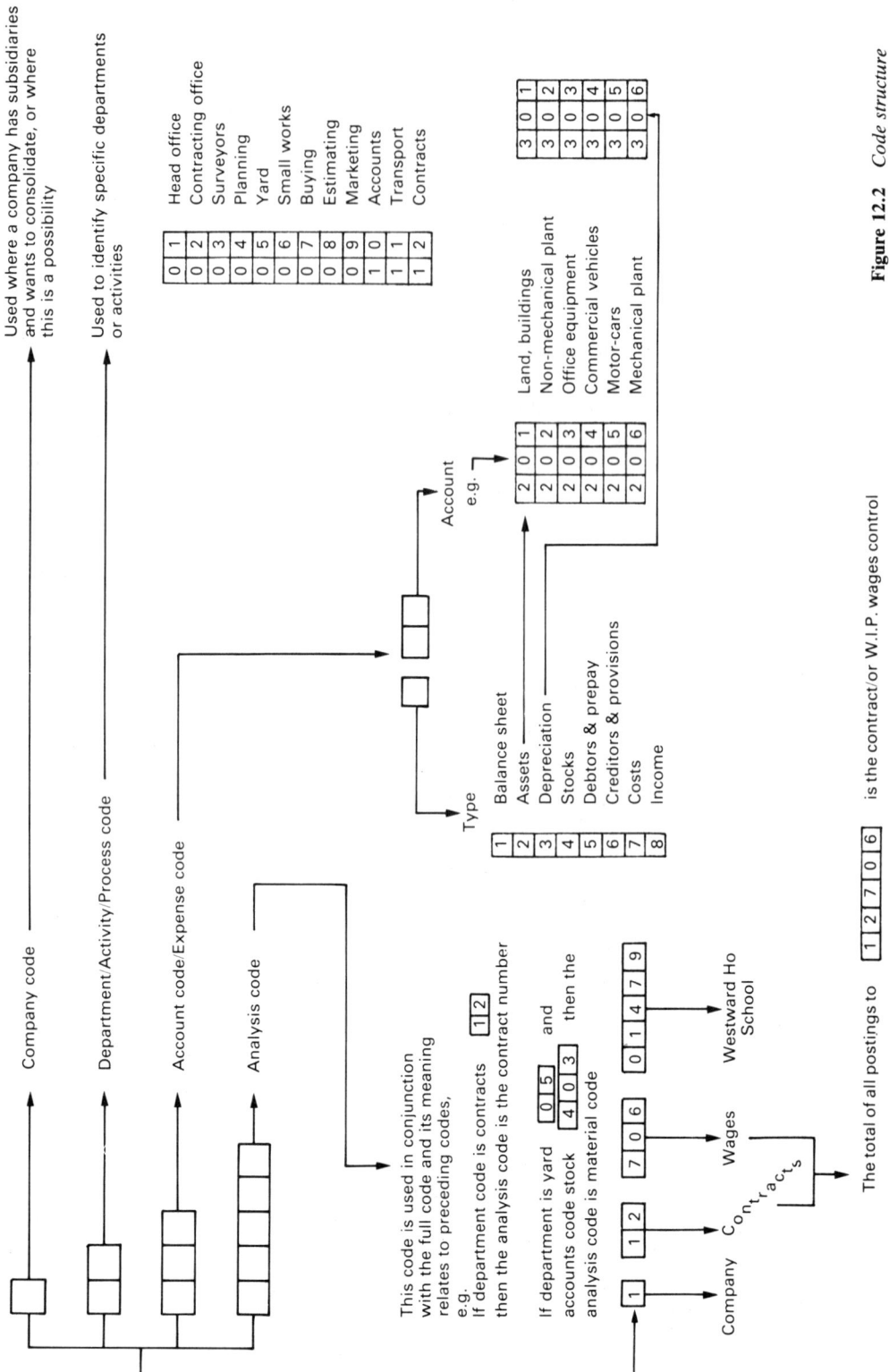

146 — *Management information systems and data processing*

Company code — Used where a company has subsidiaries and wants to consolidate, or where this is a possibility

Department/Activity/Process code — Used to identify specific departments or activities

0	1	Head office
0	2	Contracting office
0	3	Surveyors
0	4	Planning
0	5	Yard
0	6	Small works
0	7	Buying
0	8	Estimating
0	9	Marketing
1	0	Accounts
1	1	Transport
1	2	Contracts

Account code/Expense code

Account e.g.

2	0	1	Land, buildings
2	0	2	Non-mechanical plant
2	0	3	Office equipment
2	0	4	Commercial vehicles
2	0	5	Motor-cars
2	0	6	Mechanical plant

3	0	1
3	0	2
3	0	3
3	0	4
3	0	5
3	0	6

Type

1	Balance sheet
2	Assets
3	Depreciation
4	Stocks
5	Debtors & prepay
6	Creditors & provisions
7	Costs
8	Income

Analysis code

This code is used in conjunction with the full code and its meaning relates to preceding codes,
e.g.
If department code is contracts [1][2]
then the analysis code is the contract number

If department is yard [0][5] and accounts code stock [4][0][3] then the analysis code is material code

[0][1][4][7][9] → Westward Ho School

[7][0][6] → Wages

[1][2] → Company

Contracts

[1] → Company

The total of all postings to [1][2][7][0][6] is the contract/or W.I.P. wages control

Figure 12.2 *Code structure*

The third example deals with a quarrying company which developed a new keyboard system to replace the use of coded delivery tickets which were sent to head office and punched onto cards for input. The new system that was introduced used an off-line terminal to input data locally from delivery tickets onto cassettes. Overnight the data were transferred from the local terminals to the central computer via telephone lines. The machines at both ends were equipped with automatic facilities, so no people were involved in the transfer procedure. The system is now being changed once again, and the new system will involve the use of terminals in the quarries where the data will be collected on floppy discs from keyed input which will also be used to print the delivery tickets. The data on floppy discs will then be transmitted to the central computer. The system is in two stages:

1. On-line for initial data collection when printing tickets.
2. Off-line for subsequent input to the computer where the data are processed in batches.

These three examples serve to show how input devices are selected in relation to the system. The range of possible input devices and methods is, of course, enormous, varying with individual system design and types of equipment.

12.5 DATA TRANSMISSION

In Chapter 8 networks for linking computers were discussed. This included the use of modems for translating signals so that they could be transmitted through the network.

When data are transmitted, especially in an interactive environment, the efficiency of the transmission depends on two factors:

1. Speed.
2. Accuracy.

Speed of Transmission

Speed of transmission depends on the type of line used and the speed of the line. There are three types of line generally available (Figure 12.3).

1. Simplex, which is one way only.
2. Half-Duplex, which is one way at a time.
3. Full-Duplex, which is both ways at the same time.

The speed of a line is controlled by its type and the band width. New developments are increasing the speed all the time. The speed with which responses can be received on a transmission also depends on the traffic using the line.

When data are transmitted a number of steps are involved. These are:

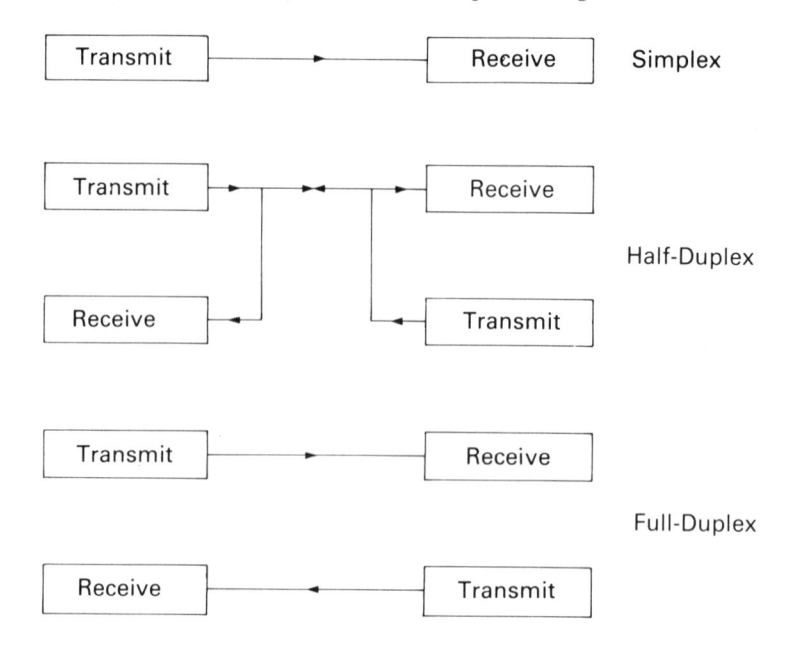

Figure 12.3 *Types of transmission lines*

1. Prepare data and press transmit key.
2. Input waits for poll.
3. Input transmitted.
4. Computer receives message.
5. Computer processes message.
6. Output ready and waiting for free line.
7. Transmit data.

These steps all take time and if there is a lot of traffic it is like driving on a busy road: everybody slows down. The polling operation of the computer is a continuous operation where the computer software repeatedly goes to each terminal or line and asks whether there are any data to be transmitted.

Accuracy of Transmission

Accuracy of the data being transmitted has to be protected. If care is taken to ensure accuracy of the collection and input stages, it would be criminal if the transmission stage were to create errors. This can occur because of something called 'noise'. Just as when you use a telephone it is rare to get a completely clear line without any crackles or buzzing, this noise can affect the message and distort the data. This is clearly shown in Figure 12.4.

Data collection and communication — 149

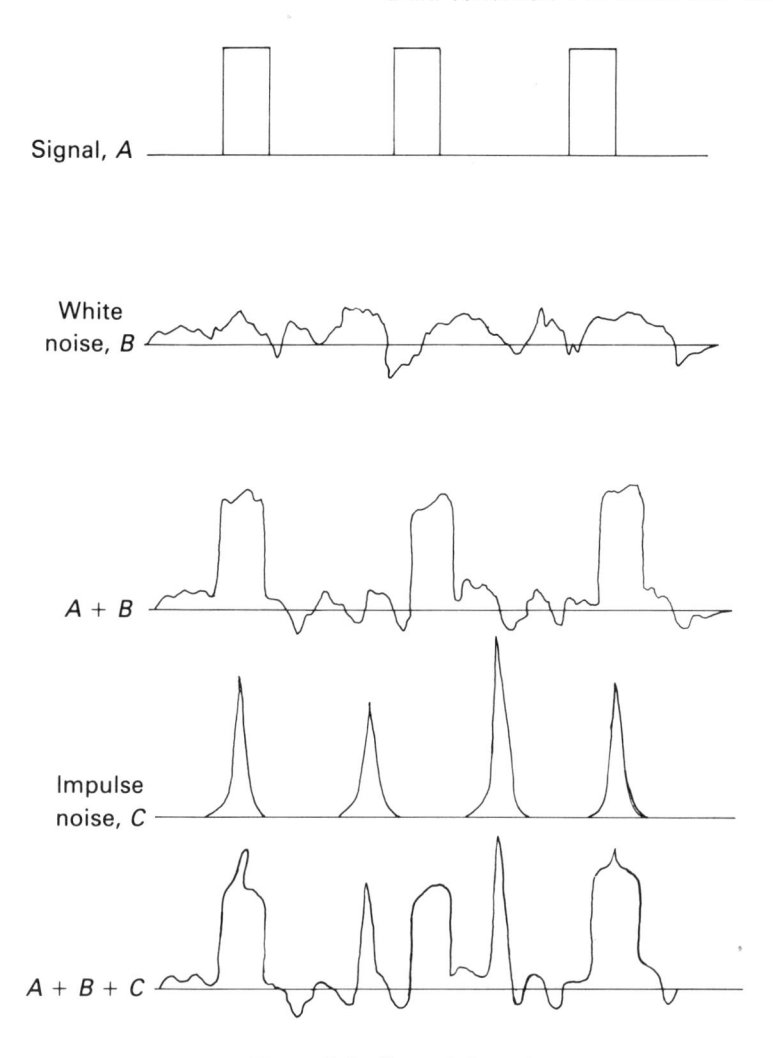

Figure 12.4 *Transmission noise*

The signal, A, is shown as a wave with the peak representing a binary 1 and the trough a binary 0. As noise affects the wave it makes it difficult for the computer to interpret the binary 1 and 0s. This is prevented by the use of amplifiers on the line which strengthen the signal in stages.

In addition the data are checked to highlight any errors and the computer automatically requests a further transmission. These checks depend on whether the transmission is asynchronous, i.e. character by character, or synchronous, i.e. in blocks (see section 9.4).

As the character or record is transmitted the terminal or modem adds signals which are calculated as an algorithm, in binary, of the character or record. When the signal is received the data are translated and these additional signals are checked to confirm the validity of the data transmitted. The two main methods used for carrying out these transmission checks are:

1. Parity checks.
2. Loop checks.

Parity checks. Parity checks are a simple technique of adding up the 1 bits in a binary word and adding an additional bit which is a 1 or a 0, to make the total sum of bits either even or odd, depending on whether the check is for even parity or odd parity (Figure 12.5).

Asynchronous (stop/go): Each character is transmitted with its own timing pulses

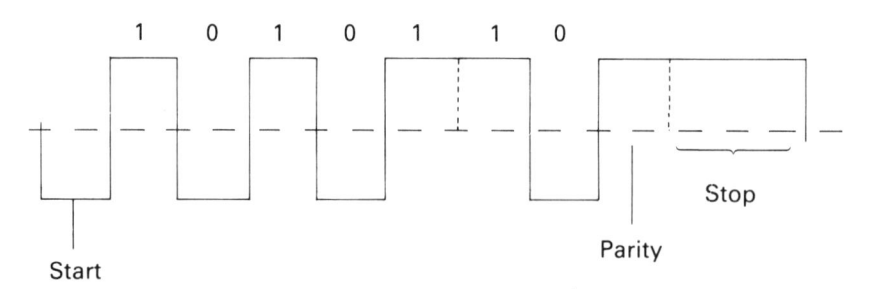

Synchronous: Several characters are stored then transmitted as a block

| SYN | SYN | SYN | SOM | Message | EOM | BCC |

Synchronizing characters — Start of message — End — Block check character

Figure 12.5 *Parity and block checks*

Binary word	Parity bit	
1 0 1 1 1 0 0 1	1	Even parity
1 1 0 0 1 1 1 1	0	
1 1 0 1 1 1 0 1	1	Odd parity
1 1 0 0 0 1 1 1	0	

The additional bit is referred to as a redundant character or bit and is dropped after the check is made.

Loop checks. Loop checks, also known as re-transmit checks, use a method of sending the data back to see whether they check with what was originally sent. This is

Data collection and communication — 151

the method used by people sending radio transmissions. It is very effective, and when combined with parity checks the level of accuracy on transmissions can be 10^{11}. If care is taken to ensure accuracy when collecting data, it would be criminal to spoil it during transmission.

12.6 DATA VALIDATION AND CONTROL

When validation of data is discussed there is a tendency to expect the computer to check data to depths of detail which are simply impossible. The word 'validate' means to ratify or confirm, and this implies that there is some rule to decide whether the data are right or wrong. The checks that the computer can do are limited to the following:

1. Field content.
2. Field size.
3. Correct codes using check digit.
4. Range checks.
5. Calculations.
6. Completeness.
7. File checks.

Field Content

Field content can be checked because each field is specified as numeric, alpha or alpha-numeric. If the data entered do not match, an error is reported.

Field Size

Field size is specified and so the computer can check that the characters fill the field. An overflow will, or should, report an error. If less than the full data is entered it will either be reported or the program could arrange for the field to be left or right zero filled.

Correct Codes

Codes can be checked using a method known as 'check digit'. The check digit is an additional digit added by a simple calculation performed by the computer. If customer codes are being issued it may be desirable to add a check digit to prevent errors. This check digit would work as follows:

   Customer number 1437 ÷ 7 Remainder = 2
   Customer number with check digit 14372

If this number is transferred as 14732, the computer will carry out the calculation and discover the remainder should be 3, i.e. for number 1473 the check digit is 3, therefore number 14732 is incorrect.

Range Checks

Range checks can be made by specifying in the program that for a particular field the content should fall within certain limits. For example, if entering prices, the range could be £20 to £90. If £17 was entered, it would be rejected as falling outside the range.

Calculations

Calculations can be checked by simple reverse calculation. For example, if a sales value is calculated by multiplying volume by price, then the calculation can be checked by dividing the result by the price, e.g.

$$110 \times 10 = 1100$$
$$\text{Does } 1100 \div 10 = 110?$$

This is a very simple method, but a very effective one. Another way of checking calculations, particularly additions, is by feeding in a control total with the data. The computer carries out the additions and checks the total it creates with the input control total. It is not always possible or desirable to produce a figure for the computer to agree with, since the computer is being used because of the complexity of the calculations. It means, therefore, that users must have confidence in the accuracy of the machine.

Completeness

Completeness means that all the records have been input and received by the computer. This is done by inputting control totals, hash totals and/or record counts. A control total is a total of real values, e.g. invoice values, etc. A hash total is a number created by adding a mixture of dates, codes and real values, hence the name 'hash total'. A record count is quite simply a count of all the records input.

File Checks

File checks involve the program checking with a file to see if the codes are correct. For example, when customer codes are entered the program can go to the customer file to see if the codes exist, before accepting the input. This is vital in interactive processing, to prevent file corruption. In batch processing the data may be accepted initially then rejected when the processing takes place.

Even with all these facilities the computer can be beaten by the human being. If the invoice is coded with a customer code which is correct and exists on the file, but is for the wrong customer, it will be accepted, because the computer has no way of checking. The computer is, therefore, subject to human error and many, if not all, of the mistakes that computers make are really made by people.

12.7 DATA COLLECTION: THE KEY TO GOOD SYSTEMS

Information systems cannot exist without the data, just as no product can exist without the raw material. Yet very often little effort is expended on the design of data collection systems, while considerable time and money are directed to sophisticated programming, complex file structures and fancy reporting systems. Most of this is, of course, wasted if the primary data are suspect.

When management use information to make decisions they must have confidence in the system that produces the information. This will not happen if errors percolate through, and if the data are incomplete.

In a major UK company a survey of information needs was carried out and the most important result was the recommendation that the systems for collecting data be re-organized and improved before any efforts were made to improve reporting procedures. The management were not immediately receptive to the idea, but when they realized the degree of error which could exist in their decision-making information, it became a top priority.

12.8 COST OF DATA COLLECTION

Data collection, input, transmission and validation are the most expensive part of every data processing system. The cost involved is usually in excess of 50 per cent of the total data processing costs.

These costs stem naturally from the hardware and software needed for transmissions and validation. In addition there are the human costs of the people involved in creating the data, checking and recycling errors.

There is also the high cost of data maintenance. Data change regularly, particularly the kind of data dealt with as constant. Data like customer address and product descriptions change from time to time, and in addition new customers and products have to be added to the files.

The costs of data collection are high, but fully justified if the resulting information systems are going to be effective and trusted. If a priority has to be set for spending in data processing, then undoubtedly it should be data collection systems.

12.9 SUMMARY AND REVISION NOTES

Data collection is the foundation of successful administration and information systems.

Data collection methods are many and varied, but fall into two distinct areas:

1. Indirect, which use existing sources of data.
2. Direct, which are specially designed.

Within these two methods data are collected on:

1. Paperwork.
2. Pre-coded documents.
3. Keyed input.
4. Direct transfer.

Input devices (see section 9.4) depend on the needs of the data collection system and should be selected accordingly.

Data transmission along the networks (see section 8.7) depends on the type of lines, which could be:

1. Simplex.
2. Half-Duplex.
3. Full-Duplex.

Data flow along these lines at varying speeds, depending on the type of line and the amount of data traffic.

Data must also be protected from noise generated on the lines so that the signals can be interpreted correctly. This is done by physical devices which strengthen the signals, and in addition the data are checked by:

1. Parity checks.
2. Block checks.
3. Loop checks.

Data validation is carried out by the computer and covers:

1. Field content.
2. Field size.
3. Correct codes – check digits.
4. Range checks.
5. Calculations.
6. Completeness.
7. File checks.

Data collection systems are the key to successful information systems and the high costs which have to be paid for good data collection are necessary.

Data collection and communication — 155

QUESTIONS

1. The auditors have asked that a section of each system specification used by your company should be devoted to the control aspects of the process of data capture through to transfer by the computer onto the magnetic storage media. Using, for purposes of illustration, a sales order system, which commences with the completion of sales order forms by sales representatives in the field, prepare the section of the systems specification referred to above. (ICMA)

2. As a systems analyst you have been investigating a sales order entry system and you have decided that the following data will be the required input:
   (a) date;
   (b) order number;
   (c) customer's number;
   (d) for each item ordered –
       commodity code
       type code
       quantity.

   State the validation checks you would specify for the order entry data. What would such checks achieve and why are they necessary? (ICMA)

3. Describe what is meant by the following:
   (a) parity check;
   (b) direct data transfer;
   (c) check digit;
   (d) pre-coded documents;
   (e) transmission noise.

4. What methods of data collection or data capture would you recommend as input to computer systems in the following situations:
   (a) stock ordering in a supermarket;
   (b) time recording in a factory;
   (c) sales order entry in a mail order business?

   Describe the main features of each of the methods you have recommended and, for the above applications, give their respective advantages and disadvantages. (ICMA)

5. 'It is silly to spend so much money on data collection. The data are there; why can't we just collect it?' Discuss.

CASE STUDY EXERCISE

Prepare a schedule of the data to be collected in your system and indicate:

1. Methods of collections.
2. Problems of data collection.
3. Validation checks you will institute.

13

Computer Operations

13.1 ORGANIZATION OF THE DATA PROCESSING FUNCTION

Data processing activities are organized in a number of different ways in different businesses. The first thing to examine is the way the function fits into the company organization structure. There are, in the main, three ways in which this takes place:

1. Separate function reports to the chief executive.
2. Under a central function, usually finance.
3. As a part of a decentralized divisional structure.

As a separate function reporting to the chief executive, it is likely that DP activities will be given more import, and the head of the function, who would probably be a director, is much more involved in the day-to-day decision-making and the long-term planning activity of the board.

When the function is part of a central function there is a danger that it will concentrate on developments related to that function and, perhaps more important, will be seen as a tool of the function, leading to internal political problems.

With the advent of, or return to, decentralized data processing (section 8.6), more and more DP activities are being handled within the division. These activities usually involve the control and use of one part of a network and do not normally include system development functions.

Data processing is usually part of a wider function which could be called management services or corporate systems, or some other name. These major functions cover a variety of activities, and a typical structure is shown in Figure 13.1.

Within the overall structure there are four main functions, two of which fall into the development area and two into the operations area:

1. Development: Organization and Methods; Systems Development.
2. Operations: Communications; Data Processing.

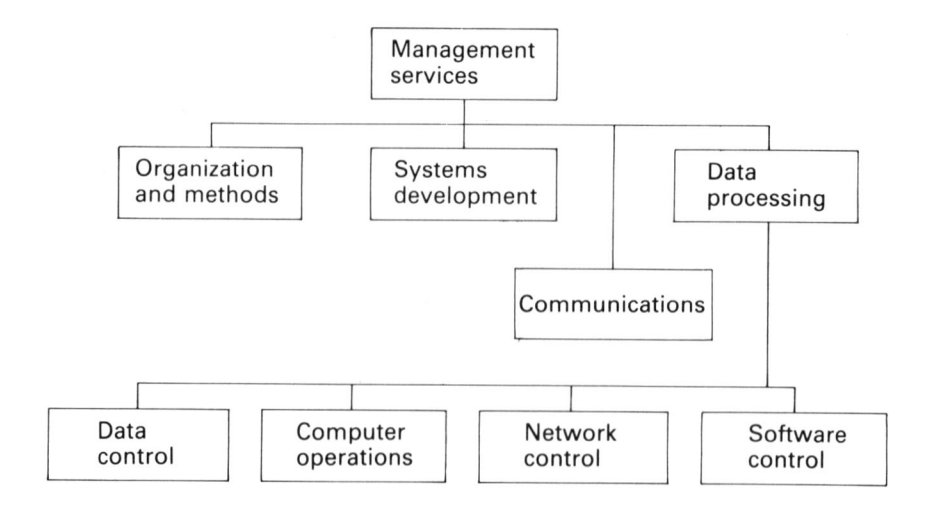

Figure 13.1 *Organization chart*

The development functions deal with problem-solving. Organization and methods deals with all aspects of administrative efficiency, including office layout, etc. Systems development deals with those aspects dealt with in Chapter 5.

The operations activities cater for the day-to-day operations designed by the development functions. These operations activities are now handled in two separate sections: communications, which deals with the operation of the communications network, including all forms of communication equipment, voice, document transfer, electronic mail, etc; and data processing, which is a name used to cover day-to-day management and control of the computer.

13.2 COMPUTER MANAGEMENT AND CONTROL

The management and control of computer operations can be separated into four distinct, but closely related activities (Figure 13.1):

1. Data control.
2. Computer operations.
3. Network control.
4. Software control.

The data processing function can be compared in many ways with a manufacturing unit. It is an information factory. Data flow in, are processed on machines, stored and dispatched as finished products in the shape of reports or signals to an outlying terminal

Within the DP factory the keyword is control. There are so many things that can go wrong that every individual working in the DP environment must be constantly vigilant and follow the rules and procedures which are laid down.

Data control is the activity which receives the data from the various collection points and arranges them for processing. This means organizing the materials required by operations for an effective production run.

Computer operations handle the planning and scheduling of work and the carrying out of the actual production runs, passing the completed products back to data control, who arrange dispatch.

Network control deal with the physical links between terminals and distributed processors and try to ensure that the network operates efficiently, balancing the flow of traffic with the system's capabilities.

Software control handle the preparation of the control instructions for the various production runs. This is referred to as job control language (JCL).

These four functions operate continuously and can best be examined by looking at a number of activities in greater detail.

13.3 PLANNING AND SCHEDULING

In a busy computer centre, planning and scheduling make the difference between efficiency and chaos. Careful timing of the whole of the operation is essential, from the receipt of data to run preparation, computer runs and output distribution.

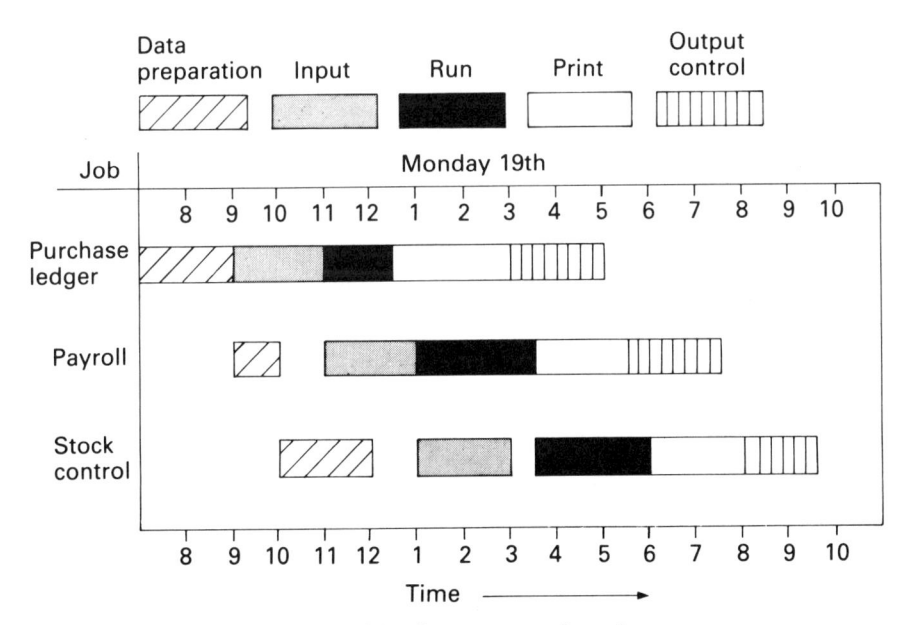

Figure 13.2 *Computer operations plan*

If one job could be run at a time then the planning would be fairly straightforward and would appear as indicated in Figure 13.2. As might be expected with a single stream of work, some jobs would have to wait for the previous stage to finish. With modern computers there is usually more than one stream of work and there could be a mixture of batch processing and interactive work.

With this degree of complexity it becomes a difficult and, in some cases, a full-time job to plan and schedule computer resources. The job of the scheduler would be to produce the daily plan and then to monitor what happens and adjust the schedule accordingly. As many people's work depends on the schedule it is a vital part of efficient computer operations.

Modern mainframe computers offer automated operations and resource scheduling. However, many operations managers who have used these facilities maintain that well trained operators perform better than the machine and react more efficiently to problems that arise. The schedule should set out the following:

1. What job is to be run and when.
2. Data needed.
3. Computer resources needed.
4. Planned duration.

Job Run Timetable

The job run timetable is very important, since it must fall into a logical sequence. Many jobs are dependent on preceding job runs. For example, in a payroll system it would be necessary to run the employee file update before the wages calculation. If this were not done there would be errors and discrepancies. Jobs requiring related files must be carefully timed so that the correct data are used.

Necessary Data

The data necessary for a job have to be specified. This means not only raw data but also existing files which will contain brought-forward information. These files will need to be extracted from the library and made available in time for the job.

Computer Resources

The computer resources that a job will use will usually consist of:

1. Main memory (specified size).
2. Disc file (specified size).
3. Tape decks.
4. Printers.
5. Card reader, etc.
6. Communication lines.

If when the job is run these resources are not available, then the job will abort or be held in suspense. It is usual for the computer to report that resources are lacking. In modern computers there is usually a priority system. This means that each job carries a priority rating and the machine automatically allocates its resources to the job with the highest priority, leaving the others until it can get to them.

Planned Duration

The planned duration of every job should be shown on the schedule. This is important because the actual time taken should be recorded and compared in order to assess performance. This recording task is now simplified by the operating system providing an accounting function which records what the computer is doing every second.

13.4 COMPUTER RUNS

A job is defined as a set of tasks with a beginning and an end which can be clearly specified. A job will be run on the computer as a separate entity. It may be linked to other jobs or it may stand alone.

A typical production run sheet is shown in Figure 13.3. This names the job and indicates other jobs on which this one is dependent. This can be checked with the schedule to ensure that the sequence is maintained. On an automatic machine the dependency would be checked and, if out of sequence, the machine would refuse to process the job. Files are indicated for both input and output, and other requirements and instructions are given.

The production run sheet will accompany a parcel of material which will include:

1. JCL cards or tape.
2. Input data.
3. Files (if from a file library outside the computer room).
4. File references and where loaded (if files are held permanently on the computer).

This material would be put together by the data control section in conjunction with the scheduler. The parcel of material on a trolley or in a special container will be passed to the computer room for the operators, ready for the scheduled run.

The operators will take the material, load the JCL into the computer, load files, and input data. During the run the job will be monitored and the operator will respond to messages he or she receives on the console, which is the operator's method of controlling the computer. It will also be necessary, when the appropriate point is reached, for the operator to load the required stationery into the printer, making it ready for printing.

When the run is complete the operator will unload files and the completed reports, including control reports, and pass the full set of materials back to data control, who will check the details to see if the job has been run successfully. Of course, things

162 — *Management information systems and data processing*

PRODUCTION RUN SHEET

WORK CODE:-   DATE:-

JOB NAME:-   DEPENDENT ON JOB(S):-

PACK(S)	FILE NAME	INPUT	OUTPUT	REMARKS

CARD INPUT:-

STATIONERY REQD.:-

CARD OUTPUT:-

PRINTER LOOP NO.:-

SPECIAL INSTRUCTIONS

SIG

OPS REMARKS

SIG

TIME STARTED
FIRST ATTEMPT
SECOND ATTEMPT

Figure 13.3 *Production run sheet*

don't always go smoothly, and special control procedures are needed to cope with problems (see section 13.7).

The JCL is a very important part of the operator's kit and is usually prepared in conjunction with the programmer, who has designed the logic of the way the programs are run. The JCL contains:

1. Identification of the job.
2. Sequence of the run, what is done when.
3. Programs to be called.
4. Files to be used.
5. Computer resources needed.
6. Responses to be made to the operator.
7. Default procedures.
8. Job priority.

The JCL is itself a form of program which controls the production run. In computers which run more than one job at once several JCLs are, of course, loaded at any one time, and these are held in memory by the computer. Without this facility it would be extremely difficult, if not impossible, to multi-program a computer.

13.5 MULTI-PROGRAMMING

When computers were first developed and operated on a single stream of programs, a great deal of waste occurred while the various parts of the computer waited until they were needed. This waste is overcome if more than one stream of programs can be worked on. Over the last ten years this facility, known as multi-programming, has become widely available and most modern mainframe and mini-computers can now multi-program.

The operating software of the computer controls the number of streams that can be processed, but other factors are:

1. Size of programs.
2. Size of memory.
3. Operating skill.
4. Efficient scheduling.

Memory Size

Memory size is, of course, a key factor and when looking at any computer configuration it is important to ensure that there is sufficient memory to do what is required. The main memory is where the computer holds all its current programs and the data on which it is working. The make-up of memory is shown in Figure 13.4.

The size of memory indicated in Figure 13.4 is available in mainframe computers and many mini-computers. However, in microcomputers the memory is limited and so the facilities are limited, and few have multi-programming.

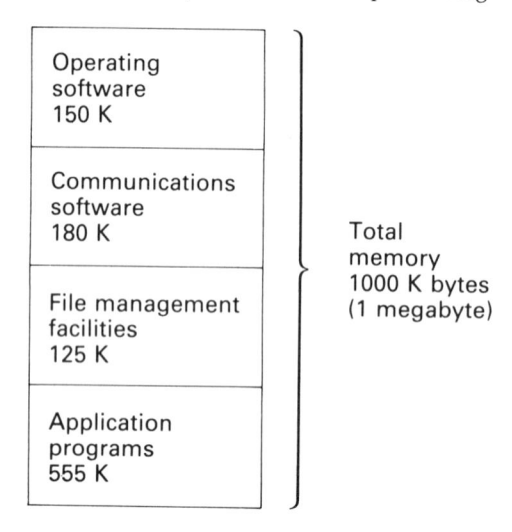

Operating software 150 K
Communications software 180 K
File management facilities 125 K
Application programs 555 K

Total memory 1000 K bytes (1 megabyte)

Figure 13.4 *Memory make-up*

Operating Skill

Operating skill is also very important for multi-programming. When more than one stream is being processed the operator is under pressure to respond to the computer's requests and questions and to load the files, etc. There are many examples where computers that could handle, say, five streams have never handled more than two because of the lack of operating skills or bad scheduling.

Efficient Scheduling

Efficient scheduling is exceptionally important for effective multi-programming. Getting the sequence right and balancing resource use don't happen in practice if they have not already been worked out on paper in the schedule. This lesson is not always learned by operations managers, and some blame the computer or the operators when the problem is scheduling.

13.6 MULTI-PROCESSING

Multi-processing is often mistaken for multi-programming. It is quite different, for while multi-programming uses a single processor, multi-processing uses two or more central processing units. These CPUs are linked so that peripheral equipment and files can be used by whichever processor needs them. With communication links the processors need not be in the same computer centre.

This form of data processing is used primarily in major computer centres using very large mainframe computers. In most data processing applications multi-processing is not necessary. It does mean, however, that it is not necessary to build exceptionally large computers now that several smaller ones can be linked and work as if they were a single machine.

13.7 CONTROL PROCEDURES

During normal data processing operations it is essential that everyone concerned knows what is happening. This means maintaining a careful log of all events, especially problems. There is a wide variety of things that can go wrong, but they will all fall into one or other of the following categories:

1. Run failures.
2. File errors.
3. Data losses.
4. Output failure.

Run Failures

Run failures occur for many reasons, including loss of power, machine failure, lack of resources, operator error, faulty programs, or missing data. When any of these events happen the operator will have to abandon the run, establish the reason for the problem and take corrective action. This action comprises:

1. Establish the reason for failure.
2. Record what happened.
3. Record what action is taken to correct the failure.
4. Re-run the job and record results.

Some operators by-pass these procedures and just re-load and re-run in the hope that all will go well, and sometimes it does. With batch and interactive processing, when failure occurs it could have affected the files held in the system, so a re-run would not correct the problem.

File Errors

File errors arise from four main causes:

1. Loading incorrect files.
2. Machine failure.
3. Incorrect re-run procedure.
4. Incorrect data.

Loading incorrect files. Perhaps the main cause of file errors is the loading of the incorrect file or the wrong version of the file. This is often not discovered until the control reports are being checked by data control and, of course, means that the whole run has been a complete waste of time. This can be overcome if file references are held within the JCL for the next run, and a check will register that the wrong file is being used. Prevention is far better than cure.

Machine failure. Machine failure, particularly the failure of a tape drive or a disc drive, can literally ruin a file. A disc 'crash', so called because the read/write head crashes onto the surface, not only spoils the file but also the disc itself. This can be coped with only by a re-run to recreate the file that has been spoilt.

Incorrect re-run procedure. Incorrect re-run procedures often corrupt a file by continuing to use a file that might have been affected by the run failure. Files can be transformed into rubbish by careless operating procedures, particularly when an operator wants to hide the fact that a re-run has been necessary.

Incorrect data. Incorrect data that get through the validation programs can, of course, corrupt the file, and these errors are usually overcome only by re-processing with correcting data.

Data Losses

Data losses are supposedly impossible. The belief is that once data enter the system everything is okay. Unfortunately, this is not true, and data can be lost at every point, from creation to final output. Losses occur through carelessness, i.e. human error, machine fault and system errors.

Human error. Human error covers such things as quite literally throwing data away by mistake, and forgetting to input data but making up the controls.

> In an automated data collection system the local terminal operator swore he had transmitted the data. At the computer centre they also were adamant that they had not received them. The data were re-transmitted and a group of customers were invoiced twice.

Such errors are not uncommon.

Machine fault. Machine faults simply cause individual characters or records to be dropped between the point where the fault occurred and the point where correction takes place. Such gaps are discovered when the controls are checked, but occasionally not until long after the run has been completed.

System errors. System errors involve the incorrect operation of programs which simply do not handle data correctly, possibly because they are of a size larger than a field.

> One system fault encountered was a particular error that increased all prices by one decimal place. The price field was five characters and a decimal point was automatically inserted to make the field £££pp. Unfortunately, one production

unit was entering prices to three decimal places, i.e. ££ppp. The computer read this as £££pp – hence the error. It was not discovered until the customers involved complained when they received the invoices.

Output Failure

Output failure can happen from machine faults and from some of the other reasons for data and file errors. One of the most obvious errors is feeding the wrong stationery; another is failure of the program to print the correct headings, or for the spacing to be incorrect. If the data are incorrect or a file corrupted, then the output will be incorrect. (Output is dealt with fully in Chapter 14.)

All the faults and errors that can occur need to be guarded against by the development of efficient control procedures, particularly:

1. Recovery.
2. Dumps and re-starts.

Recovery

Recovery procedures involve returning to the point immediately prior to the failure and, once the failure has been corrected, continuing to a successful run. Recovery therefore requires program facilities which allow the operator to check what point had been reached when the error occurred. From this point the operator needs a procedure to follow to balance the run. Some computers have automatic facilities which work for a full re-run. The software then checks what it is being asked to do with what it has already done, and accepts only the new data. The most important point about recovery is that it is properly recorded.

Dumps and Re-starts

Dumps and re-starts are expressions used when files are dumped, copied from disc to tape, used as a means of clearing the file or disc, but keeping a copy on tape. This allows for a re-start. Re-starts do not necessarily have to take place at the beginning of a run. If the computer has recorded where the failure occurred, a re-start can be done at that point. It depends to some extent on the operating software available. Dumps of files also take place as a part of control procedures and for security (Chapter 17).

13.8 PERFORMANCE MONITORING

Computer operations need to be closely monitored. This is done in two ways:

1. Operations log.
2. Computer log.

Operations Log

The operations log is maintained by the operations supervisor and records what is happening. There is a wide variety of layouts for the log, but whatever the layout, the log should contain the following:

1. Date.
2. Jobs run.
3. Re-runs.
4. Reason for re-run.
5. Problems.
6. Machine failures.

In addition to the operations log a record of files used should be maintained. If the computer centre is large enough, a librarian will manage this aspect.

The operations log is passed from one supervisor to the next, and this is important where shifts are working. People must know what is happening all the time.

Computer Log

The computer log is the record of what is happening and is maintained automatically by the computer. This is often referred to as job accounting. Where the feature is available it is very useful, but it does not replace the operations log. Job accounting does, however, provide detailed timing for jobs and shows the use of resources at any time of the day. Some larger computers will, on request, display a screen showing graphically the current use of the computer resources.

13.9 EFFICIENT COMPUTER MANAGEMENT

The judge of successful computer management must be the achievement of objectives in minimum time at minimum cost with a high level of quality. In batch processing users can judge only on whether the output is received when promised. They cannot see how many re-runs it might have taken. With interactive processing users can see immediately what response they are getting.

As more and more systems become interactive the computer centre is under pressure to perform well. With the advent of micro-computers many areas of the business are in a position to acquire these machines independently of the computer centre. Efficient computer management does, therefore, mean more than good operational control. It means providing management throughout the organization with the best computer service possible.

To achieve this broad aim it is important to take a broad view of needs, which will encompass all forms of computer resources, directed to meet management's needs. This puts data processing and computer management into a somewhat different position in the organization than the position in which most people imagine it.

13.10 SUMMARY AND REVISION NOTES

DP fits into the organization in a number of ways, the three main ones being:

1. Separate function reporting to chief executive.
2. Under a central function.
3. Within a decentralized divisional structure.

Within DP itself there are two main areas of effort:

1. Development.
2. Operations.

The operations side covers:

1. Data control.
2. Computer operations.
3. Network control.
4. Software control.

In the way it is organized DP can be seen as an information factory.

Planning and scheduling are crucial for efficient operations. Deciding what is to be done when, and the resources necessary, is fundamental to good DP management.

Computer runs should be carefully controlled and data control should assemble the job requirements in conjunction with the scheduler. These will include:

1. JCL cards or tape.
2. Input data.
3. Files (from library).
4. File references (where loaded permanently).

The JCL (job control language) is the key to modern computer operations. It is a program which contains:

1. Job identification.
2. Sequence of run.
3. Program to run.
4. Files to be used.
5. Computer resources needed.
6. Responses for operator.
7. Default procedures.
8. Job priority.

Multi-programming is the running of several jobs simultaneously through a single central processing unit.

Multi-processing is the use of two or more central processors linked to represent one very large system. Each of the processors could be multi-programming.

Control procedures are established to record and rectify problems, which tend to fall into four categories:

1. Run failures.
2. File errors.
3. Data losses.
4. Output failure.

Performance monitoring is crucial if operations are to be managed effectively. Two logs are required:

1. Operations log, completed by operations supervisor.
2. Computer log, or job accounting, carried out automatically by the computer.

QUESTIONS

1. (a) Produce an organization chart for a typical medium-sized computer department.
   (b) Describe four of the jobs that appear on your chart.
   (ICMA)

2. Describe what can go wrong during a production run and the action the operator should take to rectify the situation.

3. When a computer job is scheduled it has to be prepared by the data control staff. List what they have to prepare for the computer operator.

4. 'An efficient system of file referencing is essential for good computer operations management.' Discuss this statement.

5. Define multi-programming. Discuss the hardware and software facilities necessary to facilitate multi-programming. (ICMA)

CASE STUDY EXERCISE

Prepare a suggested organization structure for the DP activity and indicate the probable staffing. Draw up outline working procedures from receipt of data to final distribution of output.

14

Computer Output

14.1 PRINCIPLES OF USABLE OUTPUT

The output from the computer is the result of a considerable amount of thought and design and a good deal of effort. It is critical, therefore, that the output is used as it was intended. To make output usable it must be produced in the form required by the user. This is an obvious statement, but there are many examples of output which is not used because it is in the wrong form.

With the increasing use of computers in business, more and more of the information presented to managers is arriving direct from the computer. Although this is a definite advantage from the point of view of efficiency, the form in which the information arrives often leaves a great deal to be desired.

The quality of computer output varies considerably depending on the type of equipment used, the layout on the page or screen and the use of numbers in place of names.

There are also technical reasons for poor reproduction quality. These are concerned with the speed and method of printers used. Modern developments are overcoming most of these technical problems, but managers are still complaining about the poor presentation of the information they receive from the computer. Too many accountants and managers allow their output requirements to be dictated by the DP manager's so-called 'constraints' without appreciating what these constraints are. On the other hand, the DP manager wants to produce information in the simplest possible way which allows the machine to work at its fastest.

This conflict can be overcome with careful attention to the user's needs and an approach to form design which acknowledges the importance of making the output a usable document.

Form design, referred to in computer circles as 'formatting', deals with the way in which the information is printed on the stationery. This is controlled by the print

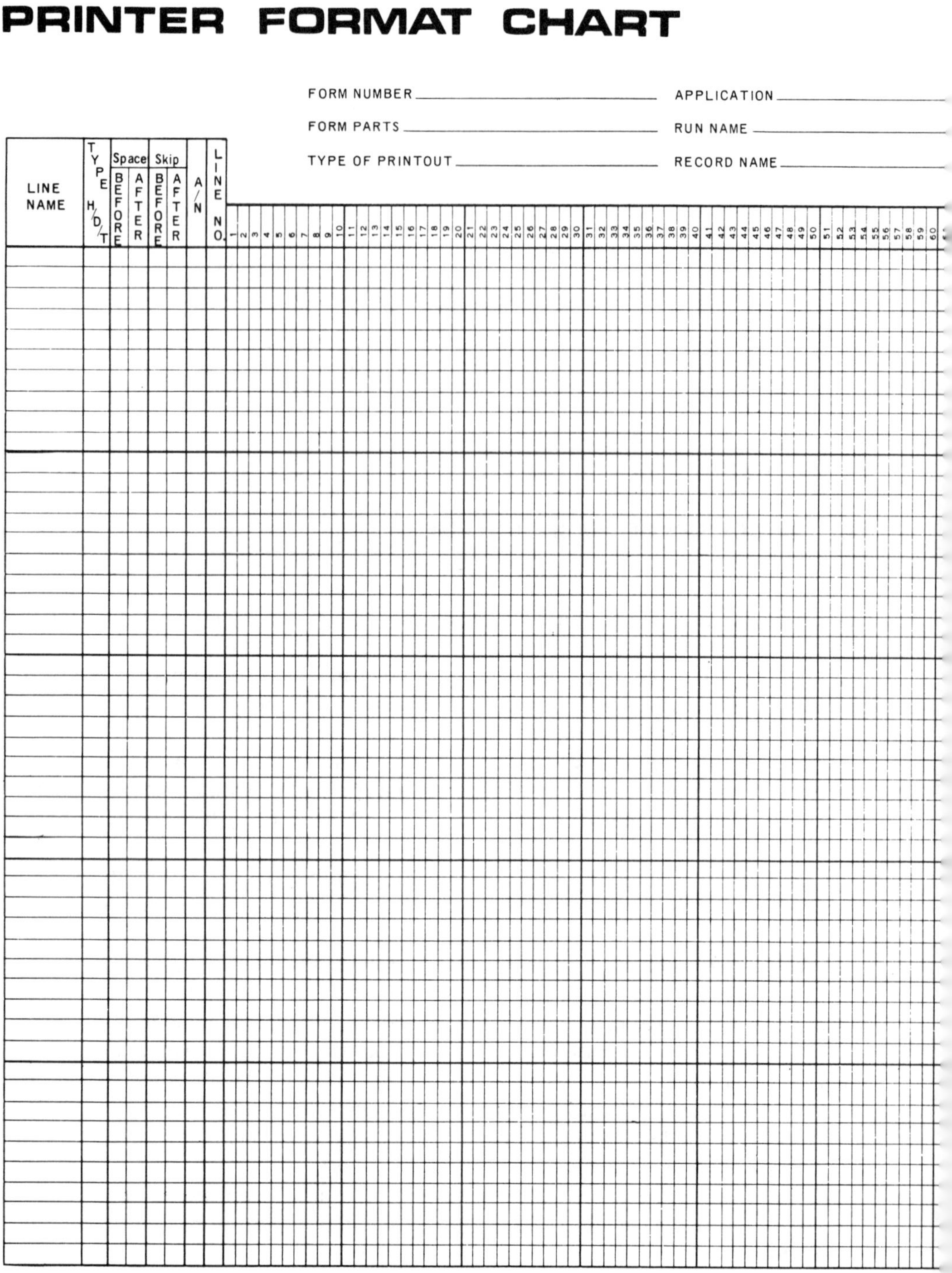

PRINTER FORMAT CHART

Figure 14.1 *Print format chart*

Computer output — 173

programs. Though this approach provides considerable theoretical flexibility, it does in practice rely entirely on the knowledge, experience and attitude of the system designer, who, though he or she may be an excellent programmer, may be an awful form designer. Very often neither the user nor the system designer has been trained in form design. This problem, together with their lack of understanding of each other's needs, leads to poor, inappropriate formats.

Computer manufacturers usually provide a special sheet given various names including 'Printout Format Sheet', 'Print Layout Sheet' and 'Print Format Chart'. An example is shown in Figure 14.1.

It can be seen that every print position is shown by the simple process of drawing horizontal and vertical lines. If the required form is drawn on the layout sheet and an example of the printout entered in the appropriate positions, the layout has been produced. The layout is then programmed and the eventual printout will match the example precisely.

If the outline of the form is required it will be necessary to have the stationery pre-printed. This is expensive and is considered cost effective only for large stationery orders. Most short runs are printed on plain paper. This problem can be overcome by xerographic printing and copying with overlays.

Formatting is not difficult, but users are rarely given the opportunity to use 'Print Format Charts'; these are wrongly considered to be the prerogative of the programmers and analysts and no ordinary person is allowed to use them. There is no technical knowledge required to produce a format, only a good idea of what is wanted. To overcome this problem the user can be provided with an 'Output Request Form' (Figure 14.2).

This form is used to ensure that the user gets what he or she wants by simply stating his or her requirements as clearly as possible. The initial section of the form for distribution and timing is important; it is there so that the computer manager can schedule the work as well as produce the required format. The output form can also be used for requesting screen formats as well as printout. The user should always request the exact form of printout required. He or she should be aware of the limitations indicated above and the cost of using pre-printed forms, but a request for computer printout should always start from exactly what is wanted.

With knowledge of what is required it is possible to examine the best method of producing the information.

14.2 METHODS OF COMPUTER OUTPUT

The output from the computer can be examined in two distinct categories:

1. Machine readable.
2. Human readable.

OUTPUT REQUEST FORM

DIV. REQUESTING	

PERSON REQUESTING		DATE REQUESTED	

DISTRIBUTION		
PERSON/DEPARTMENT	DATE REQUIRED	DATE RECEIVED

THIS REQUEST CONFIRMS MY VERBAL REQUEST OF:

OUTPUT REQUIRED

DATE PROCESSED	DATE DISPATCHED

Figure 14.2 *Output request form*

Machine-readable Output

Machine-readable output is intended for further processing or for playback on a suitable machine. In addition there are the direct output signals used on automated systems. The usual media for machine-readable output are tape and disc, both of which can be used for playback on a local machine or as a storage medium.

Human-readable Output

Human-readable output comes in four distinct categories:

1. Printed.
2. Terminal output.
3. Plotted.
4. Computer output microfilm (COM).

These four methods of output all require the same attitude towards design. Whether the output is on paper or screen it must be laid out in the best way to facilitate use. Each of these methods has certain features which affect the way the output appears, but the overall objectivity of design should remain the key factor.

14.3 PRINTED REPORTS

The vast majority of work in most computer departments finds its way to the printer, and so the printer is used much more than any other machine in the computer department. It is the one machine which causes most delays and breaks down most often. It is primarily a mechanical device with many moving parts which are called upon to perform at high speeds with high precision. It is not surprising, therefore, that those who are involved with computers want the simplest possible print run.

The real limitations of computer printers are concerned with:

1. Number of print positions.
2. Characters available.
3. Speed.
4. Ability to produce copies.
5. Paper handling.

Print positions can vary from 60 to 160, so quite naturally the number of positions available will determine the size and scope of the information that can be printed. It is usual to find that standard printers have 132 print positions, which provide sufficient flexibility for most needs.

Most printers have all the characters needed for normal usage, including ten numbers, 52 letters (upper and lower case), mathematical symbols and punctuation marks. It is possible when buying printers to select the character set which is considered most appropriate, so there should be very little limitation to what is printed.

Speed is not usually a limitation for presentation except where there is a high volume of printing, which can reduce the quality of printing. There always has to be some trade-off between speed and clarity.

Duplicate copies are often considered a limitation because they are not very good copies and are usually quite dirty. It is not usually possible to produce more than three or four copies.

There are some people who believe that the limitation on the number of copies is a distinct advantage, preventing too much paperwork from being produced and distributed.

However, to overcome the limited number of copies, the stationery manufacturers have produced two forms of masters in continuous form. These can be used for offset litho reproduction and for spirit duplication reproduction. There is, however, the problem of having to use special ink ribbon for offset and special carbon for spirit duplication.

The most widely used method of presenting computer-based information to management is undoubtedly by computer printout. This general term covers a very wide range of possibilities and in theory offers an extremely flexible approach to the design of management reports. There are, however, a number of factors which limit the effectiveness of computer printout, apart from the technical constraints discussed above. These constraints are concerned with:

1. Type of paper used.
2. Computer operations.
3. Form design.

The first important point with regard to printout is the need for the stationery used to be 'continuous'. This means that each form is attached to the next and folded in such a way that the feeding of the printer and the subsequent stacking can be handled efficiently. The way in which continuous stationery is folded is shown in Figure 14.3.

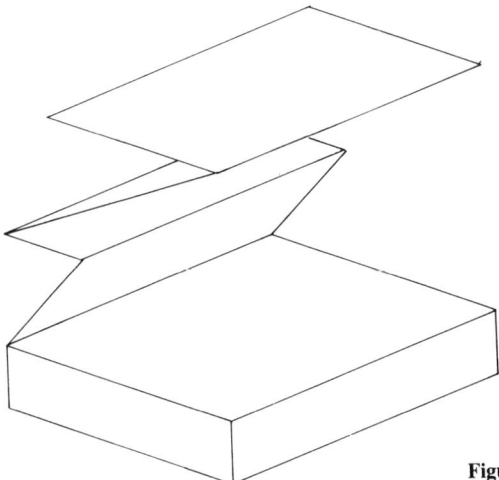

Figure 14.3 *Continuous stationery*

This essential requirement for efficient feeding of the computer causes the first of the problems met by the user. It is naturally much easier for the computer staff to distribute printouts direct from the computer in this specially folded form, which is designed for easy handling, not for easy reading. This problem can be overcome by using a 'bursting' machine, which breaks the continuous flow into separate sheets and stacks them face up. This would make reports more readable, as they could be bound on the left or the top and handled in a much easier and more natural way.

A second essential requirement of continuous stationery is the punching of sprocket holes, which are used to align paper in the printer and to transport the paper through the printer. The problem with sprocket holes is that they make the edge of the paper very scrappy and are too near to the edge for efficient filing. This problem can be overcome by trimming the sprocket holes at the same time as bursting.

There are many instances where computer departments equipped with bursting and trimming machines for handling routine documents such as invoices and cheques ignore them when producing information for management.

The third important aspect of continuous stationery is the problem of taking copies. The number of copies that can be taken direct from the printer is, for all practical purposes, limited to three or four. The print run can, of course, be done twice to give double the number of copies, but this is not really cost effective.

There are two usual ways in which copies are produced by using either interleaved carbon or 'no carbon required' (NCR) paper. In the case of interleaved carbons it is necessary to remove the carbon by the use of a decollating machine, which in the case of NCR paper is used only for separation.

Stationery manufacturers have produced continuous stationery for almost every conceivable type of document and report, from self-adhesive labels to special payroll documents which print a payslip held inside a carbon-backed envelope which allows data to be printed onto the payslip and, by removing the ink ribbon, leaves the front of the envelope blank.

The speed of printers varies considerably, but even the fastest printer is a snail compared with the speed of the computer. Because of this the printer can slow down the overall speed of computer processing, so the computer staff want the simplest possible print run.

Computer operators are responsible for loading printers with paper and aligning the stationery so that the machine prints where it should. The efficiency of the operation often controls both the speed of printing and the quality of the result. Many operators will state quite firmly that they think all output should be on standard (plain) paper, because this avoids alignment problems and paper changes. Paper changes are regarded as a necessary evil, so computer operators do not welcome the use of preprinted forms with special headings and addresses.

The more complex printing jobs, with special documents, special printing requirements and preprinted stationery, are not normally welcomed by the computer department. There is often resistance to such user-designed approaches, which sometimes takes the form of giving reasons why it cannot be done. It is possible to produce most requirements, if only the computer staff were prepared to take just a little longer and take a little more care.

14.4 TERMINAL OUTPUT

There are two types of terminal available – teletype and screen. Teletype is in effect a printer and has all the limitations of computer printers. Screens, on the other hand, have certain special features which will be dealt with more fully below. It is interesting to note that many people using screens also need a printer.

We are all used to looking at the television screen, from which we receive information in coloured visuals supported by commentary and music. The computer output screen is, however, somewhat more limited than this, although with colour graphics there is considerable scope (see section 14.5).

The screen of the visual display unit (VDU) is of a limited size. The size varies but will usually be defined as so many lines of so many characters. This provides a controlled framework for the form designer to produce the appropriate data in an easily readable form.

With modern facilities it is possible to represent data in a variety of ways and to construct reports on the screen which look similar to a printed report. Screen output is used primarily in interactive systems, where the response onto the screen is part of the processing operation. Screens are also used for interrogation of files. One problem that can exist is holding the data on the screen for relatively long periods. This requires either constant regeneration by the computer or using a buffer store in the terminal itself.

The choice of VDU as a means of output depends on the particular system, the needs of the user and the efficiency and cost effectiveness of the approach. There are circumstances in which other methods are much more effective.

14.5 GRAPHICS

Graphs and diagrams can be a very effective method of presenting information. Screen-based graphics are extremely sophisticated and allow for three-dimensional images which can be rotated. Using colour video monitors instead of the monochrome unit allows a wide range of graphics to be used.

Graphs and diagrams can also be plotted on paper. Plotters are not used as widely as printers, but offer a very flexible method of presenting information graphically.

Methods are becoming increasingly sophisticated, with programs that can rotate diagrams from plan to three-dimensional. The simpler plotters work on the basis of a pen held by an arm which moves horizontally and vertically across a sheet of paper. The plot is controlled by the use of two co-ordinates in the vertical and horizontal axes and this is why these machines are referred to as *X–Y* plotters.

Ordinary computer printers can be used to provide a crude graphic presentation by using a program which prints characters in print positions controlled by *X–Y* co-ordinates.

14.6 COMPUTER OUTPUT MICROFILM

This is a form of output which takes magnetic data from the computer and converts them to readable microfilm reproduced on roll film or microfiche. The microfiche is produced by a special machine using one of three types of conversion techniques, which are:

1. Cathode ray tube, which is the simplest and most common method used and is based on taking a photograph of the information recorded on a cathode ray tube within the machine. An image can be superimposed on the screen to produce the outlines of a form.
2. Fibre optics are used to produce a character by selectively illuminating fibres. The film is produced line by line to build up the full frame, upon which the outline of a form can be subsequently filmed and superimposed.
3. Electron beam can be used to write characters directly onto the microfilm, which is held in a vacuum chamber. The form outline is subsequently superimposed or programmed.

COM recorders can be linked directly to the computer or can operate separately by the use of magnetic tapes output from the computer. The latter approach is the method which is most widely used. Most companies using COM magnetic tape send it to external service bureaux for development.

14.7 DESIGNING COMPUTER OUTPUT

When designing computer output to present management information there are a number of points to be considered. These can be reduced to two principal factors – dimensions and order. The dimensions deal with the horizontal and vertical presentation and order deals with the way the content is organized.

Dimensions

The first decision that must be made is which headings will be on the horizontal dimension, i.e. across the top, and which will be vertical, i.e. down the page or screen. This is an important decision because the horizontal headings will be written into the program whereas the vertical headings will be part of the data held on the file.

This point can be appreciated if each line printed across the page is considered as a line of data transferred from the computer to the printer as a complete line. So the program instructs the printer to print the headings each time it moves to a new page, and then it prints each line of data.

The amount of data that can be printed horizontally is normally limited to 132 characters, including spaces, so the normal procedure is to choose the lesser number of headings for the horizontal headings. For example, if there were 100 expense headings for ten departments, it would be better to print the departments as horizontal headings and the expenses as vertical headings. Such a report would take up about five or six pages of printout, depending on the line spacing.

The content printed under each heading is decided by the user both in terms of whether it is numerical or alphabetical and whether it is single-factor or multiple-factor. Single-factor means that there is a single piece of data under each of the headings. Multiple-factor means that there is more than one factor under each heading, as in Figure 14.4.

Horizontal Headings

	Vehicle	January	February	March	April
	XYZ 123T	126.3 GW			
		19.4 ALS			
		345.6 VAL			
	PNZ 178T				
	JLM 917T				
	PXT 815S				

Vertical Headings

GW = Gross weight, ALS = Average load size, VAL = Value

Figure 14.4 *Computer report layout*

This is quite a complex way of presenting information, but it does indicate the scope available in computer output.

Order

The actual content printed under the headings comes from the computer file and is organized by the print program before printing takes place. Each of the spaces on the report where data are to appear is called a field. Each field will consist of a specified number of characters and, if the computer has more data on its file than the print program will accept, they will not appear. In most cases the computer will report an error. It is very important, therefore, to make sure that field sizes are carefully specified, and it must be remembered that, with a computer, spaces are included as characters.

Spacing is an important factor in computer reports. Once again we have to consider spacing in two dimensions – character spacing between fields across the report and line spacing between vertical lines.

Both forms of spacing are crucial to producing a readable report, and you should avoid trying to cram too many data into one page. Paging is another important spacing

182 — *Management information systems and data processing*

08 ANALYSIS Concrete Division North Lancs. – Sales delivered collected per area analysis   M/END 06/77 Page 6

Area	Depot	D/C	Quantity (metres)	Gross value	Haulage charged	Weight cement	Weight sand	Weight course aggregate	Total weight aggregate	
3	236	D	264.80	£4543.52	£741.21	63.66	191.05	328.35	519.40	Depot total
3	236	T	54.50	£1049.29	£159.34	16.22	36.77	67.58	104.35	Usage per m
			324.30	£5669.54	£900.55	61.05	231.43	402.13	633.56	
						0.25	0.71	1.24	1.95	
3	237	D	1267.40	£22290.24	£3465.28	349.18	730.28	1735.93	2466.21	Depot total
3	237	T	97.50	£1864.39	£232.69	26.91	56.14	133.54	189.68	Usage per m
			1364.90	£24154.63	£3697.97	376.09	786.42	1869.47	2655.89	
						0.28	0.58	1.37	1.95	
3	238	C	26.50	£396.02	£0.00	3.44	18.37	36.26	54.63	Depot total
3	238	D	1616.50	£27201.41	£3357.88	516.43	874.40	2209.73	3084.13	Usage per m
			1643.00	£27597.43	£3357.88	519.87	892.77	2245.99	3138.76	
						0.32	0.54	1.37	1.91	
3	240	C	11.00	£173.08	£0.00	1.94	7.15	15.04	22.19	Depot total
3	240	D	2261.10	£40656.53	£4717.99	619.27	1313.55	2959.12	4272.67	Usage per m
			2272.10	£40829.61	£4717.99	621.21	1320.70	2974.16	4294.86	
						0.27	0.58	1.31	1.89	
3	242	C	26.00	£433.41	£0.00	6.93	18.08	32.23	50.31	Depot total
3	242	D	977.10	£17113.12	£2542.46	258.58	685.37	1211.56	1896.93	Usage per m
3	242	T	32.00	£642.11	£89.15	9.07	21.95	39.68	61.63	
			1035.10	£18188.64	£2631.61	274.58	725.40	1283.47	2008.87	
						0.27	0.70	1.24	1.94	

Figure 14.5 *Computer report – normal*

08 ANALYSIS Concrete Division – Sales delivered/collected per area analysis   M/END 06/77 Page 12

Area	Depot	D/C	Quantity (metres)	Gross value	Haulage charged	Weight cement	Sand	Weight Aggregate	Total aggregate	
East	Whitby	C	224.00	£3304.08	£0.00	58.13	135.40	291.20	426.60	
		D	2393.70	£41578.71	£5771.67	674.16	1399.82	3120.21	4520.03	Depot total
			2617.70	£44882.79	£5771.67	732.29	1535.22	3411.41	4946.63	Usage per m
						0.28	0.59	1.30	1.89	
East	Hull	C	138.50	£2124.98	£0.00	35.60	83.57	180.05	263.62	
		D	1627.50	£28472.86	£4027.63	473.02	951.09	2115.75	3066.84	Depot total
			1766.00	£30597.84	£4027.63	508.62	1034.66	2295.80	3330.46	Usage per m
						0.29	0.59	1.30	1.89	
East	York	C	31.00	£422.59	£0.00	6.86	19.70	40.30	60.00	
		D	390.50	£6268.36	£1155.13	101.95	237.77	507.65	745.42	Depot total
			421.50	£6690.95	£1155.13	108.81	257.47	547.95	805.42	Usage per m
						0.26	0.61	1.30	1.91	
East	Thirsk	?	63.00	£257.04	£0.00	0.00	0.00	0.00	0.00	
		C	6.00	£85.11	£0.00	1.31	3.84	7.80	11.64	
		D	1742.00	£26093.70	£4794.82	446.63	1068.37	2264.60	3332.97	
			1811.00	£26435.85	£4794.82	447.94	1072.21	2272.40	3344.61	Depot total
						0.25	0.59	1.25	1.85	Usage per m
East	Malton	D	428.50	£7513.38	£1152.47	114.98	258.28	557.05	815.33	Depot total
			428.50	£7513.38	£1152.47	114.98	258.28	557.05	815.33	Depot total
						0.27	0.60	1.30	1.90	Usage per m

Figure 14.6 *Computer report – improved*

consideration. Unless the computer is told when to space and skip, it will continue printing regardless of where departments or other headings might finish.

Perhaps the way to look at paging is to relate pages and line spacing to the way information is to be sub-totalled and totalled. Totalling is one of those aspects of computer reports which users take for granted. It seems quite natural that if there are certain groups of vertical headings they can easily be totalled and sub-totalled. However, in computer terms there are several ways in which this can be done.

Totals can be produced horizontally and vertically. The horizontal totals can appear after each group of data or at the end of the report. The reason for this variety of approaches is that the totals are produced in the programming before printing, and can be sorted to be printed where required on the report. This does not mean that it is easy to produce sub-totals if none was originally specified. At the very minimum this means changing the programs producing the totals and the print programs.

The golden rules of presentation – clarity and simplicity – are no less applicable to computer reports than to every other kind of report. Clarity is not always a term associated with computer reports. Apart from careful attention to content and spacing, it is necessary to consider using pre-printed forms. As mentioned earlier, the printing industry can supply continuous stationery in many formats and the effect is to significantly improve appearance.

If Figure 14.5 is compared with Figure 14.6, it can be seen that the use of words instead of numbers, and using lines to separate fields and spacing, make the report much more readable.

14.8 THE USER-DP CONFLICT

One of the greatest problems that users of computer output have to overcome is the extensive use of numbers. The computer works on numbers, giving everything with a name a code. This is done for efficient computer operations, ease of data storage and accuracy. Unfortunately, for the normal user, the customer's name is more important than the customer's account number. Similarly, product names and location names are easier to read and understand than code numbers. Yet very often computer output is entirely numerical.

The codes can all be converted to names, but this has two effects on data processing:

1. Additional program steps are required.
2. More space is needed on the printout.

Programs for printing have several jobs to do. The first of these is to print the headings for the reports, then to state what should be printed in each position of the layout, including the sub-totals, spacing and summaries. If the code numbers have to be converted to names it means that description files have to be searched and the appropriate names inserted instead of the codes. This increases processing time and means that description files have to be maintained.

Printing space is often at a premium and the use of names or descriptions uses up much more space than codes. However, this can still be catered for in the formatting stage.

The computer is an excellent servant, but if everything that is printed out is going to be limited by what the computer can do, or rather what the computer staff want to do, the computer becomes the master. There are far too many companies in which the computer department controls the form and appearance of output. Until this is changed and the user controls the form in which information is received, the complaints will continue.

If computer reports are going to be made more useful it is important that the designers consider carefully the users' needs and the constraints of the computer. With care and attention to detail it will be found that the computer is quite capable of producing excellent reports which are both comprehensive and readable.

14.9 SUMMARY AND REVISION NOTES

Creating usable output means giving very careful thought to the needs of the user. Form design is a skill which is not always an inherent ability in system designers.

Users should be involved in designing the output, using format charts or providing examples of what they want.

Computer output is produced in two main forms:

1. Machine-readable.
2. Human-readable.

The human-readable output is received in four main ways:

1. Printed.
2. Terminal screen.
3. Plotted (on paper or screen).
4. Computer output microfilm (COM).

The success of printed output depends partly on the design, and partly on the printing and the paper used. The designer must take these factors into account when designing printed output.

Terminal output needs to be designed just as printed output does. The screen size is limited and must be used effectively.

Graphics on both paper and screen have to be used with care, ensuring that the output is simple and clear. With sophisticated modern colour equipment a wide range of effects can be produced.

Computer output microfilm is an effective way of transferring data from magnetic tape to film for subsequent reference. There are three main types of equipment:

1. Cathode ray tube.
2. Fibre optics.
3. Electron beam.

When designing output, of whatever kind, there are two key factors to be considered:

1. Dimensions.
2. Order.

Dimensions cover the way in which the document is laid out, the use of headings, etc. Order covers the content and the way it is inserted onto the format.

There is often a conflict between the needs of the user and the efficiency of data processing. The DP function prefers simple numeric prints on plain paper, while users want descriptive text with ruled layouts. This conflict can be overcome if both parties work together to make the output well presented and useful.

QUESTIONS

1. Discuss the importance of form design in producing effective computer systems. (IMS)

2. You have been asked to prepare a design for a computer printout. Explain the factors you will have to take into account and the limitations you will have to observe.

3. Give examples of situations in which the following computer output would be appropriate:

   (a) screen-based graphics;
   (b) COM;
   (c) printed report on plain paper;
   (d) printed report on pre-printed paper.

4. Your company has been operating a computer system for a number of years and, contrary to initial expectations, the volume of printout has risen dramatically each year. Describe the system and operational techniques which can be employed to reduce output volumes. (ICMA)

5. 'Why is it I can never get what I want from DP? They always have some damned good reason why it's not possible.' Discuss this statement.

CASE STUDY EXERCISE

Produce a schedule of the anticipated output from your system, together with an indication of the methods you will use to produce the output.

15

System Standards

15.1 THE NEED FOR STANDARDS

Standards are necessary at three distinct levels:

1. Company.
2. National.
3. International.

They are necessary at these levels for the same reasons:

1. Consistency.
2. Quality.
3. Compatibility.

At company level, standards are required for all aspects of systems design, programming and operations. These standards could be based on published standards, e.g. the National Computer Centre (NCC) standards. Alternatively, the standards could be specially written to suit the company's individual requirements.

National standards, particularly in communications, are very important for linking systems and for the design and development of computer equipment and software.

The computer industry is international, both in terms of the building of computers and software, and in terms of international links crossing national boundaries and oceans.

With the development of fibre optic communications and the transfer of data via satellites, standards have become even more important.

The need for standards can be seen more clearly when we examine the problems that can arise from lack of standards.

> A company decided to install a national network of terminals linked to a central computer. The objective was to collect large volumes of data and transfer them to the computer via an overnight automatic link.

The mainframe manufacturer offered an automatic polling system. The terminal manufacturer had a special auto-answer device and the Post Office assured the company that their dialled network could cope.

After numerous attempts the system would not work. Everyone involved said their system had been produced to the Post Office standard. However, when the details were examined they had all been made to a slightly different specification and so would not work. Eventually the terminal manufacturer amended his device and the system worked.

In another example a UK company wished to transmit information via a telecopier to a subsidiary in the USA. The machines at each end were identical and each was set up correctly. The international link just would not work. The machine at the UK end was adapted to transmit to the USA, but it would no longer work with machines in the UK.

Standards are, therefore, essential if systems are to be consistent and compatible and if they are to produce high-quality results.

Consistency is important at all levels. Many people believe that standardization limits creativity and initiative, which it does if it is interpreted as a constraint. However, if standards are seen as providing a level of consistency in the way systems and equipment are designed and built, then the result will be seen in higher quality.

Machines and equipment must be compatible before they can be linked, and numerous manufacturers have benefited by producing equipment which is compatible with machines sold by market leaders. This equipment is referred to as 'plug compatible' because it can be plugged in and operates as if it were an original.

Consistency and compatibility lead to higher quality, both in the way people work and in systems performance. Standards provide the basic rules that lead to high quality and also provide a way in which performance can be assessed.

15.2 HARDWARE STANDARDS

It is important that the hardware used in a system is compatible. Data must flow from machine to machine and must be interpreted correctly. This means that the linking mechanisms (the interfaces) are specified to the same standard.

It is possible and perfectly feasible to link the machines of different manufacturers by producing special 'black boxes' which receive data to one specification, interpret them and pass them to the next machine in the specification it requires. These black boxes or interface units are not uncommon in communication networks.

The standards are concerned with technical factors such as the amplification of the signals, the checking procedures and the coding sequence used. All these factors, together with physical requirements such as plug layouts, wiring configurations and pin lengths, have to be specified in the same way before machines can be linked.

There is, of course, a certain resistance on the part of manufacturers, who can make changes to specifications as a marketing policy, so that buyers must buy the manufacturer's peripheral equipment as well as the main machines. However, national and international telecommunications networks are forcing manufacturers to conform to established standards. The standards have not all been agreed and published, but activities are leading in this direction.

15.3 SOFTWARE STANDARDS

Software standards have been argued about for many years and the computer industry is no nearer to a solution now than it has ever been. Standards are required at all levels, namely:

1. Operating software.
2. Programming languages.
3. Job control languages.

Operating software is developed by manufacturers to suit the architecture of their particular machines, and to include features which will give them a competitive advantage. This means that no two operating systems are the same; nor are they ever likely to be. This leads to a variety of problems, the worst of which is the need to convert or re-program systems when machines are changed. This is the main reason why few companies change their main machine. Unfortunately, when some manufacturers develop new machines, they change the operating system. This means that conversion is necessary even when changing models of the same computer.

Cobol is, as its name implies, a common language, but there is ICL Cobol, UNIVAC Cobol, IBM Cobol, and so on. Each varies slightly, meaning that programs written in Cobol for one machine will not work on another. This is true of most programming languages and is even spreading to microcomputers through different versions of Basic. The differences are not always significant, but the programmer must learn the differences and this learning curve slows down programming and reduces the quality of the programs.

Job control languages differ for every make of machine and sometimes for different models. This further aggravates the problems of making changes.

It will be very difficult, if not impossible, to produce software standards to overcome the above difficulties, but there is no reason why control standards should not be established within the company for application software.

15.4 SYSTEM DESIGN STANDARDS

Apart from general industry standards, each organization should establish its own standards for the whole of the system design process, from the initial review to final evaluation (see Figure 5.2).

The system design process itself should be a standard, with each element of the process being followed in the prescribed way. The output of each element forms part of the documentation standards (see section 15.5). The technical standards which are followed within the system design process are as follows:

1. Programming standards.
2. Flowcharts standards.
3. Data control standards.
4. Form design standards.
5. Documentation standards.

In addition to these there are also operating standards (see section 15.7).

Programming Standards

Programming standards should deal with all those factors which will ensure:

1. Quality of programs.
2. Consistency of approach.
3. Efficiency of operation.
4. Continuity of understanding.

This means setting down the approach to programming and the rules that must be observed. An example extracted from a company standards manual is given below.

In preparing detailed program specifications the following rules must be followed:

1. The maximum program size of 35 K must not be exceeded.
2. All parameter input to the computer must be via parameter cards, *not* via the console.
3. A program must never use more than one tape drive.
4. Systems must never be reliant on the computer system data.
5. All peripherals should be released at end of file.
6. Wherever passwords are used, they must be systems which are independent and capable of being changed easily.
7. Agree the need for re-start procedures with the DP Manager. The aim is to produce programs which take no more than one hour on a single run.
8. Details of input and/or output on terminal or card should be passed to the DP Manager as soon as the input/output program specification is complete. Agreement must be reached on this point before actual programming commences.

File names will start with the program name. Because of this it is essential that program names are not changed, as this will cause the file name to be changed, thus creating the following extra work. No more than one program should create a file.

1. Job control will have to be altered twice – once for input of old file and once for output of new file.
2. Operating instructions will have to be changed.
3. File specification will have to be changed.
4. Names of files in tape storage equipment and tape library register will have to be changed.

Programming standards will not stand still: as additional features are used or new techniques developed, they will be added to the standards.

Flowcharts Standards

Flowcharts can be produced in a variety of ways, all of which can be effective, but standards should be established for:

1. The symbols to be used.
2. The way the flowcharts are drawn.
3. Coding and referencing of flowcharts.

Flowcharts were dealt with in more detail in section 5.6, and examples were given of symbols and types of charts. If standards are not established then new employees will continue to use methods learned elsewhere, and very soon a wide range of flowcharts will exist and confusion will reign.

Data Control Standards

Data control standards are very important, particularly when data base systems are to be designed. These standards are important in ensuring that all data transactions can be traced and audited, and follow a consistent path. An example of data control standards is given below.

Audit trail. Any transaction entering the system will be given a unique reference made up of two elements.

Computer batch no. The installation control file contains a batch number that should be referenced at the start of any input run and updated by one every time a new batch is encountered. At the end of the validation run the control file should be updated with the last computer batch number used.

Batch sequence number. Each transaction within a batch will be given a number starting at 1 with the batch header and progressing in increments of 1 through to the batch trailer.
   The combination of these two numbers gives each transaction a unique reference which should be retained by the transaction throughout its system life.

Input control. Every batch entering the system should be shown as it enters the system, giving the full batch reference, the batch detail values and printed under the heading 'New' or 'Correcting Input'. Each batch balance error, where the input total does not agree to the detail total, will be flagged on the input register by an asterisk.

Batch listings. The listing of the contents of a batch will always be preceded by a print of the batch header record. This will show the full batch reference, enabling the batch to be traced to its point of origination.

The batch listing will also print the computer batch number at the end of the reference as part of the audit trail.

Error matching. Error matching has proved the biggest problem in systems and the rules for matching have been evolved from these problems. The rules are simple and are:

1. A batch balance error will cause the batch to be rejected in its entirety. The batch will be rejected as *XX* data and not *XE* data. (*XX* is new data; *XE* is error data.)
2. Where an error occurs within a balanced batch, the record will be written to the error file and terminal file with the computer generated number. *This number will be used for error matching.*

The advantages of this method of matching are:

1. Any field within a record can be altered without altering the main reference fields.
2. The error cycle file can be maintained by this method, leaving only genuine outstanding errors on the cycle file.

(It may be necessary to restrict the set of fields to be altered in the record to those fields not affecting batch balancing.)

Error cycle file print. At any point during the month it should be possible to print the errors on the cycle file. This print must include the computer-generated reference to enable the transaction to be traced back to its point of entry in the system.

Data control standards depend on the particular circumstances in the organization and could cover a variety of validation checks and reporting controls (see section 12.5). It is important, however, to ensure that the specific organization standards are observed.

Form Design Standards

Form design standards should be agreed for several aspects of form design:

1. Form make-up, i.e. paper, print styles, size, filing, etc.
2. Spacing, vertical and horizontal field definitions, headings, etc.
3. Highlights, using heavy lines, hatching and other highlighting methods.
4. Style, whether fields will be open or boxed.

All these factors and others need to be built into the standards. (A full set of form design standards can be found in the author's book *Making Information Systems Work.*)

15.5 DOCUMENTATION

Documentation standards are a vital part of the systems design standards. Documentation is not liked by systems design staff, and unfortunately, few organizations insist on the preparation and maintenance of adequate documentation. Like procedure standards, documentation standards should start at the beginning of the system design process and continue for the life of the system. The full documentation consists of:

1. Design report.
2. System specification.
3. Program specification.
4. Test report.
5. Amendment records.

Design Report

The design report itself must contain:

1. The system objectives (a reiteration of the systems proposal).
2. The benefits (a reiteration of the systems proposal or better).
3. Basis of the system.
4. Output.
5. Input.
6. Operation of the system.
7. Detailed time scale.
8. Implementation proposals.

The basis of the system must cover the main principles on which the system (solution) is based and indicate the requirements in terms of people and equipment. This section must be written so that the reader can obtain a picture of the system as a whole as it will eventually operate.

Output of the system is a key area, as this is the result as seen by the user. The detail of each report should be provided using a Report Analysis Sheet, which states quite clearly:

1. The purpose of the report.
2. The distribution.
3. The content.
4. The format.
5. Decision relationship.

Input forms should be clearly drawn (using the form design sheet where appropriate) and details of their completion should be given.

The way in which the system operates is important, both to the computer operations personnel and to the user. They should be able to check their ability to meet the system requirements for data collection, input, processing and output. Any relationships with other systems must be spelt out in this section.

The detailed time-scale leads on from the operation of the system and should clearly state constraints in terms of the working calendar.

The implementation proposed needs to clearly state each step to be taken, who is responsible and how long it will take. If any changes have occurred since the systems proposal, particularly with regard to the cost of the project, this is the point at which such details should be set out.

System Specification

This is the blueprint for systems and will be referred to constantly during the building of the system. It should therefore contain the details required by everyone concerned.

The system specification starts with a form which records updates, and a comprehensive index. These are important for two reasons:

1. Changes.
2. Use of the specification.

Changes must not be made unless authorized by those listed. When changes are agreed, amendments should be made to specification and noted on the update form. An out-of-date specification is like a filled dustbin, full of rubbish and of no further use. The index should be fully detailed and provide ready access to the content for any user.

The general description of the system is the next section and is usually an abstract from the Design Report, but may also include any other information thought to be of value to the user of the specification, including where necessary a definition of the terms used. It will be necessary to use technical terms but, wherever possible, jargon should be avoided.

The system specification should be produced in logical order, so the next stage is the system input. The input is set out in full detail. Every transaction type is detailed, complete with layouts, card, tape, screen formats, etc. Not only are the technical details such as length of record, type, i.e. alpha, numeric, etc., provided, but also the way in which input is validated, controlled and updated.

The systems flowchart comes next. It is produced in detail and forms the basis of subsequent programming activities. The flowchart should be drawn to show how every element of the system fits into the overall design. It should be considered as a fundamental requirement of successful design.

Effective controls are a very important part of the system, so the next section sets out the controls built into the system, what they are for, when they occur and how they work. This section should also cover basic requirements for security and standby in the event of a failure in some part of the system, whether this is human or machine failure.

The output of the system is the product as far as the user is concerned; therefore it should observe the following basic rules:

1. As little as possible.
2. Printed in English; words are preferable to code numbers.
3. Produced in the order required.
4. Produced in the form required.
5. Be easily changeable.
6. Be clearly titled.
7. Dated.

Every report and document should be listed and cross-referred to the program which creates it and to the file which holds the data. Then an example is given of every item, indicating how and when it is produced and what it is for.

It is likely that some changes will have been made to the formats included in the Design Report. These should be noted. In the initial documentation the examples will be hand-drawn, but as the system is tested these will be replaced with examples from the machine.

File structure and organization are important in the design and must be clearly defined, including:

1. File specification.
2. File layout.

The file specification indicates the type of file, the record types and sizes, the total file size, sequence and security requirements.

The layout sheet provides a detailed definition of each field within each record on the file.

The file specification is held within the systems file, but the layouts are maintained in a master file layout file held by computer operations. This not only avoids errors, but also ensures that the master file in use is always up to date.

The final section of the system specification is the program overview. This is the linking device between the systems specification and the program specification. It also enables a full understanding of the system to be obtained from the systems specification. The overview (Figure 15.1) contains:

1. Program name.
2. Input files: name and brief description.
3. Output files: name and brief description.
4. Objects of program.
5. Controls.

In order to ensure that the systems specification is readable and also technically complete, appendices are used. This approach enables long and complex tables, matrices, lists of codes, etc., to be filed at the rear of the specification and cross-referred to in the text.

Program Specification

The program specification is a working document produced in sufficient detail to allow a program to be written. Whether this is produced by the systems designer, the programmer or jointly depends on the circumstances and the people. Regardless of who produces the specification, it should contain:

1. Input details. ⎫
2. Output details. ⎬ (From program overview)
3. Objects of program. ⎭
4. Procedure.
5. Program flowchart.
6. Appendices: codes, matrices, algorithms, etc.
7. Print layout sheet.

The program specification and the latest compilation are filed in numerical order. Access to these files should be restricted to authorized personnel only.

The program procedure sets out in narrative form the step-by-step method by which the program achieves its objectives. Again the principle of using appendices is employed so that the narrative is relatively free of matrices, code lists, etc. The proce-

```
                    PROGRAM OVERVIEW

    Program Name            SDO4
    Input Files             SDCTCKTDATA disc file out of TDO1
                              containing new tickets and
                              correction ticket batches

                            SDCTCKTERROR disc file – 'Memo file'
                              routine file select parameter

    Output Files            SDCDAILYRUN disc file containing new
                              ticket batches
                              correction ticket batches
                              recycled ticket batches
                              (Memo file Mini batches)

    Objects of Program
            1. To create a file containing new and recycled
               ticket details in batch sequence.
            2. To batch balance ticket batches creating a
               dummy batch balancing record for batches not
               in balance.
            3. To select 'mini' batches from the input
               SDCTCKTERROR for recycling.
            4. Generate input batch/record sequence numbers
               on the output records.

    Controls
            Accumulate counts of input and output records and
            check with control record counts.
```

Figure 15.1 *Program overview*

dure should indicate quite clearly how the program should be written and should contain no ambiguity.

The logic of the approach should be analysed using structured program techniques, before the program is written. A programmer should never start coding until he or she has a clear understanding of the logic, purpose and approach of the program.

Program flowcharts are an excellent means of showing the detailed steps within the program. If the logic has been verified then the program flowchart should be the programmer's guide as he or she writes the program.

Appendices contain any matrices, formulae, etc. which are used within the program. Wherever possible, data should not be written into the program. Separate tables should be used. The additional programming required at the development stage is more than compensated for subsequently, when changes are necessary.

During the writing and testing of the program the specification is used as the guiding instruction to the programmer. After the system becomes operational the program specification is a key to effective systems maintenance. It is essential, therefore, that as much information as possible is included in the program file. It is almost certain that the program will need to be amended by someone other than the originator, and without a comprehensive program specification this is a long and tedious exercise, if it can be done at all.

Test Report

The procedures for testing systems were fully set out in section 7.5. The test report is the documentation of these procedures. There are two main documents involved:

1. Program Test Sheet (Figure 15.2).
2. Run Test Sheet (Figure 15.3).

The program test sheet records details of the job and the peripherals used to test the program, together with console messages and notes made by the operator of any action he or she has taken. The programmer and operator note their general comments on the performance of the program.

The run test sheet records similar information but now it is for the whole run, which will include all the programs in the job.

In addition to the test sheets, the test report will contain comments on the results of the tests and the corrective action taken. There will be several test sheets for each test, and these should form a comprehensive file from the commencement of tests to the satisfactory completion.

Documentation is absolutely essential for efficient design, development and maintenance of good information and control systems. There are three very good reasons why this is so:

1. Continuity.
2. Changes.
3. Security.

System standards — 199

PROGRAM TEST SHEET

JOB NAME	
JOB STEP - PROG NAME	

CARD READER	

PRINTER		LOOP		STATIONERY	

TAPE G90		FILE NAME		VSN		Can tape be scratched	
TAPE G91		FILE NAME		VSN		Can tape be scratched	

Should any tape deck be set down	

TLCD 00	
TLCD 01	
TLCD 02	
TLCD 03	
TLCD	
TLCD	
TLCD	

TERMINAL	
DE 523	
CASSETTE	
1200 FT TAPE	
PRINTER	
VDU	
COP	

CONSOLE MESSAGES	OPERATOR ACTION

PROGRAMMER NOTES

OPERATOR NOTES

Figure 15.2 *Program Test Sheet*

200 — Management information systems and data processing

| RUN TEST SHEET | | JOB REF. | | JOB NO. | |

JOB NAME		ACTUAL RUN TIME	
PRIORITY		ESTIMATED RUN TIME	
DATE SUBMITTED		TIME SUBMITTED	
PROGRAMMER		TELEPHONE	

CORE	
MAGNETIC TAPE UNITS REQD.	
CARD READER	
PRINTER	
TLCD 00	CYLINDERS CREATED =
TLCD 01	CYLINDERS CREATED =
TLCD 02	CYLINDERS CREATED =
TLCD 03	CYLINDERS CREATED =
	CYLINDERS CREATED =
	CYLINDERS CREATED =
DE 523 TERMINAL	
CASSETTE TAPES	
1200 FT TAPE	
PRINTER	
VDU	
COP	

PROGRAMMER REMARKS
ARE PRODUCTIVE FILES USED — YES/NO (DELETE AS APPLICABLE)
NO FILES REMAIN ON DISC — FILES USED —

OPERATOR REMARKS

Figure 15.3 *Run Test Sheet*

Continuity can be achieved only with complete specifications. If the systems designer leaves, then it should be possible for his or her replacement to pick up the specification and continue to maintain the systems.

Changes (amendments) are required for a variety of reasons. Without a comprehensive specification the effects of changes cannot always be predicted. The specification is the only place where the effects of a change can be traced through the whole system.

Security, both of data and of the system, can be maintained only by reference to the procedures set out in the specification.

The investment in applications software can amount to several million pounds, and the only visible evidence of the software is the documentation plus a copy of the programs on tape or disc. These, therefore, should be protected.

15.6 MAINTAINING THE SYSTEMS INVESTMENT

No information system stands still if it is to be effective and serve management. This means that changes will take place continuously, and these must be properly managed and controlled if the investment is to be maintained.

This maintenance task can be achieved only if sound standards are established and followed. These standards must cater for a variety of types of changes:

1. Software changes: new releases from manufacturer; modifications; application software to –
   (a) correct errors,
   (b) enhance the system,
   (c) improve operating efficiency.
2. Operational changes: new peripherals; extended networks; new job control programs; distribution of output.
3. System changes: improvements to meet users' needs; re-organizations; improvements in control.

All these changes have to be properly communicated and controlled, and this calls for standards to determine what is done and when it is done.

Amendments will always be required, for a wide range of reasons. The system should be designed to cater readily for amendments when they are necessary. There are five guiding rules for dealing with amendments:

1. Check why the amendment has been requested.
2. Determine the extent of the problem.
3. Decide whether or not an amendment is necessary.
4. If an amendment is necessary consider how it can be done, producing alternatives if required.
5. State the cost of carrying out the work and, based on the degree of need for (benefit of) the amendment, schedule it for action.

Priorities should be established to ensure that amendments are dealt with efficiently. The normal priorities are:

1. First priority, modifications: changes required to meet the objectives of the system and to correct deficiencies.
2. Second priority, improvements: to meet user requirements not originally part of the system.
3. Third priority, operating efficiency (computer): to improve the operation of the system without changing the system.
4. Fourth priority, system changes: changes in the specification of the system.

The management of amendments is done by recording every amendment on a special document which is returned and entered into the amendment system (Figure 15.4). During the amendment procedure, amendments can be co-ordinated to minimize the changes made to the systems and consequently to the systems documentation. It is not unusual for contradicting amendments to be requested, and it is essential to co-ordinate all requests. Amendments must be carefully evaluated before they are carried out.

15.7 OPERATING STANDARDS

Apart from good operating procedures (Chapter 13) there are several aspects of operations for which standards should be established. These cover:

1. Job control.
2. Program libraries.
3. File management.
4. Output distribution.

Job Control

Job control concerns the way the job is run on the computer and should be established by the programmer and the operations supervisor during the final systems testing phase. Once established the job control should only be changed by reference back to the programmer. Operators must never attempt short cuts; they invariably go wrong.

Program Libraries

Program libraries must be handled with great care. There should be three libraries:

1. Load library.
2. Temp library.
3. Test library.

System standards — 203

SYSTEM AMENDMENT REQUEST

GROUP SYSTEMS PROJECT TEAM

DATE		FROM		TO	COMPUTER *	NUMBER	
					SYSTEMS *		

AMENDMENT REQUIRED

REASON FOR AMENDMENT

COMPUTER AND SYSTEMS USE ONLY

EFFECT OF AMENDMENT

PROGRAMS INVOLVED	
ESTIMATE OF WORKLOAD	
STATIONERY INVOLVED	
AMENDMENTS REQUIRED TO MANUALS	PROCEDURE / OPERATOR
TRAINING REQUIRED	

EXTENT OF AMENDMENT	GROUP	DIVISION	REGION	AREA *

AGREED AND AUTHORIZED BY		DATE	

*DELETE AS APPROPRIATE SEND SECOND COPY TO OTHER DEPT.

Figure 15.4 *System amendment request*

Live programs are held in the *load library* and all live work is done using these programs.

Programs which have been tested but not yet accepted by operators are held in the *temp library*. Programs being amended or new programs are held in the *test library*. Transfers between libraries must be handled with care (Figure 15.5).

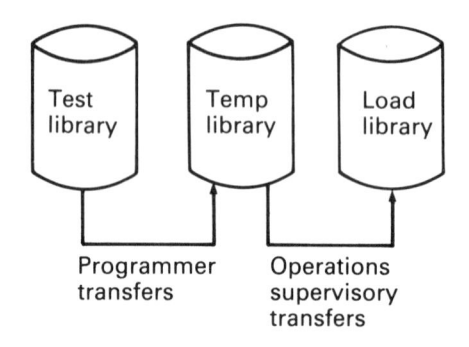

Figure 15.5 *Program libraries*

File Management

Files have to be managed with care and skill, and this includes files held outside the computer as well as those on the machine. The standards should cover:

1. File names.
2. Reference codes.
3. Dates.
4. Versions and copies (see Chapter 17).
5. Library records:
   (a) when used;
   (b) by which jobs;
   (c) programs within jobs.
6. Controls.
7. Authorization for access, deletion, etc.

It is important that once these standards have been established they are rigorously maintained. Inadequate file management is one of the primary causes of errors and re-runs.

Output Distribution

Output distribution must be carefully managed, particularly with regard to changes in personnel, both leaving and starting, and re-organizations. Output request documents should be used to request additional information or to request that reports be stopped.

When a company recently examined its output distribution records it found eight reports being sent to staff who had retired and three to staff who had died.

An output distribution record should be maintained showing, for each request:

1. Frequency of output.
2. Recipients.
3. Columns for dates sent.
4. Section for comments.
5. Date report stopped.

15.8 ENFORCING STANDARDS

Standards are all too often ignored by data processing management. The results can be quite easily seen in inadequate performance. Standards must be not only established, but enforced. Ignoring company standards should constitute a breach of contract. If staff wish to change a standard they can do so via normal channels, and this is vital, because standards need to change to keep up with technological changes.

If standards are properly defined and written they should aid staff, and the true test of a standard is whether or not it helps. Unless standards are provided in the first place there will be no guidance for staff, so the quality, consistency and continuity which are so important in data processing will just not exist.

15.9 SUMMARY AND REVISION NOTES

Standards are required at three levels:

1. Company.
2. National.
3. International.

They are needed for:

1. Consistency.
2. Quality.
3. Compatibility.
4. Continuity.

Hardware standards are important for linking machines together, particularly in communication networks. Special 'black boxes' are often built to overcome the problem of incompatible interfaces.

Software standards are needed at three levels:

1. Operating software.
2. Programming languages.
3. Job control languages.

System design standards are required to cover four areas:

1. Programming standards.
2. Flowcharts standards.
3. Data control standards.
4. Form design standards.

Documentation of all aspects of system design is essential and should include the following:

1. Design report.
2. Systems specification.
3. Program specification.
4. Test report.
5. Amendment records.

Documentation is vital for:

1. Continuity.
2. Changes.
3. Security.

Maintenance of the systems investment is essential, particularly as the investment could run into millions of pounds. Maintenance is required at three levels:

1. Software changes.
2. Operational changes.
3. Systems changes.

Operating standards cover all aspects of operations, but particularly:

1. Job control.
2. Program libraries.
3. File management.
4. Output distribution.

It is not enough to produce standards: they must be enforced. If they are not, performance will suffer.

QUESTIONS

1. 'The worst part of any project is completing all the documentation at the end.' Discuss.

2. Explain what is meant by the following:

   (a) plug-compatible interface;
   (b) international standard;
   (c) 'black box' interface.

3. Define a system specification and indicate the content you would expect to find in a well written system specification.

4. State the case for documentation standards. Imagine that you are attempting to persuade a data processing manager who does not believe in using documentation.

5. Prepare a brief outline of a procedure for dealing with amendments to systems, stating how you think priorities should be handled.

PART THREE
Systems Evaluation and Audit

16

System Evaluation

16.1 ASSESSING SYSTEM PERFORMANCE

Good systems meet five principal criteria:

1. Flexibility.
2. Reliability.
3. Economy.
4. Simplicity.
5. Helpfulness.

These five criteria should have been built into the original specification and will be a means by which the system achieves the overall objectives agreed and stated in the design report.

System performance is not measured in terms of the speed of the central processing unit or the number of programs run. The only true measure of a system is its achievement of the original objectives while at the same time meeting the five criteria mentioned above.

Flexibility

Flexibility is vital in a good system. All organizations are dynamic entities. Changes occur for a wide range of reasons, and a good system must be able to adapt to meet these changes. Information systems must be adaptable or they will fail. Flexibility in the way the system is designed is crucial. This is achieved by planning to allow for change in the original design, thus making changes easier to manage. Two ways to achieve this are:

1. Modularity. This means designing the system in small modules and programming accordingly. When change occurs it is easier to adapt a module than it is to adapt the whole system.
2. Data-free programs. If programs are written with dependent data elements, e.g. VAT rates, then when the rates change the program must be changed. This can be avoided by using a table of rates in the file and getting the program to 'look up' the table. The processing takes longer but changes are much easier to handle, since only the data in the table have to be changed.

Both these approaches have to be built into the original design.

Reliability

Reliability is crucial to performance and can be ensured only by thorough checking and testing, avoiding taking short cuts in both design and operations. Good standards help to make the system reliable, as do good validation and security routines (see Chapter 17).

Economy

Economy does not mean always choosing the cheapest method, but rather selecting the method which is cost-effective. There are many hidden costs in the design, development and operation of systems, the most important of which is the time of the people involved. Costs should be carefully monitored once the system is working and compared with the original planned costs.

Simplicity

Simplicity in design will find its way through the system. Anyone can design a complicated system but it takes real skill and experience to design simple systems which are easy to operate and control. Modularity helps, but perhaps the main key lies in the use of flowcharts which make complexity visually apparent. Systems are abstract: you cannot see a system. It is therefore not apparent that it is complex. If the system is put down on paper in the form of flowcharts, then suddenly the complexity is obvious.

Helpfulness

Helpfulness is, of course, the reason for the system. Unless the system helps in the planning, operation and control of the business, it is superfluous. At the initial design stage the system should have been justified, and it is important that the evaluation check that the reasons for which it was justified have been met.

16.2 PERFORMANCE ANALYSIS

The performance of the system must be analysed to see if the criteria have been achieved. This analysis is carried out in five stages:

1. Objective achievement.
2. System costs.
3. Security and control.
4. Benefits to the business.
5. Future needs.

Objective achievement means listing the original objectives and assessing each on the following scale:

1. Fully achieved.
2. Mainly achieved.
3. Partly achieved.
4. Nearing achievement.
5. Not achieved.

This should be completed by the users, not by the system designers. The systems team can then produce a report indicating the reasons for the performance and action that has been, or is being taken, to improve performance.

Computer costs come in three principal forms – hardware, software and operations. In spite of significant developments in both hardware and software and in automated operating procedures, computer costs are still rising. The amount of equipment and the number of people involved in computer systems development and operating seem to increase regularly, with commensurate increases in cost.

Many computer installations cost two or three times as much as they should for the work they do. Computer manufacturers and suppliers have had a field day. The analysis would establish the validity of current levels of cost and would seek to indicate areas for improvement based on the achievement of the objectives at lower cost.

There is, however, a danger that in seeking to cut computer costs the machine and systems on which the company depends are made more vulnerable. The places in which to seek improvements are inefficient data collection systems, inefficient operating procedures and badly organized and controlled systems development and maintenance. It is here that enormous waste can be found.

When looking for reduced costs it is important to determine the degree of dependency on the computer, and the implications and cost of failure should be clearly established. Security and control procedures should be checked and evaluated (see Chapter 17). The investment in the computer will be extensive and, because of systems dependency and its implications, the investment must be protected. It is usual to find that the investment in existing software far outweighs the investment in equipment.

Virtually every computer installation produces benefits for the organization. The benefits may be inadequate or may cost too much, but it is rare to find computer installations which do not provide any benefits. Organizations do, however, change, and these changes will mean that the benefits once produced may no longer be relevant. Surprisingly, computer systems do not adapt easily to rapid business changes unless they have been designed specifically to cope with change.

The benefits of the computer-based systems should, wherever possible, be measured in money terms. This can nearly always be done if the effort is made. Benefits such as 'improved efficiency' are only real if they are measured in real terms. Once benefits have been stated in real terms they can be compared with the costs of the computer service. Needless to say, the benefits should exceed the costs; where they do not, attention should be paid to finding ways to make sure they do.

The past can only be analysed; it cannot be changed. We can, however, make changes to the present in order to improve the future. This means that we have to know what future needs will be, so that changes and improvements can be made which are directed towards meeting them.

16.3 KEY SUCCESS CRITERIA

To make the performance analysis more straightforward it is important that during the initial design phase a schedule of key success criteria is produced. This must be closely related to the system and must use real values wherever possible. This schedule can then be used for the performance analysis mentioned earlier.

It does, of course, take some courage to produce such a schedule, and many systems people would prefer to work to vague promises rather than specific performance criteria (Figure 16.1).

KEY SUCCESS CRITERIA

System: On-line accounts Date: 19.7.81

	Item	Timescale	Value
1	To produce accurate accounts at less cost	10th work day	£25 000
2	To provide on-line credit control	Continuous	£295 000
3	To allow accounting exercises using modelling facilities	Continuous	£75 000
4	To reduce administration staff costs	–	£90 000
5	To simplify paperwork and reduce cost	–	£18 000
6	To provide the above within the budget	1 Jan. '82	£118 000

Project leader

Figure 16.1 *Key success criteria*

The statement would be supported by notes on each of the criteria detailing how the saving is to be produced. The management involved will have approved the design report containing the statement of key success criteria and so will have approved the criteria. This is an important point, because no system, no matter how well designed, will produce savings. It is the people who use the system who create the savings, and if they do not have a commitment, the system will not meet the performance criteria.

16.4 EVALUATING DESIGN TECHNIQUES

Within the system design function the operation of the system can be evaluated on a technical basis. This must not be confused with performance evaluation. It is perfectly possible for a system to meet the key success criteria and yet not be technically a good system. The technical elements to check are:

1. Design efficiency.
2. Operating efficiency.
3. Maintenance efficiency.

Design Efficiency

Design efficiency is concerned with the logic of the system and the way in which the various elements and modules relate to each other. Good standards and clear thinking are crucial features.

> In an on-line accounting system two prime elements, the 'on-line nominal' and the 'budgeting' systems, had to come together to prepare the accounts. The design could be called efficient if the system could be linked automatically without human intervention to make adjustments and corrections. The design concepts are shown in Figure 16.2.

Design efficiency would also depend on the way data flowed through the system with the minimum of manipulation and transfer. The file structures and ease of use, including access, would be a further factor. All these design points would impinge on operations.

Operating Efficiency

Operating efficiency is measured by three factors:

1. Simplicity of operation.
2. Timing.
3. Ease of recovery.

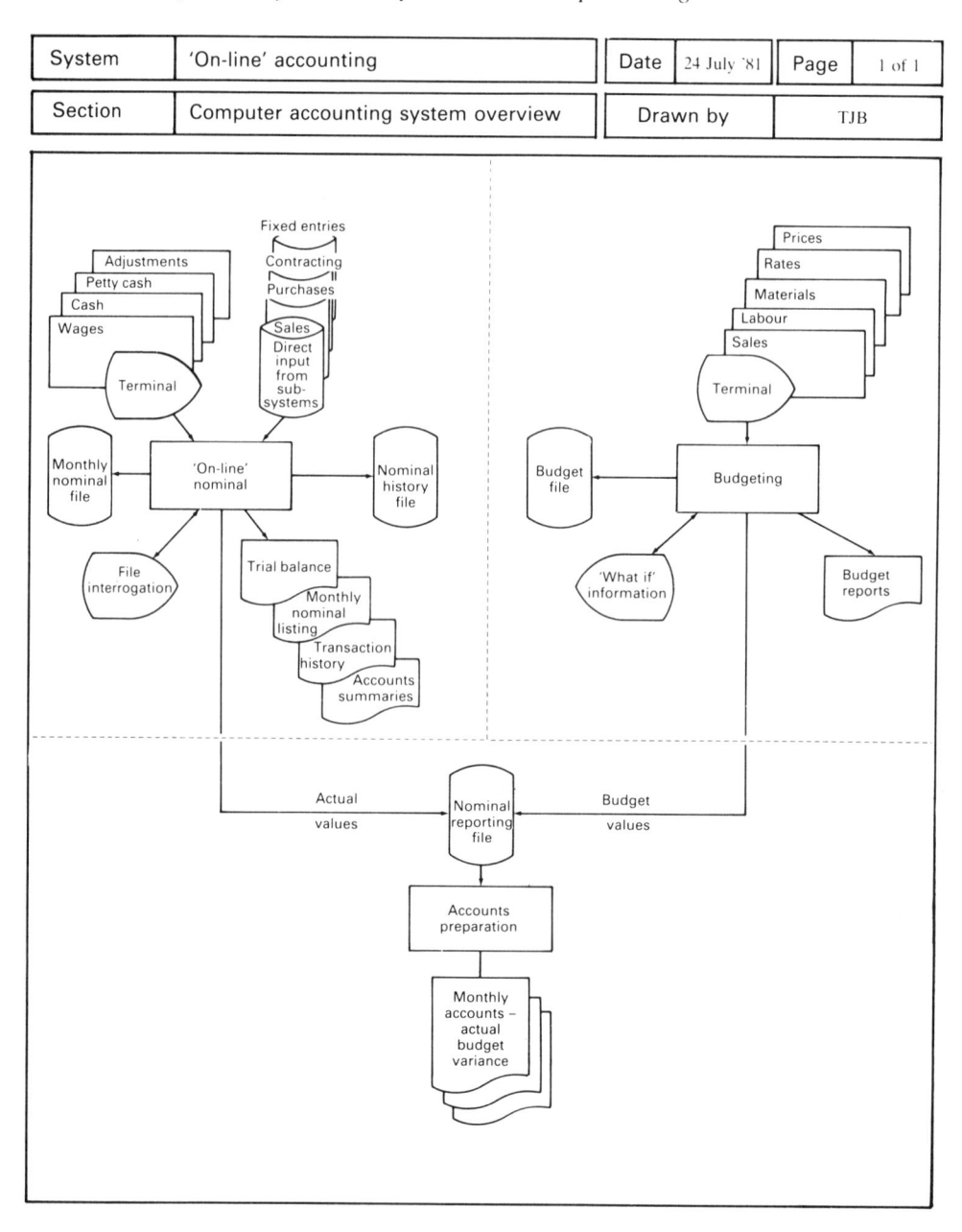

216 — *Management information systems and data processing*

System	'On-line' accounting	Date	24 July '81	Page	1 of 1
Section	Computer accounting system overview	Drawn by		TJB	

Figure 16.2 *Design concepts*

Simplicity of operation. If the system is easy to operate then it will tend to create fewer problems and fewer errors. If the logic of the design is sound, jobs will fall automatically into the correct sequence and file management will be made easier. Unfortunately, many system designers ignore or play down the operational needs in the design.

Timing. Timing both in running the system and in the response to users is perhaps the most apparent measure of system efficiency. If a user on a terminal receives a slow response it is very frustrating. In batch processing such frustration has to be borne by computer operators waiting for a job to finish. The longer a job runs, the more likely it is that errors will occur. Small modules which are quick and easy to run often beat the big, slow system.

Ease of recovery. If a system is easy to recover when a fault occurs it will operate more efficiently. Recognizing that faults can and will occur and designing methods of recovery are crucial features of good systems design. It may appear at the design stage to be unnecessary and wasteful of time and effort, but the benefits will be reaped later.

Maintenance Efficiency

Maintenance efficiency can be monitored by recording the amendments that have been requested and the time spent carrying out the amendments. Naturally some amendments cannot be foreseen, but many of them arise from inadequate design.

16.5 EVALUATING OPERATING TECHNIQUES

There are occasions where apparent systems inefficiency is in fact due to inadequate operating procedures. If good standards have been established then the efficiency can be measured against the standards. The key yardsticks are:

1. Fault analysis.
2. Re-run time.
3. Resource usage.

Fault Analysis

No matter how large or small, or how busy the computer department is, every single fault should be recorded and analysed, with details of:

1. Type of fault.
2. Implications.
3. Time lost.
4. Frequency of fault.

This analysis will cover all types of faults, hardware and software, and such a record is important in diagnosing and curing recurrent problems.

Re-run Time

Re-run time should also be monitored, showing:

1. Reason.
2. Time lost.
3. Job.
4. Implications.
5. Action.

The re-run records are a crucial factor in measuring and improving operations efficiency. With modern computers the machine can be programmed to maintain these records and will often be able to assist in diagnosing the cause.

Resource Usage

Resource usage is a critical measure of efficiency. The balancing of computer resources, whether done manually or automatically, should be monitored and reported. Here again the computer is invaluable in recording the use of every peripheral and in identifying systems which use resources inefficiently. Misuse can also arise from inefficient operating procedures and poor scheduling.

16.6 COMPUTER EFFICIENCY AUDIT

A computer efficiency audit is an intensive and comprehensive examination of the computer systems and operations which seeks to answer a number of questions:

1. Is the computer being used in the right way?
2. For the right reasons?
3. Is it cost effective?
4. Is the computer system secure?
5. Are the controls adequate and effective?
6. Is the development strategy in concert with the organization's strategy?
7. Does the organization have the computer knowledge and skills it needs?

Few, if any, large organizations could administer and control their activities without the use of computers. Over the past 20 years the importance of the computer to the large organization has increased gradually and often unnoticed until the present time, when most large organizations are computer dependent. Remove the computer and the organization would collapse.

Once the organization embarks on a policy of using computers it sets off along a one-way road which permits very little opportunity to return. The organization can change the direction of its computer policy, but rarely, if ever, can it reduce its commitment to high-technology equipment and highly skilled people.

This dependence on computer-based systems brings with it problems of security, control and cost. The computer is a particularly vulnerable device. There are numerous ways in which its effectiveness can be impaired, from outright physical attack to simple human error. The importance of such failure can be catastrophic. Few, if any, computer proposals state the implications and cost of failure, but they should, and efforts should be made to protect the computer.

The vast majority of installations are so vulnerable to external and internal interference that in the near future computer crime is going to increase rapidly. This will include not only fraud, but also extortion. What would a company be prepared to pay in protection money to avoid an attack? In some cases the cost of such an attack could run into millions of pounds.

This vulnerability must be protected by security measures, both physical and systems-based controls. The physical protection includes access to the machine, not only to the computer centre but to local terminals. Physical protection could mean using magnetic access cards, shatterproof windows and protection from fire and theft.

Systems-based controls are essential and will be used to make access to the systems difficult by using special code numbers, so that even if someone gains access to a terminal, they cannot use it without having the codes. Within the systems there must be the control to recognize and prevent errors. As vulnerability increases so must protection, and this of course costs money.

The control of computers and their development in the organization are largely in the hands of a specialist group. It frustrates senior management to discover that ever more money must be pumped into the computer facilities. Computer expenditure proposals often show little quantifiable benefit and nearly always include phrases such as 'we don't really have much choice'.

Add to these dangers the danger of cost escalation and we begin to wonder why we bothered with computers in the first place. The reason is that properly designed and controlled computer systems are powerful tools for administration, planning and control; however, many fail to live up to their promises.

It is unfortunate, but true, that most computer installations exceed their original cost budgets or fail to produce the results promised. It is often necessary to obtain more equipment or more staff to get the system working. This may be due to the over-optimism of the company's own computer people or underselling on the part of computer suppliers.

The only way to make sure that the computer installation does what is expected is to concentrate on good design and tight control. Ensuring that this takes place and that the computer is serving the needs of the business is a difficult task, especially as the company's own computer people have a vested interest and their colleagues in other disciplines do not have sufficient computer knowledge to challenge them.

New developments in smaller, easier-to-use computers are rapidly changing the world of the computer manager, but many of them are resisting these developments, or trying to stop other managers getting involved.

The time has now been reached when every organization should review its use of computers and the direction it should take in the future.

Every organization using computers needs a computer development strategy. Such a strategy should relate the organization's needs to its use of computers. However, few, if any, large organizations are in a position to start from the beginning; they already have large investments in computer hardware and software.

The importance of the computer to most large organizations cannot be overstated. It is vital, therefore, that the policy and strategy are right for the business. With the promise of tremendous advances in computer technology and the prospect of the electronic office, every organization must ensure that it makes the right decision.

Computer efficiency audit provides a basis from which future developments stem. Unless the present systems provide the right foundation there is little prospect of future growth.

16.7 SUMMARY AND REVISION NOTES

Systems performance is measured in a general sense by evaluating five criteria:

1. Flexibility.
2. Reliability.
3. Economy.
4. Simplicity.
5. Helpfulness.

(Students may find it useful to use the mnemonic FRESH to remember these criteria: good systems are FRESH systems.)

Performance analysis involves examining five factors:

1. Objective achievement.
2. System costs.
3. Security and control.
4. Benefits to the business.
5. Future needs.

Key success criteria should be defined in the original design report and should form the basis of systems evaluation.

Design techniques should be assessed by looking at:

1. Design efficiency.
2. Operating efficiency.
3. Maintenance efficiency.

Operating techniques are evaluated by examining:

1. Faults.
2. Re-run times.
3. Resource usage.

Computer operations should be subject to an efficiency audit which will seek to answer the following questions:

1. Is the computer being used in the right way?
2. For the right reasons?
3. Is it cost effective?
4. Is the computer system secure?
5. Are controls adequate and effective?
6. Is the development strategy in concert with the organization's strategy?
7. Does the organization have the computer knowledge and skills it requires?

QUESTIONS

1. Explain what you think is meant by the phrase 'an efficient system'. Describe the key attributes of an efficient system.

2. 'The system works well, but no longer achieves the objectives for which it was designed.' State how this could happen and the action you would take to rectify the situation.

3. Explain the importance of the following:

    (a) record of faults;
    (b) analysis of amendment requests;
    (c) modularity;
    (d) key success criteria.

4. 'Data-free programs lead to efficient and easy systems maintenance.' Discuss.

5. State what is meant by each of the following and indicate the implications for overall systems efficiency:

    (a) design efficiency;
    (b) ease of recovery;
    (c) resource usage.

17

Systems Audit

17.1 INFORMATION: A VITAL RESOURCE

Information and its value was defined earlier (Chapter 2). It was stated that the value depended on the effective use of information. This in turn depends on management's confidence in the information they receive. Their confidence is based on the reliability and accuracy of the information.

Throughout this book emphasis has been placed on designing and building systems which provide reliable, accurate information, where and when it is needed. However, no system, however good, can be left for too long before it is checked to see that it is performing efficiently. There are many ways in which a system can be damaged, both deliberately and accidentally. It is essential, therefore, that all systems are regularly audited.

In many organizations the information held within the system is of vital operational and strategic importance to the organization. The possibility of such information falling into the wrong hands, or the damage that might be caused if the information were lost, are not often thought about. The cost of either event occurring could be extremely high, and organizations really have no alternative but to protect their information resources.

17.2 SYSTEMS DEPENDENCY AND VULNERABILITY

There are many areas in which the thought of existing without the computer is frightening: we would simply lose control. The traffic in New York could not be controlled without the computer; hospitals could not function effectively; neither could the railways or the airlines; the banking system in the western world would collapse, as would many of the large companies, whose production lines and processes would be thrown into chaos. The computer and its servants are assuming a place in society which their inventors never imagined. The dangers of dependency are immense, especially dependency on machines which relatively few people understand. Even computer programmers and operators do not know how the electronics within the machine function.

Of course, programmers do not need this knowledge to write programs, but it indicates the string of dependencies that the many groups of people involved in computing have on each other. This dependency does, of course, lead to vulnerability of computer systems, to fraud, error, misuse and damage.

In recent discussions at the American National Computer Conference in New York the following areas were highlighted for attention.

1. Control and protection of input and output from error, theft and modification.
2. Access to computer files.
3. Unauthorized use of programs.
4. Unauthorized changes to programs.
5. Physical protection of magnetic files, tape and disc.
6. Adequate controls.
7. Auditability.

These are all concerned with the protection of the systems themselves, but there is also a need to protect computer resources from physical damage. The best auditing and control procedures possible will be of little use if the computer centre is burned down.

17.3 PHYSICAL PROTECTION AND SECURITY

The protection and security of computer systems can be examined at two levels:

1. Physical.
2. Systems (section 17.4).

Physical security is concerned with:

1. Access to facilities.
2. Fire.
3. Theft.
4. Power interruptions.
5. Sabotage.
6. Environmental.

Access to Facilities

Access to premises is the starting point, because if access is difficult or impossible, except for authorized personnel, the possibility of theft or damage is reduced. There are various ways in which access can be controlled, including magnetic card locks, reception areas, security guards, etc.

Fire

The effects of fire can be guarded against with fireproof premises, cupboards and security copies of files stored off the premises. Special fire detection and control systems can be installed which can put the fire out by using a chemical gas to suffocate the flames. Sprinkler devices can also be used, but water does as much damage as, if not more damage than, fire.

Theft

Theft is a real hazard, both direct theft of magnetic tapes or discs, and indirect theft via terminals. The first is controlled by access security, the second by systems security. There have been a number of cases of staff stealing files and offering to sell them back.

Power Interruption

Power interruptions caused by power cuts, strikes or simple voltage fluctuations can be protected against by installing the appropriate equipment. It is important to remember that RAM files are volatile and will be affected by power interruptions.

Sabotage

Sabotage, though less likely, is nevertheless a threat. Computer centres have been sabotaged by terrorists, staff taking industrial action or disgruntled employees.

Environmental Protection

Environmental protection is needed to cope with the potential damage of heat, cold, humidity, dust and magnetism. Again, if the appropriate equipment is installed and standards are established, such as no smoking and wearing overalls, these problems can be overcome.

Contingency Plans

Even though these threats can be guarded against to some extent, 100 per cent security is never possible and so it is essential that every organization has contingency plans in the event of a serious disruption taking place. Contingency plans should cover:

1. Copies of files and software.
2. Access to data-processing resources.
3. Contingency procedures.

Copies of files should be made regularly, ideally daily, and these should be held with copies of software off the premises, preferably in secure premises. Most banks offer such a service.

Of course, copy files are of limited value if there are no machines to put them on. It is usual to have an arrangement with another company to borrow their machine and vice versa. These are known as reciprocal arrangements. Some organizations are so dependent on computer systems for order taking or control that they have their own stand-by facilities at another site. With the growth of distributed systems, protection is increased, because if one site is taken out another site can be used. However important these aspects of security are, the main threats come from the breaching of systems controls.

17.4 SYSTEM CONTROLS AND SECURITY

Systems security can be separated into:

1. Data security.
2. File security.
3. Program security.
4. System design controls.

Data Security

Data are vulnerable at three points in the system:

1. Input.
2. Processing.
3. Output.

Input. When data are input full records must be kept which show clearly where the data originated, i.e. the prime documents, the person inputting the data, and where the data are going within the system. For batch systems, batch controls should be kept: the date, reference number and content are vital items to be recorded. For interactive systems where data are input direct to the computer, often with no prime document, a detailed transaction log must be produced by the computer.

Processing. During processing, as data are moved around the computer, it is essential that the controls affected by the move are checked before and after the move. This calls for additional programming but will ensure the integrity of the data (see section 17.5).

Output. Output controls are associated with file security, but in addition it is important to ensure that the computer does not provide data to unauthorized users, either on paper or on screen. It is important, therefore, that every item of data output should be recorded, showing:

1. What has been output.
2. To whom it was given.
3. When.

Even if some unauthorized person gains access, this control procedure should identify the fault.

File Security

Data are held in the computer as some form of electronic signal in the main processor, or as a sensitized spot on some magnetic medium external to the computer. There is always a possibility that the data could be wiped off the file, over-written, mixed up with other data or simply lost.

There are a variety of engineering devices within the computer to provide a degree of protection, but human error cannot be foreseen by the computer. It is essential, therefore, that data files are removed at regular intervals and held in a relatively secure form, normally magnetic tape.

At least two copies of these files should be kept – one on the premises and one elsewhere, preferably in a bank. The normal procedure is known as 'grandfather, father, son', which means holding a copy of each file as follows:

1. The last updated file position – son.
2. The transactions to reach 1.
3. The previous updated file position – father.
4. The transactions to reach 3.
5. The previous updated file to 3 – grandfather.

If this procedure is followed (usually standard practice) it is possible to recreate the file position that might be lost or damaged by re-running the previous file and transactions. Where batch processing is used, the files should be copied at the end of each run. In transaction processing regular copies have to be taken on a time basis, i.e. hourly, daily, weekly, etc. With copies of the files available, containing the appropriate controls, it is possible to recover from situations which would be a disaster in most manual systems. However, simply keeping copies is not the answer unless the data held on the copies can be checked with the controls. It has been known for a file to be regenerated from a partially read security file, thus creating an incomplete file. When files are being changed (file maintenance) it is important to control the implications of the changes. Basically four types of action take place:

1. New/insert record.
2. Amendment to existing details.
3. Display current details.
4. Delete record.

When a validation program links with a file maintenance system, part of the controls should be a count of the different types of transaction that are going to affect the master file.

In the main update itself the program must produce the following controls:

1. Number of records b/fwd.
2. Breakdown of transactions input.
3. Rejections.
4. Total update records.
5. Number of records c/fwd.

In some files, where information other than static information is held, it may be necessary to expand the controls under each of the categories to show either absolute values or hash values or, in the case of a file where an amendment does not affect the file structure, the date of the last update.

Program Security

Program security is important. We have already seen that there are three program libraries held on the computer – a test library, a temporary library and a load library. Access to and use of these libraries must be carefully controlled.

The first step is to restrict access to a very limited number of people. The next step is for the computer to record and produce a control report for every access to the program libraries, showing:

1. Who accessed the library.
2. Which programs they extracted.
3. When.

This report can then be reviewed and, if necessary, questions asked.

In addition to controls on library access it is crucial to protect programs from unauthorized use. This is difficult if people with authority wish to misuse the programs for their own purposes. One of the controls that can be used is to produce a control system which links to the computer accounts system and shows, for every program:

1. When it was last used.
2. The job.
3. The work the program does.

228 — Management information systems and data processing

This is particularly important for transaction processing systems and can lead to rather interesting reports showing programs being used in the middle of the night for odd purposes.

It must also be possible to run a program through an audit system to establish what the program does, particularly in relation to file update or data input and output.

System Design Controls

System design controls should be built into the system. At any point within a system it should be apparent if a malfunction has occurred. To this end it is important that within any system there are control points. Control should appear at the beginning and end of each system and also at any point in the system where data are extended or change their nature, e.g. merges, validation, extensions, etc.

A control flowchart should be produced showing where each control point is and its role in the system (Figure 17.1). It should go without saying that all these controls are fully documented so that they can be audited at some future date.

17.5 OPERATIONAL CONTROLS

In Chapter 13 the problems concerned with effective operating control were fully discussed. It is important to reiterate here the need for observance of these controls. Standards must be produced and followed if operations activities are to be secure.

Perhaps one of the most important considerations is the proper separation of duties. This is done to avoid one person being able to tamper with the program, then run the program and change the controls. The rules are:

1. Programmers must not be allowed to operate.
2. Neither operators nor programmers are allowed to authorize controls.
3. People responsible for input must not be involved in output control.
4. Programmers must not have access to live files.
5. Operators must not have access to programs, except for loading.
6. File libraries, whether on-line or on tape, must not be accessible by programmers.

The objective of separating duties in this way is to make misuse difficult without collusion of several people. This reduces risk considerably; it does not, however, eliminate it.

17.6 AUDITABILITY

Auditability refers to the way the system is designed so that it can be audited. This means being aware of the auditors' requirements at the design stage, and incorpora-

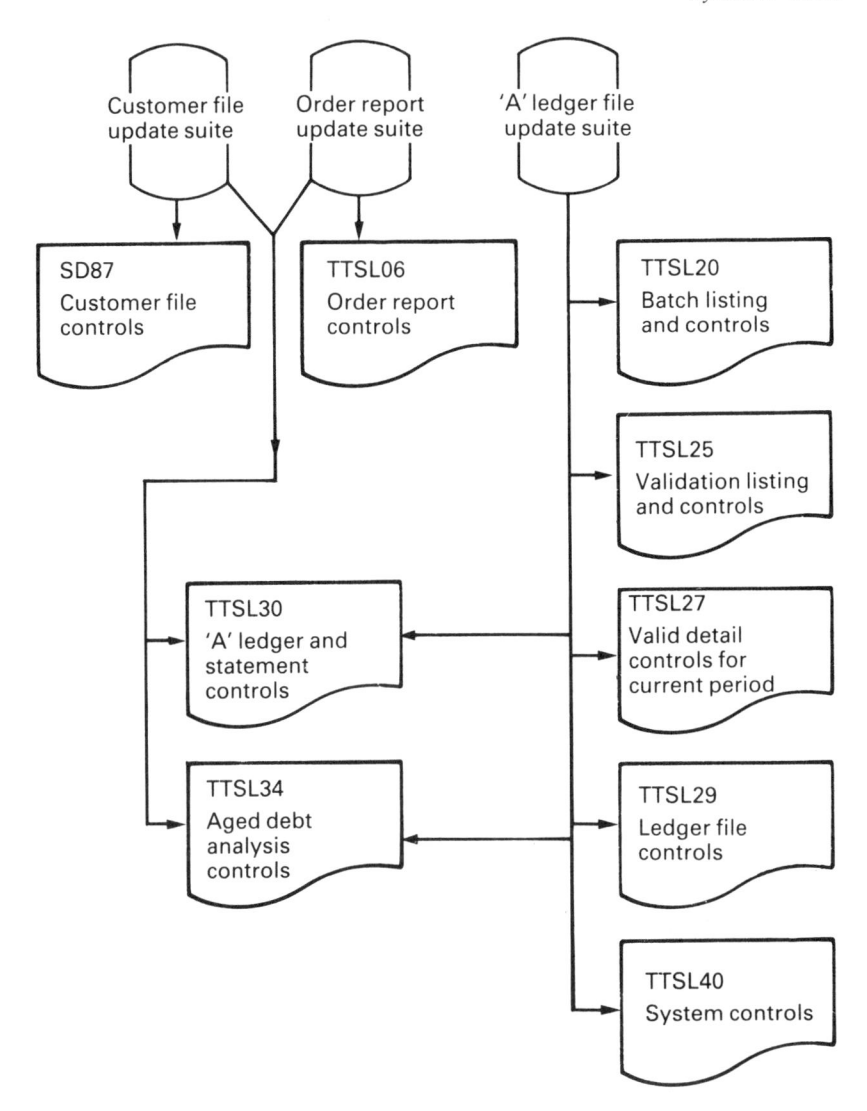

Figure 17.1 *Control flowchart*

ting the appropriate codes, validation checks, records and controls necessary to permit an audit.

One way of ensuring that the system is auditable is to involve the auditors in the initial design phase. They must at least approve the design report, and then comment and make suggestions when the system specification is produced.

Auditing is a continuous task and all system changes must be carefully examined to ensure that they do not prevent an audit from taking place.

In one company this occurred when a system amendment was carried out that did in effect contravene an audit requirement. The system rejected transactions which were outside a certain price range. It was necessary for the rejection to be checked by a supervisor and for a document to be signed authorizing the price. On second input, with the supervisor's code, the computer accepted the price. The amendment stopped the rejection and replaced it with a report stating that prices had been accepted outside the range. The auditors objected, saying that this was not acceptable to them as there was no way to audit who had authorized the special price.

In another case the auditors objected to a procedure for using a suspense account. The situation was as follows.

On input a transaction with an incorrect analysis code, but with all other codes correct, was accepted and used in the accounting system, but placed in an analysis suspense. The suspense account was printed out and all items re-coded and transferred from suspense to the correct accounts. The auditors believed that this offered an opportunity for misuse of the suspense account. The problem was overcome by including a personal reference of the input clerk for entering costs to the suspense and a personal reference of the person transferring the entries out.

It is the ability to recognize who has done what and where transactions originated, and their destination, which consitutes an auditable system. This, however, only audits data, and it is also important to audit what the system does, i.e. the programming steps. This means that the auditor has to be able to check what every program does and how it can affect files. The auditor must also be able to print files to check the correct content.

When carrying out the audit the auditor will not check every transaction but will want to take a sample which is statistically large enough to give a high level of confidence in the system's performance. He or she will then check the sample thoroughly to ensure that all is well.

In large, computer-based systems, particularly where data base management systems are in use, the auditor will want to use auditing programs to do the work. He or she may want to input an audit sample and follow it through the complete system, checking every step of the processing. This type of auditing is called integrated testing and is being developed by large auditing companies.

When a system is designed originally it is a good idea to check with the auditor how he or she intends to design the audit system so that the required facilities can be built in. This is not only good sense, but can save in audit fees. The primary requirement will undoubtedly be a clear audit path through the system.

17.7 AUDIT PATH

An audit path or trail is a way in which the auditor can check transactions by leaving control signals as the data proceed through the system, rather like leaving marks on trees when going through a dense forest.

The ability to select a transaction at random at any point in the system and trace it to either its entry or exit, or both, is fundamental to effective auditing. This requires considerable understanding of the way in which computer-based systems work and the variety of interpretations that can be placed by programmers on seemingly simple and direct instructions. The responsibility of ensuring that the systems are auditable rests with the designer, who should insist on the design and programming standards that are required. Those involved in the programming and operation of computer systems should be allowed no discretion in interpretation of such auditing standards. However, such standards should be prepared with a view to the programming and operational constraints and the general level of machine efficiency.

The audit system must provide a means for auditing the following aspects:

1. Systems:
   (a) user needs;
   (b) design methods;
   (c) project control;
   (d) testing procedures;
   (e) maintenance procedures.
2. Processing:
   (a) organization of transactions;
   (b) data entry;
   (c) data communications;
   (d) processing procedures;
   (e) storage and retrieval of data.
3. Computer operations:
   (a) input/output controls;
   (b) library controls;
   (c) division of duties;
   (d) physical searching procedures;
   (e) stand-by and back-up.

Meeting these auditing and security requirements places a burden on the system designer, but it is a burden he or she must accept if the systems are going to serve the organization.

17.8 SUMMARY AND REVISION NOTES

Information is a vital resource, and time and money must be spent to protect it from misuse, damage or loss.

As organizations become dependent on systems, so they become vulnerable to any change in those systems. The main threats are:

1. Theft and modification of input and output.
2. Access to computer files.

3. Unauthorized use of programs.
4. Unauthorized changes to programs.
5. Physical damage to or theft of files and equipment.

Protection and security are produced at two levels:

1. Physical.
2. Systems.

Physical security covers fire, theft, power interruptions, sabotage and environmental damage. Systems protection deals with:

1. Data security.
2. File security.
3. Program security.
4. System design controls.

Operational controls cover the way the data are managed through the system, with the object of preventing:

1. Unauthorized access.
2. Misuse or corruption of data.
3. Theft.

Auditability depends on good initial design, which should cater for the needs of the auditor to make thorough checks.

The audit path provides the auditor with a means of following the transaction through the system and checking its movements in any direction.

QUESTIONS

1. Your organization is about to install a computer system but your auditors have written to you expressing their concern over the proposal, as they fear that the audit trail may be lost. Draft a reply to your auditors responding to their concern and, in addition, pointing out ways in which the computer can assist the audit process. (ICMA)

2. Due to a combination of an inexperienced operator and an electrical fault, the main master file of 150 000 policy holders' records was destroyed. Describe what precautions should have been taken so that the above situation could be retrieved in the case of:

   (a) a tape-based installation;
   (b) a disc-based installation.
   (ICMA)

3. State how you would ensure that a system remains auditable after its initial implementation and show how changes would be handled.

4. A file containing highly confidential information is held on magnetic tape. Discuss in detail the procedures which should be adopted to:

   (a) ensure the confidentiality of the data on file;
   (b) protect the data from loss or damage.
   (ICMA)

5. Define the following and state the implications for the system:

   (a) integrated audit facility;
   (b) unauthorized access;
   (c) environmental damage;
   (d) power interruption.

Case Study

Reward Chemicals Ltd

Reward Chemicals Ltd is a subsidiary of Reward International. The company was started in 1933 by John Willow, who was a chemist working as a research assistant in a laboratory. He had produced a chemical compound which he discovered could kill the weeds on his lawn (actually his landlord's lawn) without killing the grass. In fact it seemed to feed the grass and make it greener. He called his wonder chemical *Grassguard*. The success of the company has been based on this original product, which is still one of the best-selling lines.

In 1969, after several narrow escapes from bankruptcy, John Willow sold the company to Reward International and retired. The new owners re-organized the company and pumped a sizeable sum of money into research. The result is that today Reward Chemicals Ltd is a medium-sized company employing 600 people at the Selby factory, producing a range of products which have become household names, including: Grassguard, Flyswot, Rootgrow, Floranosh and Greenery.

In recent months the returns to RI company headquarters (referred to as RICH) have shown a rather unhealthy trend, with costs rising rapidly, problems with quality and rather high material variances.

The directors of Reward Chemicals Ltd have been informed that RICH are sending a team to investigate the problems and recommend action.

The managing director of Reward Chemicals has blamed the costing system for not providing accurate information quickly enough. In turn the factory accountant has blamed the production manager for not making sure the information is collected as and when it should be. In fact everyone seems to be blaming everyone else.

The managing director of Reward Chemicals Ltd, Edward Oak, has been asked to help the team and to provide the following information:

1. Organization structure and functional responsibilities.
2. Product information and current prices.
3. Product cost information.
4. Factory accounts.

ORGANIZATION STRUCTURE

Figure C.1 indicates the way the company is organized.

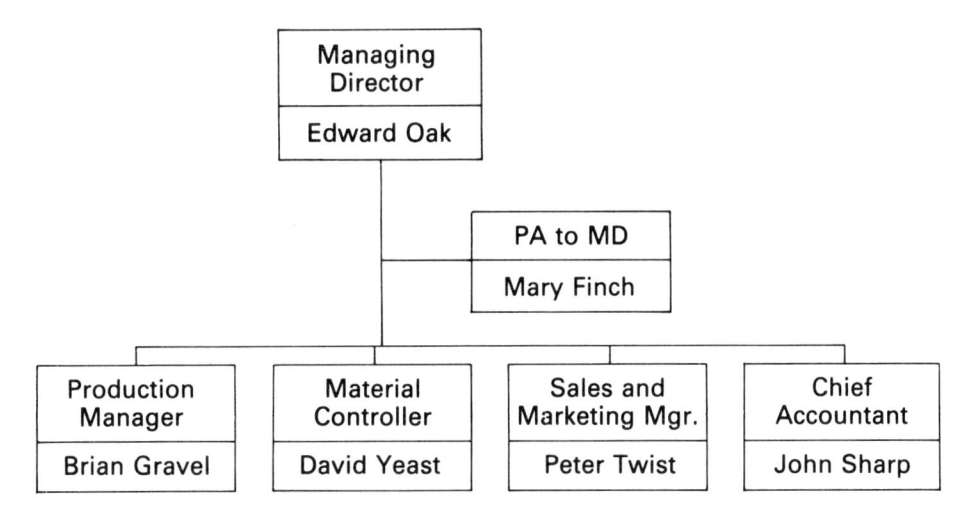

Figure C.1 *Organization structure*

Managing Director

Edward Oak is 58, a qualified chemist who was appointed from a competitor when Reward International bought the company in 1969. He is a good manager and involves his team of managers in all aspects of the management of the company. He has been criticized by RICH for his easy-going approach, but so far his results have always been good and so he has been left alone to go his own way.

Production

Dr Brian Gravel is a highly qualified chemist who runs the production via a team of production supervisors. Each production supervisor manages one of the eight production lines normally in operation. He also controls the research laboratory, which is his consuming passion. He has been trying for 15 years to develop a spray that will be an insecticide, a fungicide and a fertilizer all in one, for use on roses, another of his consuming passions. The production organization is shown in Figure C.2.

The primary lines produce the base chemicals for the product range and can be separated into:

1. Herbicides (weed killers).
2. Insecticides.
3. Fertilizers.

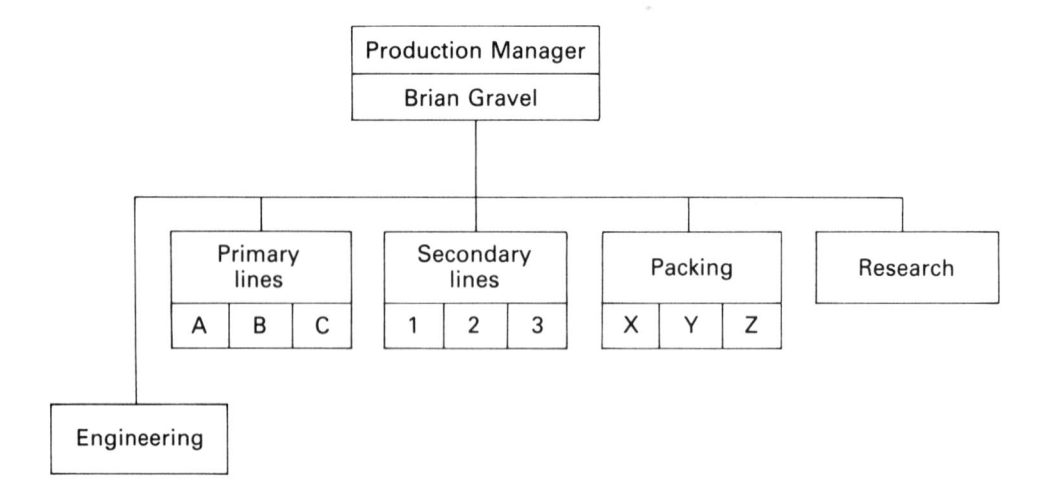

```
                    ┌─────────────────────┐
                    │ Production Manager  │
                    │    Brian Gravel     │
                    └─────────────────────┘
                              │
      ┌────────────┬──────────┴──────────┬────────────┐
      │            │                     │            │
┌───────────┐ ┌───────────┐      ┌───────────┐ ┌───────────┐
│ Primary   │ │ Secondary │      │ Packing   │ │ Research  │
│ lines     │ │ lines     │      │           │ │           │
├───┬───┬───┤ ├───┬───┬───┤      ├───┬───┬───┤ └───────────┘
│ A │ B │ C │ │ 1 │ 2 │ 3 │      │ X │ Y │ Z │
└───┴───┴───┘ └───┴───┴───┘      └───┴───┴───┘
      │
┌─────────────┐
│ Engineering │
└─────────────┘
```

Figure C.2 *Production organization*

The secondary lines are used for mixing primary products with additional ingredients and processing them prior to final packing. The packing lines are separated into three main lines:

1. Dry packing.
2. Aerosol.
3. Bottles.

There is some degree of automation, but compared with some companies it is labour intensive.

Material Controller

The material control function deals with the buying of all materials and packing, quality control and dispatching. David Yeast, a young, enthusiastic chemist (working part-time for a PhD) uses a small desktop computer to help with planning, buying and stock control. He has recently produced a planning procedure, indicated in Figure C.3.

This is the system which he operates on his new computer. The system is not fully operational, but he claims that when it is he will be able to control material flows precisely.

Sales and Marketing Manager

Peter Twist is a typical salesman – extrovert, somewhat flamboyant, with an optimistic streak which usually means that his sales forecasts have to be reduced. He is, however, a firm believer in giving his customers the very best product at a competitive price. If a customer complains, he takes it as a personal insult.

He controls sales and marketing via a team of regional salesmen under a sales manager, and an advertising and promotion executive. The bulk of sales are to garden centres, although 20 per cent of total turnover is taken by a large chain store.

Peter provides a monthly sales forecast for David Yeast. He bases this on his monthly reporting system from his regional sales team.

Sales are administered via the sales order processing department, who operate a manual system based on a five-part internal order, which is subsequently used for delivery and invoicing. The system works smoothly enough, although there are times when shortages in certain products cause delivery delays.

Chief Accountant

The Chief Accountant, John Sharp, runs the administration and accounting departments. His job can be subdivided into three main sections:

1. Cash management.
2. Administration.
3. Information.

The cash management involves making sure that the overdraft is maintained at the level agreed with RICH. If he exceeds the overdraft the company is charged an additional 2 per cent interest penalty by RICH. If he is below his overdraft for more than two months running, then it is automatically reduced.

Administration is concerned primarily with purchase accounting, sales accounting and payroll, together with the management of the office services, the typing pool, the

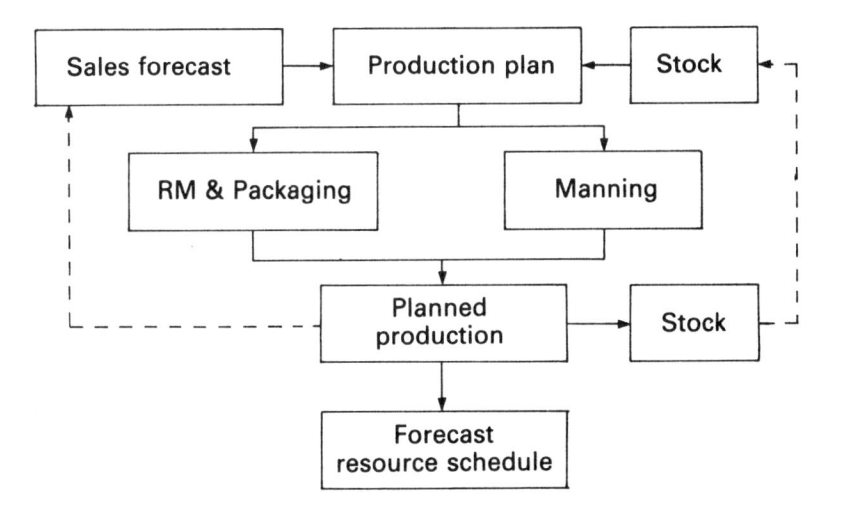

Figure C.3 *Planning procedure*

canteen and security. (The PA to the MD looks after personnel, including health and safety.)

Information is produced monthly for the management meeting and for special requests as and when they are made. The monthly report (see the last section of this case study) contains:

1. Profit statement.
2. Product analysis.
3. Production costs and overheads.
4. Stock summary.

The report is produced for the management meeting which takes place on the third Friday in the following month.

PRODUCT INFORMATION

The product range is separated into the three categories of primary products:

1. Herbicides ⎫
2. Insecticides ⎬ Killers
3. Fertilizers: Feeders

The products within each group and the form and size are given in Table C.1.

Product Descriptions

Grassguard and Greenery are exactly the same material except that Grassguard is spraydried to produce it in the powdered form.

Killall is a much more potent weedkiller used when clearing land. It is long-lasting and the ground cannot be planted for six months. Excellent for keeping gravel drives weed free. The powder is mixed with water and the liquid is diluted.

Flyswot is a general insecticide for use indoors or outdoors. It is a pleasantly perfumed spray.

Waspkil is a special derivative of Flyswot for wasps and other stinging insects.

Both Flyswot and Waspkil can discolour and damage fabrics.

Pestoff is a general insecticide for use on flowers, particularly roses. It is as near as Brian Gravel has got in his search for his all-in-one spray.

Rootgrow is a general fertilizer for root vegetables like potatoes, parsnips, carrots, etc.

Floranosh is a general fertilizer for the flowerbed and for indoor plants.

Popup is a new product which has been developed by Reward Chemicals. It is another spin-off from Brian Gravel's search and has been very well received in its small initial launch. Larger sizes are being considered. It really lives up to its name and plants fed with Popup have really outgrown the other plants, even those fed with Floranosh.

Table C.1 Product range

	Form	Size	Pack	Selling Price
Herbicides				
Grassguard	Powder	1 kg	Bag	310p
	Powder	5 kg	Bag	1280p
	Powder	10 kg	Bag	2150p
Greenery	Liquid	750 ml	Bottle	300p
	Liquid	2.5 l	Carton	675p
	Liquid	5 l	Carton	1150p
	Liquid	10 l	Drum	2000p
Killall	Liquid	250 ml	Bottle	110p
	Liquid	500 ml	Bottle	200p
	Liquid	1 l	Bottle	375p
	Liquid	2.5 l	Container	860p
	Powder	5 kg	Bag	1700p
Insecticides				
Flyswot	Spray	100 g	Aerosol can	90p
	Spray	200 g	Aerosol can	175p
Waspkil	Spray	100 g	Aerosol can	95p
	Spray	200 g	Aerosol can	185p
Pestoff	Spray	100 g	Aerosol can	85p
	Spray	200 g	Aerosol can	165p
	Liquid	250 ml	Bottle	180p
	Liquid	500 ml	Bottle	340p
Fertilizers				
Rootgrow	Powder	1 kg	Bag	975p
	Powder	5 kg	Bag	4800p
	Powder	10 kg	Bag	9075p
	Powder	25 kg	Sack	16750p
	Powder	50 kg	Sack	42150p
Floranosh	Liquid	100 ml	Bottle	105p
	Liquid	200 ml	Bottle	200p
	Liquid	1 l	Bottle	880p
	Liquid	2.5 l	Plastic container	2190p
	Powder	10 kg	Bag	8750p
Popup	Spray	100 g	Aerosol can	185p
	Spray	200 g	Aerosol can	350p

PRODUCT COST INFORMATION

The products are produced from a range of raw materials and intermediates, the current prices of which are given below (per kilo).

Raw Materials

XN12	27p
PN21	33p
Pitnec	62p
N28	119p
X87	410p
X128	620p
Sodalic	227p
DNP1	1122p
DNX	438p
DZ	220p
X187	110p

Additives

Polylip	100p
Oxylink	35p
Nyloput	100p
Xnoth	95p
Alsec	300p
Scent p2	400p
Scent p6	300p
Fastec	1500p
Gropic	400p

Packaging

All packages are purchased preprinted from Reward Packages, a subsidiary company of Reward International.

Product recipes are all per 10 litres of finished product, which is equivalent to 10 kg dry.

All products are manufactured wet up to the point at which they are spray-dried. The product structure is indicated in Figure C.4. Recipes are given in Table C.3.

Table C.2 *Packaging*

	Size	Price
Bags	1 kg	5p
	5 kg	18p
	10 kg	25p
Sacks	25 kg	35p
	50 kg	45p
Bottles	100 ml	10p
	200 ml	12p
	250 ml	13p
	500 ml	18p
	750 ml	22p
	1 l	25p
Cartons	2½ l	20p
	5 l	35p
Drum	10 l	95p
Aerosol cans	100 g	18p
	200 g	22p

MONTHLY REPORT

The monthly report contains the following information:

1. Profit statement (Figure C.5).
2. Production and overhead costs (Figure C.6).
3. Product analysis (Figure C.7).
4. Stock summary (Figure C.8).

The profit statement is produced from the summary of product sheets and the production and overhead cost sheet. The information on sales is provided by the sales and marketing department, who provide the information on quantities sold.

Production and overhead costs are extracted from the purchase accounting and payroll systems.

The stock summary is provided by the material controller and valued by the accountants.

The cashflow statement is produced by the chief accountant.

Table C.3 Recipes

		Kilos	Cost (£)	Standard cost per kilo (£)
Intermediates				
Herbico	XN12	2	0.54	
	PN21	3	0.99	0.396
	Pitnec	2	1.24	
			2.77	
Herb. X	Herbico	4	1.58	
	N28	3	3.57	1.156
	X87	1	4.10	
			9.25	
Insecto	X187	3	3.30	3.14
	X128	2	12.40	
			15.70	
Fertic	Sodalic	5	11.35	5.626
	DNP1	3	33.66	
			45.01	
Fertic Z	Fertic	6	33.76	
	DNX	2	8.76	
	DZ	2	4.40	4.692
			46.92	
Finished				
Greenery	Herbico	7	2.77	
	Oxylink	2	0.70	0.442
	Xnoth	1	0.95	
			4.42	
Killall	Herb. X	8	9.25	
	Polylip	1	1.00	1.125
	Nyloput	1	1.00	
			11.25	
Flyswot	Insecto	9.5	29.83	3.183
	Scent p2	0.5	2.00	
			31.83	
Waspkil	Flyswot	8	25.46	
	Alsec	1.5	4.50	3.146
	Scent p6	0.5	1.50	
			31.46	
Pestoff	Insecto	10	31.40	3.14
Floranosh	Fertic	9.5	53.45	5.545
	Gropic	0.5	2.00	
			55.45	
Rootgrow	Floranosh	8.5	47.13	6.963
	Fastec	1.5	22.50	
			69.63	
Popup	Fertic Z	7.5	35.19	
	Fastec	2.5	37.50	7.269
			72.69	

Case study — 243

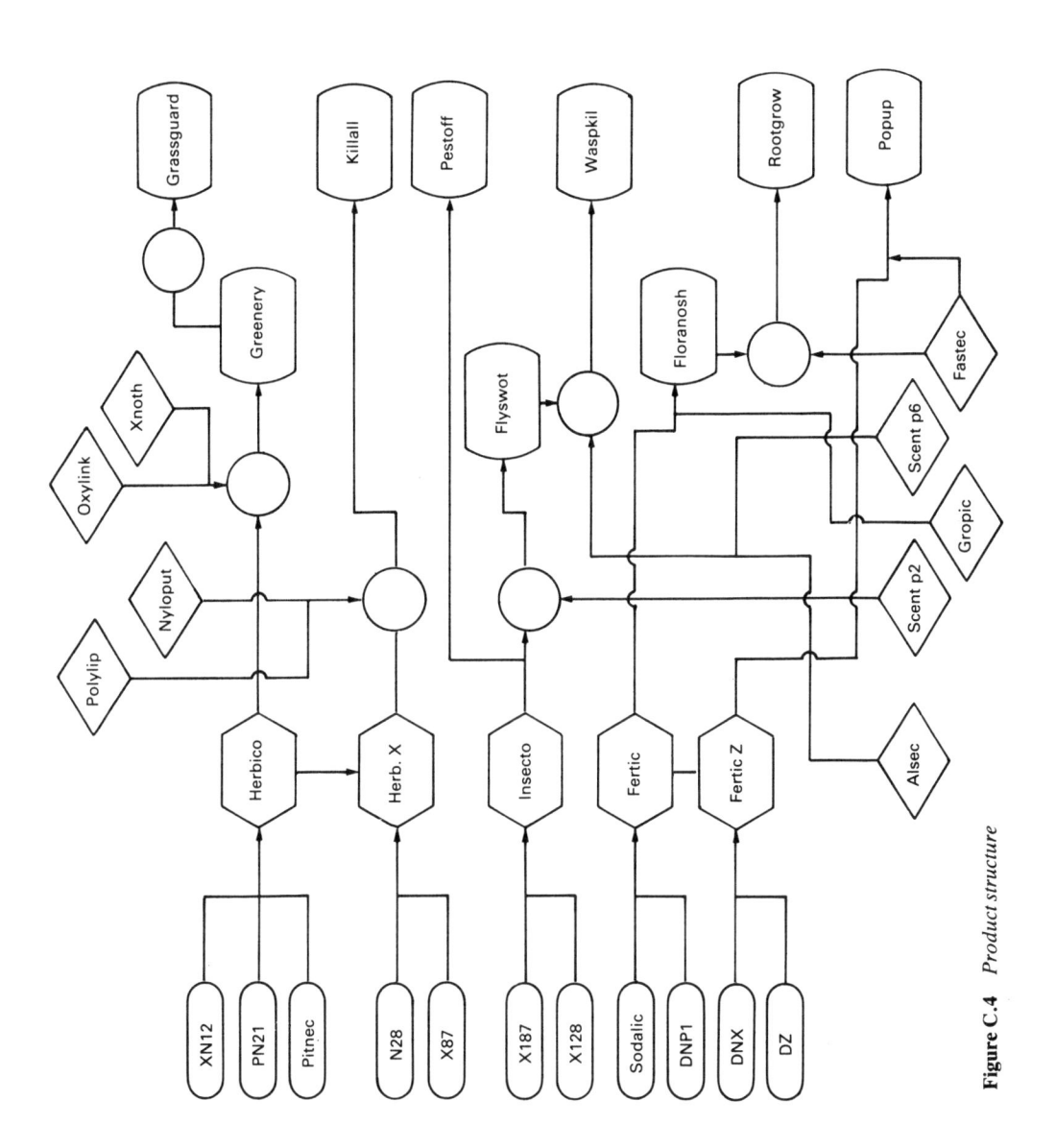

Figure C.4 *Product structure*

244 — Management information systems and data processing

	PROFIT STATEMENT OCTOBER					
	Month			Year to Date		
	Budget £	Actual £	Difference £	Budget £000s	Actual £000s	Difference £000s
INCOME						
Herbicides	600 000	426 110	(173 890)	7 000	6 825	(175)
Insecticides	48 000	27 997	(20 003)	500	421	(79)
Fertilizers	530 000	423 962	(106 038)	6 500	5 985	(515)
TOTAL INCOME	1 178 000	878 069	(299 931)	14 000	13 231	(769)
MATERIAL COSTS						
Herbicides	133 800	95 791	38 009	1 575	1 531	44
Insecticides	26 000	15 228	10 772	272	231	41
Fertilizers	354 090	286 270	67 820	4 386	4 065	321
PRIME GROSS MARGIN	664 110	480 780	(183 330)	7 767	7 404	(363)
Production	196 000	186 295	9 705	2 362	2 219	143
Research	67 000	62 011	4 989	790	821	(31)
Engineering	90 000	101 000	(11 000)	950	1 103	(153)
Material Control	52 000	54 000	(2 000)	580	620	(40)
Sales and Marketing	75 000	77 060	(2 060)	875	985	(110)
Admin. and Accounts	60 000	58 150	1 850	650	630	20
MD Office	24 000	23 050	950	260	250	10
PROFIT BEFORE INTEREST	100 110 20 000	(80 786) 25 000	(180 896) (5 000)	1 300 220	776 255	(524) (35)
NET PROFIT	80 110	(105 786)	(185 896)	1 080	521	(559)

Figure C.5 *Profit statement*

PRODUCTION AND GENERAL OVERHEADS OCTOBER					
Department		Employees	Budget £	Actual £	Var. £	%
PRODUCTION LINES						
Primary	A	70	36 000	34 107	1 893	5.3
	B	72	32 000	31 025	975	3.0
	C	63	31 000	33 016	(2 016)	(6.5)
Secondary	1	42	18 000	17 210	790	4.4
	2	41	19 000	17 110	1 890	9.9
	3	48	21 000	20 187	813	3.9
Packing	X	34	12 000	12 097	(97)	(0.8)
	Y	37	13 000	11 343	1 657	1.3
	Z	39	14 000	10 200	3 800	27.1
			196 000	186 295	9 705	5.0
Research		20	67 000	62 011	4 989	7.4
Engineering		30	90 000	101 000	(11 000)	(12.2)
Production		496	353 000	349 306	3 694	1.0
Overheads						
Material Control		40	52 000	54 000	(2 000)	3.8
Sales and Marketing		30	75 000	77 060	(2 060)	(2.7)
Administration and Accounting		31	60 000	58 150	1 850	3.1
Managing Director's Office		3	24 000	23 050	950	3.9
		600	211 000	212 260	(1 260)	0.6
			564 000	561 566	2 434	0.4

Figure C.6 *Production and overhead costs. Notes: department costs are primarily labour and consumable materials, including energy; Sales and Marketing includes advertising and promotion.*

Case study — 245

PRODUCT ANALYSIS   OCTOBER

Product	Size	Quantity	Sales income £	Std. cost £	Actual use at std. £	Material use difference £
Grassguard	1 kg	15 000	46 500	7 380	7 890	(510)
	5 kg	9 000	115 200	21 510	23 750	(2240)
	10 kg	4 000	86 000	18 680	18 780	(100)
			247 700	47 570	50 420	(2850)
Greenery	750 ml	11 000	33 000	6 067	7 100	(1033)
	2.5 l	7 500	50 625	9 788	10 111	(323)
	5 l	2 750	31 625	7 040	8 200	(1160)
	10 l	1 850	37 000	9 935	9 875	60
			152 250	32 830	35 286	(2456)
Killall	250 ml	6 000	6 600	2 468	3 000	(532)
	500 ml	4 000	8 000	2 970	3 110	(140)
	1 l	1 000	3 750	1 375	1 295	80
	2.5 l	750	6 450	2 260	2 105	155
	5 kg	80	1 360	465	575	(110)
			26 160	9 538	10 085	(547)
HERBICIDES			426 110	89 938	95 791	(5853)
Flyswot	100 g	11 000	9 900	5 478	6 100	(622)
	200 g	7 500	13 125	6 420	6 200	220
			23 025	11 898	12 300	(402)
Waspkil	100 g	2 100	1 995	1 039	1 100	(61)
	200 g	150	277	127	186	(59)
			2 272	1 166	1 286	(120)
Pestoff	100 g	600	510	296	310	(14)
	200 g	800	1 320	678	785	(107)
	250 ml	200	360	183	236	(53)
	500 ml	150	510	263	311	(48)
			2 700	1 420	1 642	(222)
INSECTICIDES			27 997	14 484	15 228	(744)
Rootgrow	1 kg	3 000	29 250	21 039	19 875	1164
	5 kg	600	28 800	20 997	19 215	1782
	10 kg	300	27 225	20 964	21 070	(106)
	25 kg	200	33 500	34 884	29 816	5068
	50 kg	75	31 612	26 145	27 218	(1073)
			150 387	124 029	117 194	6835
Floranosh	100 ml	14 000	14 700	9 163	9 310	(147)
	200 ml	12 000	24 000	14 748	15 250	(502)
	1 l	6 000	52 800	34 770	36 810	(2040)
	2.5 l	2 000	43 800	28 120	26 200	1920
	10 kg	1 150	100 625	64 055	62 100	1955
			235 925	150 856	149 670	1186
Popup	100 g	9 000	16 650	8 162	8 300	(138)
	200 g	6 000	21 000	10 043	11 106	(1063)
			37 650	18 205	19 406	(1201)
FERTILIZERS			423 962	293 090	286 270	6820
SUMMARY						
Grassguard			247 700	47 570	50 420	(2850)
Greenery			152 250	32 830	35 286	(2456)
Killall			26 160	9 538	10 085	(547)
Flyswot			23 025	11 898	12 300	(402)
Waspkil			2 272	1 166	1 286	(120)
Pestoff			2 700	1 420	1 642	(222)
Rootgrow			150 387	124 029	117 194	6835
Floranosh			235 925	150 856	149 670	1186
Popup			37 650	18 205	19 406	(1201)
			878 069	397 512	397 289	223

Figure C.7 *Product analysis*

OCTOBER STOCK SUMMARY RAW MATERIALS AND FINISHED GOODS					
Product	*Unit*	*Quantity*	*Product*	*Unit*	*Quantity*
Grassguard	1 kg	2000	XN12	kilos	7000
	5 kg	1500	PN21	kilos	9000
	10 kg	1000	Pitnec	kilos	6000
			N28	kilos	2000
Greenery	750 ml	3000	X87	kilos	1000
	2.5 l	2000	X128	kilos	900
	5 l	1000	Sodalic	kilos	800
	10 l	950	DNP1	kilos	1000
			DNX	kilos	3000
Killall	250 ml	2000	D2	kilos	2000
	500 ml	2000	Polylip	kilos	1100
	1 l	800	Oxylink	kilos	900
	2.5 l	750	Nyloput	kilos	1000
	5 kg	100	Xnoth	kilos	2000
			Alsec	kilos	1500
Flyswot	100 g	6000	Scent p2	kilos	200
	200 g	3000	Scent p6	kilos	300
			Fastec	kilos	–
Waspkil	100 g	800	Gropic	kilos	100
	200 g	100			
Pestoff	100 g	300			
	200 g	300			
	250 ml	100			
	500 ml	90			
Rootgrow	1 kg	100			
	5 kg	50			
	10 kg	–			
	25 kg	–			
	50 kg	20			
Floranosh	10 ml	1000			
	200 ml	1000			
	1 l	750			
	2.5 l	600			
	10 kg	250			
Popup	100 g	800			
	200 g	300			

Figure C.8 *Stock summary page 1*

\multicolumn{11}{c	}{PACKAGING STOCK OCTOBER}
Type	Size	Grassguard	Greenery	Killall	Flyswot	Waspkil	Pestoff	Rootgrow	Floranosh	Popup
Bags	1 kg	2000						2000		
Bags	5 kg	4000		300				575		
Bags	10 kg	3000						275	750	
Sacks	25 kg							100		
Sacks	50 kg							–		
Bottles	100 ml								900	
Bottles	200 ml								150	
Bottles	250 ml			3000			400			
Bottles	500 ml			2000			300			
Bottles	750 ml		6000							
Bottles	1 l			3000					1000	
Containers	2.5 l		3000	1000					800	
Containers	5 l		2000							
Drums	10 l		1100							
Aerosol cans	100 g				4000	2000	500			1000
Aerosol cans	200 g				3000	900	700			500

Figure C.8 *Stock summary page 2*

Index

Note: *italic* page numbers indicate illustrations.

Access (to computer area), 224
Accuracy (of information), 26, 29
Activity analysis, 32
Adaptive systems, 5, 6, 9, 27–28, 29
Administration, computers used in, 83
ALGOL (ALGOrithmic Language), 115
Amendments, system, 201–202, *203*
Analog computers, 98–99, 109
Application software, 56, 114
Architecture, computer, 97
ASSEMBLER programming language, 116
Audit
   computer efficiency, 218–220, 221
   information systems, 222–231
Audit path/trail, 230–231, 232
Auditability, 228–230, 232

Bar coding, 102–103, 143
BASIC (Beginners All-purpose Symbolic Instruction Code), 115, 190
Batch processing, 49, 50, 51
   programs for, 120, 122
Benchmark tests, 59
Benefits, computer systems, 67, 67–68, 213–214
Block printers, 108
Blocks (of data), 126
British Telecom, network services, 92–93, 94
Bubble memory, 105
Budget, as model, 8
Bureaux, computer, 54–55
Bursting machines, 178
Buses, computer hardware, 99, *100*
By-product information, 17, 19

Calculating (of data), 131–132
Case study, 234–247

Changeover
   procedures for, 76, 79
   reactions to, 78–79
Character recognition, 102
Characters, types of, 125
Check digits, 151–152
Closed systems, 3–4, 9
COBOL (COmmon Business Oriented Language), 114, 120, 190
Coding, 143–145, *146*
COM (computer output microfilm), 180, 185
Communications
   computer use of, 106, 109
   computers used in, 83–84
   development of, 11–12
Comparing (of data), 132
Compiling (of programs), *112*, 112, 121
Computer operations
   definition of, 159
   efficiency of management of, 168
   evaluation of, 217–218, 220
   management and control of, 158–159, 169
   performance monitoring, 167–168, 170
   planning and scheduling of, *159*, 159–161, 169
Computer systems
   assessment criteria for, 62–65
   dependency on, 222–223, 231
   elements of, 90–92, *91*, 95
   evaluation and ranking of, 59–60
   selection of, 53–55, 60
Computers
   business uses of, 83–84, 94
   efficiency audit for, 218–220, 221
   resources required by, 160–161
   strengths of, 88–89, 95
   types of, 84–88, *85*, 94
   weaknesses of, 89–90, 95

Index — 249

Contingency plans, 225
Continuous stationery, *177*, 177, 178
Contracts, computer supplier, 57
Control, computers used in, 84
Control flowchart, 228, *229*
Control information, 14–15
 problems with, 15
Control loops, 7, 9
 control standards for, 7, 9
 measuring devices in, 7, 9
 nesting of, 18–19, *18*
 regulators in, 7, 9
Control procedures, 165–167, 170
Control systems, 6–7, 9
 examples of, 17
Converging technology, 88
Costs
 computer systems, 64–65, 66–67, *67*, 219
 data collection, 153
 failure, 69, 79, 219
 in performance analysis, 213
 in selection criteria, 64–65
 in system evaluation, 212
CPU (central processor unit), 86, 96, 109
Cybernetics, 6–7

Daisy-wheel printers, 107
Data
 definition of, 124, 137
 forms of, 124–126, 137
 losses of, 166–167
 manipulation methods for, 131–134, 137–138
 security of, 225–226
 transmission of, 147–151, 154
 validation and control of, 151–153, 154
Data administration, 136, 138
Data base, design principles for, 134–136, 138
Data base software, 121, 122
Data collection, 90–91, 140–141
 cost of, 153
 importance of, 140, 153
 methods of, 141–143, 154
Data control, 159
Data control standards, 192–193
Data conversion, 77, 79
Data dictionary, 136
Data hierarchies/networks, 126–127, 137
Data merge, *132*, 132
Data output, 91
Data processing, 83–207
 definition of, 91
 organization/management of, 157, 169
 types of, 49–50, 51
Data-free programs, 212
DBMS (data base management system), 135, 138
Decision analysis, 32
Decision-making, information and, 12, 19, 21–22, 29
Deleting (of data), 133
Design, computers used in, 84
Design report, 39, 194–195

Deterministic systems, 5, 6, 9
Digital computers, 98, 99, 108
Direct input, 103
Disc systems, 101, 104, 106, 109
Distributed processing, 92, 95, 225
Documentation
 computer system, 42, 77, 78, 80, 194–201, 206
 importance of, 198, 201, 206
Dot-matrix printers, 108
Dumps, 167
Dynamic allocation (of computer memory), *113*, 114

Economy (of systems), 37, 212
Electrostatic printers, 108
Electrothermal printers, 108
Environmental protection, 224
EPROM (erasable programmable read only memory), 105
Error matching, 193

Facilities management, hardware provision by, 55
Failures
 cost of, 69, 79, 219
 run, 165
Fault analysis, 217–218
Feedback (of information), 19
Fields (of data), 125, 181
File errors, 165–166
File management, 91, 204
File organization, 129–131, 137
File structures, 127–129, *128*, 137
Files, security of, 226–227
Fire precautions, 224
Firmware, 111
Flexibility
 of computers, 89
 of systems, 28–29, 37, 211–212
Flowcharting, 43–48
Flowcharts
 control point, 228, *229*
 program, 47, *48*, 117, *118*
 reasons for, 43–44, 47, 51
 standards for, 192
 symbols for, 44, *44*, *47*
 systems, 44–47, *45*, *46*
Form design, 171–174, 180–184
 standards for, 193–194
FORTRAN (FORmula TRANslation), 115
FRESH mnemonic, 220

GIGO (garbage in, garbage out), 124, 144
Go–no go statement, *74*, 75
Golfball printers, 107
Graphics, as output, 179, 185

Hardware
 assessment criteria for, 62–63
 costs of, 64, 66
 elements of, 97, *98*, 108
 functions of, 99–100, *100*

250 — Index

operating functions of, 99–100, *100*, 109
selection of, 53–55, 60
standards for, 189–190, 205
Hash totals, 152
Helpfulness, systems, 37, 212
Hierarchial data bases, 135–136, *136*
Hierarchy, of sub-systems, 4–5, 9, 23

In-house systems development team, 56, 58
Indexed file organization, 129–130
Indexed sequential file organization, 130
Informal information-flow systems, 16–17
Information
  decision-making and, 12, 19, 21–22, 29
  definition of, 11, 19
  evaluation of, 26–27
  organizations and, 13–15
  presentation of, 28–29
  research into needs for, 22–23
  types of, 13–15, 33, 34
  value of, 11–13
  as vital resource, 222, 231
Information flows, 15–17, *16*, 19, 33, 34
Information handling, 15
Information loops, 17–19
Information needs analysis, 32
Information services, computers used in, 84
Information systems
  analysis of, 32–33, 34
  control of, 33–34
  flexibility of, 27–28
  objectives of, 24–26
  strategy for, 31–34
  structure of, 23–24, *24*, 33, 34
Information technology developments, 33, 34–35
Ink-jet printers, 108
Input, methods of, 141–143, 154
Input devices, 100–103, 109, 145, 147, 154
Inserting (of data), 132
Installation costs, computer system, 64, 67
Interactive processing, 49–50, 51
Interactive software, 120–121, 122

JCL (job control language), 159, 163, 169, 190
Job control, 202
Job run timetable, 160

LANs (local area networks), 94
Laser printers, 108
Line printers, 107
Loop checks, 150–151

Machine code, 111
Magnetic ink character recognition, 102, 143
Magnetics discs/tape, 101, 103–104, 106, 109
Mainframe computers, 85
Maintenance
  costs of, 65, 67
  information systems, 42, 201–202, 206
Management
  agreement to systems installation, 69–70, 79
  information needs of, 15, 22–23

Management information systems, 3–80
  definition of, 15
Manuals, computer system, 77, *78*
Manufacturers (of computers), dealing with, 56–57, 60
Mark recognition, 102–103
Material control, example, 25
Memory control, example, 25
Memory allocation, *113*, 113–114
Memory devices, types of, 104–105
Memory size, 104, 105, 163, *164*
Merging (of data), 132
Microcomputers, 86
Microfilm, as output, 180, 185
Microprocessors, 86–87
  in control systems, 7
Minicomputers, 86
Models, business system, 8–9
Modem, described, 93
Modular programming/system design, 120, 122, 212
Multi-drop network, *93*, 94
Multi-processing, 164–165, 169
Multi-programming, 163–164, 169
Multiple-level files, 128

Nested control loops, 18–19, *18*
Network control, 159
Networks, 92–94, *93*, 95
Noise, data transmission affected by, 148, *149*, 154

Objective achievement, in performance analysis, 213
OEM suppliers, 86
Open systems, 3, 4, 9
Operating information, 14
Operating manuals, 77
Operating software, 56, 113–114, 190
Operating standards, 202–205
Operating systems, 6
Operational control procedures, 165–167
Operational controls, 159, 228, 232
Operational weaknesses (of computers), 90
Operations, *see also* Computer operations
Optical character/mark reading/recognition, 102
Organization
  data processing, place in, *158*
  definition of, 6, 9
  systems within, 6, 9
Output
  design principles for, 171–174, 180–184, 186
  distribution of, 204–205
  duplicate copies of, 177
  human-readable, 107, 176–180, 185
  machine-readable, 106, 176
  methods of, 106–108, 109, 174, 176–180, 185
  user requirements and, 184–185
Output failure, 167
Output request form, 174, *175*

Packages, software, 56, 58, 60, 75–76
Packet switching, 106
Paging, 181, 184

Index

Parity checks, 150
Partitioning (of computer memory), 113
PASCAL programming language, 115
Payroll software packages, 56
PC microcomputers, 86
Performance analysis, 213–214, 220
PL/1 (Programming Language 1), 115
Planning (of computer systems), 68, 68–69
Planning information, 13–14
Planning systems, 6
Point-of-sale data capture, 141
Point-to-point network, 93, 94
Power interruptions, 224
Presentation (of information), 28–29
Print format chart, 172–173, 174
Printed reports, 176–178
Printers, 107–108, 109–110
Probabilistic systems, 5, 6, 8, 9
Procedure manuals, 77, 78
Production, computers used in, 84
Production run sheet, 161, 162
Program flowcharts, 47, 48
Program libraries, 202, 204
Program overview, 196, 197
Program security, 227–228
Program specification, 197–198
Program test sheet, 198, 199
Programmers, 111
  effective organization of, 119, 119
Programming
  flowcharts for, 47, 48, 117, 118
  principles of, 116–119, 122
  standards in, 191–192
Programming languages, 87, 112, 114–116, 121, 190
Programs
  correction of, 118–119
  running of, 119
  testing of, 73, 117–118, 198
  writing of, 117
PROM (programmable read only memory), 105
Protection, computer operations, 223–225, 232
Punched cards/paper-tape, 101, 106
Purchase (of computer), 53–54
Purchasing system, 3, 4, 25, 26

RAM (random access memory), 105
Random addressing, 131
Reciprocal arrangements, as contingency plans, 225
Records, data, 125
Recovery procedures, 167
Related file structures, 128, 128
Relational data bases, 135
Reliability
  computer, 89
  information system, 26–27, 37, 212
Reports
  computer printout, 176–178
  design of, 171–174, 180–184
  presentation of, 28–29, 184
  quality of, 171
  writing of, 39, 70–71, 79

Re-run time, 218
Resource usage, as measure of efficiency, 218
Re-starts, 167
Ryhthm control method, 17
Rigid systems, 5–6, 9
Roll printers, 108
ROM (read only memory), 105, 133
RPG (Report Program Generator), 115
Run failures, 165
Run test sheet, 198, 200
Run testing, 73
Running (of computer), 161–163, 169

Sabotage (of computer facility), 224
Security, computer operations, 219, 224, 225–228, 232
  in performance analysis, 213
Selecting (of data), 132
Sequential file organization, 129
Serial printers, 107–108
Silicon chip memory, 104–105, 109
Simplicity, systems, 37, 212
Simulation models, 8
Software
  costs of, 64, 67
  data base, 121, 122
  definitions of, 97, 111, 121
  interactive, 120–121, 122
  pattern of, 116
  selection of, 55–56, 60
  standards for, 190, 206
  tailor-made, 58, 60
  types of, 112–116, 121–122
Software control, 159
Sorting (of data), 131
Speed, computer, 89, 133
Standards
  computer operations, 202–205, 206
  enforcement of, 205
  hardware, 189–190, 205
  need for, 188–189, 205
  software, 189–190, 206
  systems design, 190–194, 206
Star network, 93, 94
Stationery, computer printout, 177, 178
Storage capacity (of computer), 89
Storage facilities (of computer), 103–105, 109
Stored-instruction devices, computers as, 111, 121
Structured programming, 120, 122
Sub-optimization, 25, 29
Sub-systems, 4–5, 9, 23, 26
Success, key criteria for, 214–215
Suppliers (of computers), dealing with, 56–57, 60
System, performance analysis for, 213–214
System amendment request, 202, 203
System design controls, 228, 229
System flowcharts, 44–47, 45, 46
System models, 8–9
Systems
  definition of, 3–4, 9
  organizational, 6, 9
  performance assessment of, 211–212, 220

252 — Index

sub-systems and, 4–5
types of, 5–6, 9
Systems analysis, 43, 51
Systems design, 36–51
  concept diagram for, *216*
  definition of, 36, 50
  design efficiency of, 215
  evaluation of, 215–217, 220
  maintenance efficiency of, 217
  operating efficiency of, 215, 217
  principles of, 36–37
  project life cycle for, 38, *38*, 50
  project management for, 42, 51
  stages of, 38–42, *41*, 50
  standards for, 190–194, 206
Systems framework, 23–24, *24*, 33, 34
Systems implementation, 40
Systems installation, 66–80
  justification of, 66–69, 79
  management agreement and, 69–70, 79
Systems planning, *68*, 68–69
Systems proposals, 39
Systems specification, 40, 195–196, *197*
Systems testing, 73, *74*, 75, 79

Tape systems, 101, 103–104, 106, 109
Teletype units, 102, 179
Terminals, output at, 102, 179, 185
Testing, computer systems, 72–76
Theft, prevention of, 224
Time sharing (of computers), 54
Timeliness (of information), 26–27, 29
Training, 71–72, 77, 79
Transaction processing, 49
Transferring (of data), 133
Transmission lines (for data), 147, *148*, 154
Transmission noise, 148, *149*
Turn-key companies, 55

Undersell (by computer suppliers), 57
User education, 71–72, 79

VDUs (visual display units), 102, 107, 179
Video discs, 105
Voice recognition, 103
Vulnerability, computer operations, 219, 222–223, 231

Word processors, 85, *87*, 87–88